GIMP Essential Reference

DISCARD

New
Riders

The New Riders Professional Library

Cisco Router Configuration &
Troubleshooting
Mark Tripod, 0-7357-0024-9

Debian GNU/Linux:
Installation and Configuration
John Goerzen and Ossama Othman,
0-7357-0914-9

Developing Linux Applications
Eric Harlow, 0-7357-0021-4

Python Essential Reference
David M. Beazley, 0-7357-0901-7

GTK+/Gnome Application
Development
Havoc Pennington, 0-7357-0078-8

KDE Application Development
Havoc Pennington, 1-57870-201-1

Linux Essential Reference
Ed Petron, 0-7357-0852-5

Linux Firewalls
Robert Ziegler, 0-7357-0900-9

Linux System Administration
M Carling, Stephen Degler,
James Dennis, 1-56205-934-3

Lotus Notes & Domino Essential
Reference
Tim Bankes and Dave Hatter,
0-7357-0007-9

MySQL
Paul DuBois, 0-7357-0921-1

Network Intrusion Detection:
An Analyst's Handbook
Stephen Northcutt, 0-7357-0868-1

Solaris Essential Reference
John Mulligan, 0-7357-0023-0

Understanding Data Communications,
Sixth Edition
Gilbert Held, 0-7357-0036-2

GIMP Essential Reference

Alex Harford

New Riders

201 West 103rd Street, Indianapolis, IN 46290

GIMP Essential Reference

International Standard Book Number: 0-7357-0911-4

Library of Congress Catalog Card Number: 99-65219

Printed in the United States of America   006.6

First Printing: November, 1999   869

Harf

03 02 01 00 99   7 6 5 4 3 2 1

Interpretation of the printing code: The rightmost double-digit number is the year of the book's printing; the rightmost single-digit number is the number of the book's printing. For example, the printing code 99-1 shows that the first printing of the book occurred in 1999.

Trademarks

Warning and Disclaimer

Publisher
David Dwyer

Executive Editor
Laurie Petrycki

Acquisitions Editor
Katie Purdum

Managing Editor
Sarah Kearns

Development Editor
Jim Chalex

Project Editor
John Rahm

Copy Editor
Daryl Kessler

Technical Editors
Zach Beane
Guillermo S. Romero

Indexer
Angie Bess

Compositor
Wil Cruz

To Mom and Dad

About the Author

Alex Harford is an electrical and computer engineering student at the University of British Columbia. An Internet veteran and experienced Linux user, he has been using the GIMP for all of his web development work since being introduced to Unix and Linux while working at Dowco.Com Internet. He is a member of the Vancouver Linux Users Group.

About the Technical Reviewers

Zach Beane has been working with GIMP since its earliest release in 1996. He is active in providing help for GIMP users in newsgroups, web pages, and IRC. In 1997, he started the GIMP News web page at `http://www.xach.com/gimp/news/`, and now maintains the News section of `http://www.gimp.org`.

Guillermo S. Romero is currently studying Telecommunications Engineering with a speciality in Data Transmision at the EUITT branch of Universidad Politécnica de Madrid.

He has worked for *PC Actual* (a BPE's magazine), and is presently employed by *Linux Actual* and *Solo Linux and Mas PC* (Prensa Técnica's magazines). The articles and courses within these magazines are mainly about graphics (2D/3D) and Linux, focusing on the GIMP, POV-Ray, and Blender programs.

Contents at a Glance

Contents

Acknowledgments

When looking back on a project of this size, it is difficult to remember everyone who helped me along the way. First of all, I would like to thank all of the developers who have put their time into creating such a quality program. The GIMP has an excellent group of people behind it, at both the developer and user level (although the lines often blur).

Also, the hackers at the Free Software Foundation and others involved with the GNU/Linux system need to be thanked. This includes rms, ESR, and Linus. Anyone involved with the creation of the Slackware distribution obviously needs to be thanked.

Thanks to Philip Greenspun (`philg@mit.edu`) for the great stock photographs found at `http://photo.net/philg`.

On a more personal note, I would like to thank the people at New Riders Publishing, especially Jim Chalex and Katie Purdum for keeping me going on this. Also, the technical editors, Zach and Guillermo, were great at keeping me on my toes.

Finally, I would like to thank my friends and family. I would especially like to thank my parents and my girlfriend for all their support. I would also like to say hi to the guys from 1st Shu.

Tell Us What You Think!

As the reader of this book, *you* are our most important critic and commentator. We value your opinion and want to know what we're doing right, what we could do better, what areas you'd like to see us publish in, and any other words of wisdom you're willing to pass our way.

As the Executive Editor for the Linux team at New Riders Publishing, I welcome your comments. You can fax, email, or write me directly to let me know what you did or didn't like about this book—as well as what we can do to make our books stronger.

Please note that I cannot help you with technical problems related to the topic of this book, and that due to the high volume of mail I receive, I might not be able to reply to every message.

When you write, please be sure to include this book's title and author, as well as your name and phone or fax number. I will carefully review your comments and share them with the author and editors who worked on the book.

Fax:	317-581-4663
Email:	newriders@mcp.com
Mail:	Laurie Petrycki
	Executive Editor
	Linux/Open Source
	New Riders Publishing
	201 West 103rd Street

GIMP Essentials

1

1.1   Introduction to the GIMP

The GIMP is one of the "killer apps" that was born from the Open Source software movement. It is an image manipulation program for Unix-like operating systems that rivals, and in some cases outdoes, Adobe Photoshop. This program was created by Spencer Kimball and Peter Mattis (S&P) at the eXperimental Computing Facility at the University of California at Berkeley. Their project has grown and split into two distinct entities: the GIMP, which is an acronym that stands for the GNU Image Manipulation Program, and GTK+, the GIMP ToolKit.

This first program, the GIMP, was released to the world under the GNU General Public License. The source code was distributed, and many people were impressed with the quality of the code. People began submitting patches and improvements to the GIMP, and the program has grown very quickly.

The version numbering scheme is the same as the Linux kernel. The major number remains the same except for very major releases. Currently, the GIMP is in version 1. The second "digit," or minor number, represents whether the version is stable or in development. Even numbers represent stable versions, odd numbers means that it is a development release. For instance, the minor number for the stable version is currently 2, so that version number is 1.2. The development version minor number is 3, so that version number is 1.3. Each version also has a patch level. In stable releases, this represents a bug-fix. For the development version, this is a point at which the developers feel ready to release a newer version. An example stable version number would be 1.2.2; a development version number would be 1.3.6.

When the developers want to release a stable version, a code freeze is put in place, at which point no new features can be added. The only changes that can be made are to bugs in the code that would make the program crash. After all the bugs are found, the program becomes a stable release, and a new development version is started. The code is usually retained from version to version, except in very unusual cases.

The second part of S&P's project is called the GIMP ToolKit, or GTK+. Originally the GIMP and the ToolKit were rolled into one program, but because the toolkit was very useful as an individual program, it was split into a separate library. The GIMP ToolKit enables people to do complicated X programming with a standard library that is fast—and best of all—free. Many programs now use GTK+ for their X library, including XMMS (an open source MP3 player), and GNOME, a desktop environment for X. The GIMP ToolKit also uses the version number system of the Linux kernel. Development versions of the GIMP ToolKit will usually end up "breaking" stable versions of the GIMP.

1.2 System Requirements

The GIMP is fairly processor and memory intensive. The minimal requirements to run the GIMP are as follows:

- A Unix-like operating system with X11. Windows and BeOS versions are being developed currently.
- An 8-bit display.
- 20MB of free hard drive space.
- A mouse or other pointing device.
- GTK+.
- 8MB of RAM.

The following setup is recommended for using the GIMP:

- A modern, Unix-like operating system. Any version released in the last four years should work.
- 16 bit or higher display, running X.
- 200MB of free hard drive space.
- At least 16MB of RAM.
- GTK+ and other graphics libraries.
- A good floating-point processor. K7 processors seem to be the best choice for the home user. Alpha and other RISC processors will provide even better performance.

These requirements are for running the GIMP, however slowly. The GIMP Web site (`www.gimp.org`) states that "a realistic low-end machine to run the GIMP on would be approximately a 486 66/DX2 with 16 megs real RAM and at least 40 virtual and 200 megs of free hard drive space."

With hardware prices dropping rapidly, this setup would be easily available. To edit large photographs, you should use a Pentium machine with at least 64MB of RAM—128MB would be better. A video card with at least 4MB of RAM is recommended for good color and resolution. A machine with multiple processors would definitely help.

1.3 Menu, Name, and Book Conventions

Throughout this book, several specific terms and assumptions have been used, and it is useful to become familiar with them.

The first is dealing with pointing devices. It is assumed that you are using a mouse with three buttons. If not, some actions may have to be done differently. Whenever you are instructed to click with the mouse, the left mouse button is assumed. Right mouse clicks will be explicitly instructed.

When describing items found in menus, several conventions are used:

- The GIMP's Toolbox is referred to as the <Toolbox>. For example, to open a file through the Toolbox, click <Toolbox>/File/Open.

- Right-clicking on an image is referred to as <Image>. So, to duplicate an image, click on <Image>/Image/Channels Ops/Duplicate. The <Image> menu can also be accessed by clicking on the arrow in the top-left corner.

- Menus inside these are separated by slash marks (for example, <Toolbox> /Xtns/Screen Shot.)

1.3.1   Frequently Used Terminology

Here are some terms with which you should become familiar:

- **Alpha.** A term that is common when discussing graphics. It represents the transparency in an image. An image can have a range of Alpha values, going from fully transparent to fully opaque.

- **Anti-aliasing.** Used to describe smoothing in an image. Many different operations use anti-aliasing, but they all refer to the technique used to make images look smoother and less pixelated. It is most noticeable when dealing with text.

- **Bit depth.** A mathematical term used in describing the number of colors available in an image. An 8-bit display means that the display can show 2^8, or 256, different colors. A 24-bit display can show 2^{24}, or 16.8 million, different colors. Refer to Table 1.1 to see the various bit depths and their available colors.

Table 1.1   Bit Depths and Available Colors

Bit Depth	Available Colors
1	2
2	4
4	16
8	256
16	65,536
24	16,777,216
32	16,777,216

- **Feathering.** Similar to anti-aliasing. Feathering is used to smooth out transitions over a large distance. The radius of the feathering can be changed, whereas in anti-aliasing it cannot.

- **Threshold.** Describes the extent of an effect. Something is either *inside* the threshold, or it is not—there is no in-between.

1.3.2 Book Conventions

The following conventions have been used to help you read this book quickly
and easily:

- **Mono-faced words**. Any word(s) appearing in `this typeface` indicates
  code to be typed, text displayed onscreen, or URLs.

- **Cross-references**. These can take two forms: *in-text* or at the *end of a section*.
  The in-text references will simply refer you to a specific page where related
  information can be obtained. The section-ending references look like this:

  ▶**See Also** "Cross Reference" (page 150)

- **Hotkeys**. Hotkeys are frequently used in the GIMP to perform operations
  more quickly. They appear in square brackets (for instance, [Ctrl+Z]).

1.4 Color Models

Another concept to be familiar with is the color models in the GIMP. There
are four different color models you should be familiar with to understand the
concepts behind this book[1]:

- **RGB**. This is the most common color model. It combines Red, Green, and
  Blue to create any possible color.

- **HSV**. The HSV model uses Hue, Saturation, and Value to describe colors.

- **Grayscale**. This model is for black and white images.

- **Indexed**. This color model is quite different from the others. It creates a
  table of colors that are contained in the image.

1.4.1 RGB

RGB is the most common color model in the GIMP. It is an additive model,
where each channel adds up to form any color. Because the GIMP is made to
be used mostly for computer graphics rather than pre-press work, RGB is the
default color model.

Every pixel in an RGB image has three specific properties that determine its
color. Every pixel has a specific amount of red, green, and blue. The color black
has 0 for each channel, for example, and white has a value of 255 for each
channel. A true red color would have a value of 255 for the red channel, and 0
for green and blue. Yellow would have values of 255 in the red and green
channels, and 0 in the blue channel.

---

[1] *Sharp readers will notice that the GIMP does not have CMYK support. This is because it was written
for computer graphics, rather than for pre-press work.*

1.4.2   HSV

The HSV color model is similar to RGB, but each of its channels represents the Hue, Saturation, or Value. This is a more intuitive approach to describing color.

- **Hue**. This channel determines the actual color of the image. It uses a 360-degree color wheel to determine the color. Red is at 0 degrees, for example, and cyan is at 180 degrees.

- **Saturation**. Saturation determines the purity of a color. It is represented as a percentage. A color with full saturation is a pure color. A pixel that has no saturation has no color; it is grayscale.

- **Value**. This channel represents the brightness in an image. It is also a percentage value. A pixel with full value will be bright; a pixel with 0 brightness will be black.

1.4.3   Grayscale

The grayscale color model is a method of displaying black and white color models. It only has one channel—value. This allows it to display 255 shades of gray, with 0 being black, and 255 being white.

1.4.4   Indexed

The indexed color model is not intuitive at all. It creates an index of all the colors in an image and puts them into a Look Up Table (LUT). It allows for only 256 different colors, but these colors can be taken from the 16.8 million available to an RGB image. Indexed images may seem useless with only 256 colors, compared to RGB images with 16.8 million. The advantage to this is that these files are often smaller than if they are saved in RGB format. If you design graphics for Web pages, you probably know that different machines display indexed images differently. This can be a problem. For more information about the Web palette, see page xxx.

1.5   Resolution

Resolution is the final topic that needs to be discussed before we start using the GIMP. This is an especially important topic if you are going to be printing the images you create. The most important distinction to make is the difference between the resolution of your monitor and the resolution of the printed image. *Monitor resolution* is described in pixels per inch (ppi). Most monitors use a resolution of 72ppi. This means that if you have an image that is 72 by 36 pixels, onscreen it is 1×0.5 inches (25.4×12.7mm). Note that this is not always true. Some people may be running at different resolutions. For instance, it is quite common for people with smaller monitors to be running at a higher resolution to give them more space on their screen.

Printer resolution is described in dpi (dots per inch) and lpi (lines per inch). The dpi is the more important resolution to be aware of. If you are going to be printing high-quality images, talk to your printing shop about optimal resolutions. Printers have much higher resolution than monitors, so you will be dealing with very large images to get good quality. Most printers found in homes will have resolutions of around 300dpi, whereas commercial printers may go as high as 2400dpi. If printing a 2×2-inch image at 300dpi, you will be working with an image that appears to be approximately 8.3×8.3 inches on your monitor.

Finding an optimal resolution is always a tradeoff between speed and quality. Working with high-quality images will always slow down your computer, and the images will take up a lot of room on your hard drive. Working with images that are small and fast, on the other hand, will give you low-quality printed images. Experimentation is best for finding optimal resolutions, but if you are doing pre-press work, consult your printing shop.

Navigating the GIMP

2

In this chapter, we will begin to examine the GIMP in more detail. You will find the GIMP's interface similar to Adobe Photoshop, particularly Version 3. By the end of this chapter, the interface and the most rudimentary techniques should be familiar to you. If you have used the GIMP before, you may want to skip this chapter.

2.1   Getting Started with the GIMP

When you first load the GIMP, the Toolbox appears (see Figure 2.1). This is where you will begin to use the GIMP. After you learn the shortcuts, you won't often need to use the Toolbox. Until you do, this window will be frequently accessed.

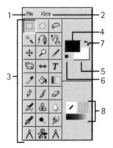

Figure 2.1   *The GIMP Toolbox with the Rectangular Selection Tool chosen, as well as black and white for the colors. Note the File and Xtns menus at the top.*

The layout of the Toolbox is simple. At the top are the File (1) and Xtns (2) menus. These are drop-down menus with other operations inside. On the left of the Toolbox are the icons for the various tools (3). For more information on these tools, see Chapters 11, 12, and 13. The currently selected tool will be indented and darker than any other. By default, the Rectangular Selection Tool is chosen.

You can switch tools by clicking on them. To the right of the tools are the active colors. The color on top is the foreground (4), and below is the background color (5). The active color is indented. By default, the foreground color is black and the background color is white. The small black and white squares to the left (6) reset the colors to the default black and white. The double-headed arrow to the right (7) swaps the foreground and background colors. This operation is also available via the hotkey [X]. The current brush and pattern are shown (8) at the bottom-right of the Toolbox.

2.1.1 Creating a New Image

Follow these steps to create a new image:

1. Click on the File menu in the Toolbox.
2. Click on New [Ctrl+N].

A dialog box will appear with several options, as seen in Figure 2.2.

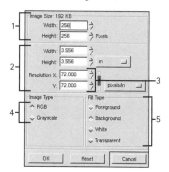

Figure 2.2 *The New Image dialog box.*

1. The first option is image size (1). The height and width can be chosen independently. The file size based on one layer is shown here.
2. Real size can be chosen here (2). The size depends on the resolution (3), so choose that first.
3. The next choice is whether the image is going to be RGB or grayscale (4). Note that you cannot create a new Indexed image. Most of the time, you will want to create an RGB image. If you need to work in black and white, however, choose grayscale. (For more information on image types, see "Image Types," page 62.)
4. The last choice you have is the background color (5). The choices are Background, White, Transparent, or Foreground.
5. Click OK at the bottom of the dialog box, and a new window will be created.

When the new window is created, as in Figure 2.3, you will be able to edit it. There are several things to notice here:

- **Rulers (1).** The rulers along the sides are measured in pixels.

- **Yellow dotted lines.** If you enlarge the window size slightly, you will see these dotted lines around the edges more clearly. These show the size of the layer you are working on. Usually the dotted lines will be the size of the image, but they can be resized if necessary (see "Resizing Layers," page 42).

- **Scrollbars (2).** These appear along the sides if your image is larger than the window you are working in.

- **Image Menu button (3).** This button is used in case you only have two mouse buttons.

- **QuickMask toggles (4).** These buttons switch between QuickMask and Normal mode.

- **Cursor Position (5).** The coordinates of the cursor are shown here.

- **Status Bar/Cancel button (6).** This shows the status of plug-ins that are running, and the Cancel button can abort them.

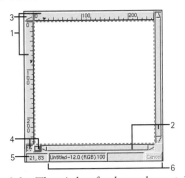

Figure 2.3   *The window for the newly created image.*

2.1.2 Basic Drawing Techniques

Since you have a new image open, you might as well draw in it. Select a tool in the Toolbar. The Pencil will be a good one, see (3) in figure 2.1. Lines are drawn by clicking and dragging with the mouse. (Is there a paint program that doesn't work this way?) Very simple and straightforward.

2.1.3 Color Selection

The Color Selection dialog box is very straightforward. It has some options that are very useful, if not always obvious.

To access the Color Selection dialog box, double-click on the foreground or background color ((4) in Figure 2.1) on the Toolbox.

The Color Selection dialog box appears, as shown in Figure 2.4. There are four different ways of selecting color:

- The GIMP method
- Watercolor method
- Triangle method
- GTK method

2.1.3.1   The GIMP Method

This represents a three-dimensional color cube[1]. In the large window, you are shown the current layer of this cube for a constant hue. In the smaller vertical bar (1) (refer to Figure 2.4), the range of layers for different hues is shown. If you click and drag along this vertical bar, you will see that the hue is the only HSV value that changes. The two squares at the top of this dialog box show the current color (2) and the previous color (3). The column of sliders and numbers along the right side show all of the color values: H for hue (4), S for saturation (5), V for value (6), R for red, G for green, and B for blue (7). Note that hue has a range from 0 degrees to 360 degrees, and saturation and value are percentages, ranging from 0 to 100. R, G, and B range from 0 to 255. There is also an area where color can be entered as a hex triplet (8), for use with Web pages.

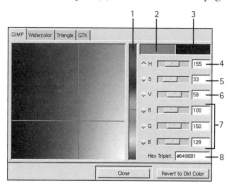

Figure 2.4   *The Color Selection dialog box with hue selected as the Z axis on the Color cube.*

---

[1] *To fully understand this, it helps to have some background on the HSV and RGB color models. See page 5 for more information on Color Models.*

By default, hue is taken to be the Z axis in the color cube. This means that the vertical bar displays varying hue. This makes the saturation change along the Y axis, or vertically in the large palette. Value displays along the X axis, or horizontally in the large palette. The color cube can be displayed on different axes as well. To do this, click on the button beside the option you want to use as the Z axis. For example, clicking on the button beside saturation would display it as the Z axis. Hue would then become the Y axis, and value would remain as the X axis.

Follow these steps to choose a color:

1. Click on the large palette to find the approximate value you need.
2. Fine-tune it in one of the following ways:
   a. Use the sliders.
   b. Enter numerical values for the desired color.
   c. Enter a hex value for the desired color.
3. Click the Close button at the bottom.

If you are unhappy with this color, click Revert to Old Color to cancel the changes.

2.1.3.2   The Watercolor Method

This method lets you choose colors by simulating a paint palette, shown in Figure 2.5. In the large window (1), the colors available are shown. Click with the mouse button to add color to the "brush." This is shown in the smaller preview area (2). Avoid dragging with the mouse; this can cause some strange colors. Once you are happy with the color, click the Close button. If you want to create more colors, click the New button. A color history (3) is shown as well, and colors can be selected from that. The amount of paint picked up on the brush is controlled via a slider bar (4).

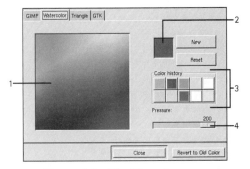

Figure 2.5   *The Watercolor menu.*

2.1.3.3 The Triangle Method

The triangle menu (shown in Figure 2.6) is based on the color wheel. The color is chosen in the large circle (1) around the perimeter of the triangle. Then the specific shade of color is chosen in the triangle (2). The selected color is shown in the bar below (3).

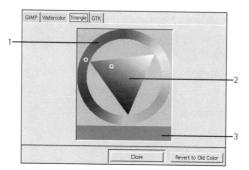

Figure 2.6   *The Triangle menu.*

2.1.3.4 The GTK Method

This menu (shown in Figure 2.7) permits the GTK method of choosing colors. It is used in scripts (see page 257) to select colors as well. It is similar to the GIMP method, but the color wheel (1) is different. The large color wheel here represents hue and saturation. As you move circularly around the wheel, the hue changes from 0 degrees to 359 degrees. If you move radially along the wheel, the saturation changes. The purest colors are on the outside edge; the least pure are found near the center. The value is then chosen through the bar along the side (2). The new color is shown at the bottom (3). Specific colors can also be entered with the slider bars (4), or using keyboard input (5).

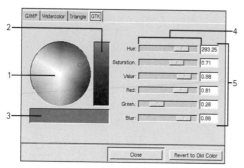

Figure 2.7   *The GTK menu.*

2.1.4 Tool Options

Now that you have the basics down, learning the different options behind the tools is important. There are three different ways to get to the options for a specific tool:

- Double-click on the tool's icon in the Toolbox.
- Right-click on the image to get into the Image Root menu, or click on the arrow in the top-left corner of the image. Go into the Dialog menu, and then click on Tool Options.
- Click on the File menu in the Toolbox, go to the Dialog menu, and click on Tool Options.

The same window will appear for each method. The last two methods might seem like a waste of time, but assigning a hotkey to either one of them can save time. See page 117 on the GIMP's hotkeys to learn how to do this. For information on specific tool options, see Chapters 10, 11, and 12.

2.1.5 Undo and Redo

Undo and Redo are indispensable tools. The hotkey for Undo is [Ctrl+Z]; for Redo the hotkey is [Ctrl+R]. Memorize these. If you wish to access them from a menu, they are found in the <Image>/Edit menu. Because storing what the image was like before the undo can take up RAM, the GIMP allows you to change the levels of Undo. See the "Interface Settings" section on page 17.

2.2 Preferences

The GIMP is highly customizable. The first place you will encounter this is in the Preferences menu. It is found in either the <Toolbox>/File/Preferences or <Image>/File/Preferences menu.

The following selections are available in the Preferences menu:

- New File
- Display
- Interface
- Environment
- Session
- Monitor
- Directories

2.2.1 New File Settings

The defaults when creating a new file are entered here. The following options are available:

- **Default Image Size and Unit.** This is entered in pixels for the bitmap size. The real size can be entered in various units, although inches are the most common.

- **Default Resolution and Unit.** The default resolution is selected here. The unit can also be chosen, but pixels/inch is the most common.

- **Default Image Type.** Either RGB or Grayscale can be chosen here.

2.2.2 Display Settings

In the Display section, you can change display options. The following options are available:

- **Transparency Type.** Determines the color used to represent transparency. The following choices are available:
  a. Light Checks
  b. Mid-Tone Checks
  c. Dark Checks
  d. White Only
  e. Gray Only
  f. Black Only

- **Check Size.** The following choices are available:
  a. Small
  b. Medium
  c. Large

- **Cubic Interpolation.** Used when scaling images. It is slower, but looks better. If you have a slower computer, leave this option off.

2.2.3 Interface Settings

The next section in the Preferences menu is the Interface. Here you have control of part of the user interface of the GIMP. The following options are available:

- **Preview Size.** This determines the sizes of previews for the Layers menu and various plug-ins that use previews. Larger previews take up more CPU resources, and also more screen real estate, but they look better. Previews can be turned off to save resources.

- **Levels of Undo.** Increasing the levels of Undo helps when editing images, but uses up a lot more RAM. If you have a computer that lacks RAM, consider reducing this value.

- **Recent Documents List Size.** Determines the number of recent files shown in the File menu.
- **Show Tool Tips.** This toggle turns tool tips on and off. Show Tool Tips causes a description to appear over buttons. Again, this uses system resources, and can be disabled.

In the Image Window subsection, the following options are available:

- **Resize Window on Zoom.** This causes the window to exactly fit the image size when you zoom in or out. If the window will be bigger than the screen, the size won't change; scrollbars will be used instead.
- **Show Rulers.** Toggles the display of rulers on and off.
- **Show Statusbar.** Toggles display of the status bar on and off.
- **Speed of the "Marching Ants".** "Marching ants" is the dotted line around selections you have made. The number here is counter-intuitive. It represents the millisecond delay before they are updated. A larger number means that the "ants" move more slowly.
- **Image Title Format.** Determines how the title of the image windows appears in the window manager. The following options are available:
  a. Custom
  b. Standard
  c. Show Zoom Percentage
  d. Show Zoom Ratio
  e. Show Reversed Zoom Ratio
- **Perfect-but-Slow Pointer Tracking.** This improves the method used to track the cursor, but it is slow. This can be left turned off.
- **Disable Cursor Updating.** Normally, the GIMP changes its cursor depending on what tool you are using. This option does use system resources, so it can be disabled.

2.2.4 Environment Settings

The Environment section of the Preferences menu controls how the GIMP uses the system resources, and how it interacts with them. In this section, the following settings are available:

- **Conservative Memory Usage.** When this is unchecked, the GIMP loses speed, but also decreases memory needed.
- **Tile Cache Size.** This changes the amount of space the GIMP can use on the hard drive. When this setting is increased, it prevents the GIMP from swapping to disk.
- **Maximum Image Size.** Determines the maximum size of an image the GIMP can deal with.

- **Install a Color Map.** This is necessary when using the GIMP on an 8-bit X server. If this is not checked, the window manager and other programs will use up all of the colors available to the system, and the GIMP will be useless. Installing a color map ensures that the GIMP has as many colors as it needs. This may make other programs look strange when they are not active, but it will not cause any harm.

- **Colormap Cycling.** This setting is not very obvious. It disables the "marching ants" dotted line; in its place it uses a solid color for the selection line.

- **Thumbnails.** Turns the writing of image previews on and off. This is useful, and should be turned on.

2.2.5 Session Settings

This section controls the Session Management options. The following options are available:

- **Save Window Positions on Exit.** This will keep track of the windows' positions, and place them in the same position when the GIMP is restarted.

- **Clear Saved Window Positions.** This button erases the stored window positions.

- **Always Try to Restore Session.** This toggle makes the GIMP restore the session when it is restarted.

- **Save Device Status on Exit.**

2.2.6 Monitor Settings

This section controls the monitor resolution settings. You can view or set the monitor resolution from either of the following:

- **From X server.** Your resolution will be listed here.

- **Manually.** The resolution can be set manually here.

2.2.7 Directories Settings

This section is very simple. It displays the locations of the various directories that the GIMP uses. The following directories can be changed:

- Temp

- Swap

The following directories are shown in the drop-down menu and can be changed after clicking on the + sign:

- Brushes

- Gradients

- Patterns
- Palettes
- Plug-Ins
- Modules

New directories are added by clicking on the New button. A directory's priority can be raised via the arrow buttons. Directories can be deleted from the list by clicking on the trash can.

2.3 Window Operations

In this section, the various operations for working within an image are discussed. The operations are very easy to learn, and they are used repeatedly. They are all found in the <Image>/View menu. The following window operations are discussed in this section:

- Resizing windows
- Zooming
- Using rulers and guides
- Views

2.3.1 Resizing Windows

Resizing windows is probably one of the first things to learn about working with large images. You must remember that not all window managers are created equally (see Appendix C, "Window Manager Versus the GIMP"). It is difficult to describe the exact process to resize a window because it is not controlled by the GIMP. Usually, but not always, there will be handles on the bottom corners of the window that can be dragged. A single line might appear previewing the size of the new window, or the window may seem to update automatically. If the image is larger than the window, use the scrollbars to move around inside the window. If you have a mouse with three buttons, click and drag with the middle button to pan.

2.3.2 Zooming

Zooming the image can be done several different ways. The first is with the Zoom tool. The second, and probably the most often used, is with the - and = keys (the minus and equal keys, respectively). - will zoom the image out, and = will zoom in. Pressing the 1 key will display the image at real size, or 100%. The zoom factor can also be chosen in the <Image>/View/Zoom menu. The various ratios are displayed there.

Zooming is described by ratios. 1:1 means that one screen pixel is one image pixel. 3:1 means that the image is three times bigger. Nine (3²) pixels represent one image pixel. It is best to zoom in powers of 2 (1:2, 1:1, 2:1, 4:1, and so on). Arbitrary numbers cannot be entered; doing so would be useless[2].

2.3.3 Using Rulers and Guides

Rulers and guides are extremely useful for aligning layers and selections precisely. They are a boon to anyone creating logos for the Web, where precision in drop shadows or different letters is necessary. Ruler and guide operations are found in the <Image>/View menu. There are several options when using rulers and guides:

- **Toggle Rulers On and Off ([Shift+Ctrl+R]).** If you need to use every bit of your screen that is available, this option may be necessary.
- **Toggle Statusbar On and Off ([Shift+Ctrl+S]).** This option turns off the status bar if you need even more screen real estate.
- **Toggle Guides ([Shift+Ctrl+T]).** *Guides* are horizontal or vertical lines placed on an image. Guides are placed by clicking on a ruler and dragging the cursor into the image. Rulers must be toggled on to use them. Guides are blue dotted lines (normally), and they turn red when they are being moved, or have a selection or layer on them.
- **Snap to Guides.** Guides can be toggled to have layers and selections "snap" to them. Snap to Guides will not work when guides are toggled off.

2.3.4 Views

There are several other miscellaneous operations in the View menu:

- **Toggle Selection ([Ctrl+T]).** This turns the "marching ants" on and off.
- **Dot for Dot.** When this is turned on, pixels are used as the units in the rulers. Turned off, the default real unit is used (usually inches).

---

[2] *There is no reason why other graphics programs allow people to do this, since it requires the program to invent pixels to fill in areas. This is a huge waste of resources, and it also gives false information about an image. Zooming in powers of 2 makes sense because at 2:1 zoom, each pixel actually occupies four pixels (a 2 × 2 square) onscreen. At 4:1, each pixel occupies 16 pixels onscreen. The program does not need to invent false information to display the pixels.*

- **Window Info ([Shift+Ctrl+I]).** This operation displays the following information for the current image:

  a. Dimensions of the image in pixels and real units.

  b. Resolution.

  c. Default unit.

  d. Zoom factor, or scale ratio.

  e. Display type (RGB, Grayscale, or Indexed).

  f. Visual class and visual depth. These are determined from the X server itself. It describes the color depth at which it is being displayed (8 bit, 16 bit, 24 bit, or 32 bit).

  g. Shades of Color hasn't been implemented yet.

- **New View.** This is very useful if you are working on a very large image, such as a scanned photograph. This option creates another window that is an exact copy of the existing one. Anything done to the first image will show up on the second. This feature allows you to zoom in on one image to pixel level detail for fine adjustments, while viewing the changes on the other, less magnified, image. Note that changes appear only after the mouse button is released, not as the mouse is drawing on the image.

- **Shrink Wrap ([Ctrl+E]).** This shrinks the window to fit the image exactly. If the image is larger than the screen, it will not work.

2.4   Creating and Editing Selections

There is much to learn about working with selections: There are many different operations for selections. It is best to start by learning the basic selections, and then move on to more complicated ones. Once you have a firm grasp on creating complicated selections, continue on to using the more interesting operations like feathering. The techniques described in this chapter apply to all selection tools. For more detailed information on a specific selection tool, see page 153.

2.4.1 Basic Selection Techniques

Selections in the GIMP are fairly straightforward once you learn the theory behind them. There are two modes for selections:

- **Active Selections.** This is what happens when the selection has been first created. Dragging a selection tool (for example the Rectangular Select) will create an active selection. The cursor then changes to the move arrows although the selection tool is still active. If you move this selection, a floating selection will be created. If you click without moving the selection, the selection will be canceled.

- **Floating Selections.** The floating selection will appear in the Layers and Channels menu (see "Layers and Channels," page 37). Floating selections act like regular layers, except that selections cannot be made inside them. Note that this behavior is different from that of GIMP 1.0. You can draw, erase, and even apply filters inside the floating selection. The floating selection will act as a regular layer until is anchored or made into a new layer.

You can anchor a floating selection by doing any of the following:

- Click inside the floating selection area with a selection tool.
- Click on the Anchor Layer button in the Layers and Channels menu.
- Choose Anchor Layer from the <Image>/Layers menu ([Ctrl+H]).

The floating selection can also become a new layer by itself: Just click on the New Layer button in the Layers and Channels menu.

A good technique to remember is this: Whenever a slightly complicated selection is made, save it to a channel. This helps avoid making the same selection many times (see "Save to Channel," page 30).

2.4.2 Copying and Cutting

Copying and cutting both are very straightforward. Copying is accomplished as follows:

1. Make sure to activate the selection, whether it is in a layer or inside a floating selection.

2. To copy something, click on <Image>/Edit/Copy ([Ctrl+C]). This will copy the selection to the clipboard. Only the current layer that has the selection will be copied. If you wish to copy a composition of the visible layers, choose <Image>/Edit/Copy Visible. This will achieve the same result as though you had merged the visible layers, copied the selection, and then separated them again (see "Merging Layers," page 42).

To cut something, follow these steps:

1. Activate the selection.

2. To cut a selection from a layer, choose <Image>/Edit/Cut ([Ctrl+X]). This will remove the selection from the current layer and place it in the clipboard.

When copying and cutting with images that have transparency, be aware that only the parts of the image with paint on them can be selected to be copied or cut. Any part of the selection with transparency in it will be ignored.

2.4.3 Pasting

Pasting is very straightforward as well. When there is something in the clipboard from copying or cutting, this item can be pasted into the image. Paste the item by clicking on <Image>/Edit/Paste ([Ctrl+V]). Whenever an image is pasted this way, it becomes a floating selection. At this point, it must be anchored to the current layer or become a new layer.

Another option is to use Paste Into, found in the <Image>/Edit menu. This operation allows you to paste into an active selection. Anything outside of this selection will not be visible. When Paste Into is used, a floating selection is created. Because of this, if you already have a floating selection, it is canceled, and the new pasted floating selection is created. When you use Paste Into, the new floating selection must always be anchored into the current layer to achieve the effect. If you create a new layer, all of the paste buffer will appear, not just inside the active selection.

2.4.4 Naming Selections

If you are doing a lot of copying, cutting, and pasting, you will want to take advantage of the Named buffer. This allows you to name your selections so that you can have multiple selections. Copy Named ([Shift+Ctrl+C]), Cut Named ([Shift+Ctrl+X]), and Paste Named ([Shift+Ctrl+V]) are all found in the <Image>/Edit menu.

When you use Copy or Cut Named, a window will pop up asking for the name of the buffer. Enter a name for this selection, and it will be saved in the Named buffer.

When Paste Named is used, a window will pop up with the listing of everything in the Named buffer. Click on the Paste, Paste Into, or Paste as New button to insert it into the image. Click on Delete to remove the selection from the Named buffer.

The last Cut or Copy Named is also placed in the regular buffer, so the regular Paste will work to insert it into the image.

2.4.5 Advanced Selections

Using more complicated selections can be difficult. There are many different options available with each mouse-click.

For all selection tools, keystrokes and mouse-clicks must be done in this order:

1. Hold down the Shift and/or Ctrl key(s) before clicking the mouse button.
   a. Use Shift+click to create a union between the existing selection and the new one (see Figure 2.8). The cursor will show a + sign at the bottom to represent this.

b. Use Ctrl+click to leave the difference between the selections (see Figure 2.9). The cursor will show a - sign at the bottom to represent this.

c. Hold down both keys and click to create the intersection between the two selections (see Figure 2.10). The cursor will show a ∩ sign at the bottom to represent this. (For the Bezier Select and Intelligent Scissors, this must be done while clicking inside the chosen area in editing mode.)

2. Click the mouse button.

3. Release the key(s) and drag the mouse to create a selection.

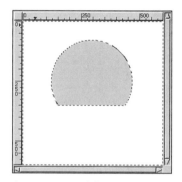

Figure 2.8 *A union (Shift+click) between a rectangular selection and a circular one.*

Figure 2.9 *A difference (Ctrl+click) between the same rectangular selection and a circular one.*

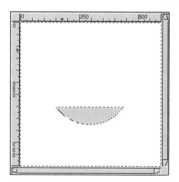

Figure 2.10 *An intersection (Shift+Ctrl+click) between the rectangular selection and a circular one.*

The Rectangular and Elliptical Select (see page 154) tools also use the keys (Shift, Ctrl or both) to constrain the shape of the selection.

To constrain the shape and replace current selections, follow these steps:

1. Click the mouse button.

2. Press the key (Shift or Ctrl).

3. Drag the mouse to create the proper selection.

To use both effects at once, follow these steps:

1. Hold down the required keys (Shift, Ctrl, or both).
2. Click the mouse button.
3. Release the keys.
4. Press and hold the required keys for the constraining effect.
5. The mouse can then be dragged for the needed selection.

If you make a wrong selection, it is possible to cancel the selection while you are still dragging. Hold down the right mouse button before releasing the left mouse button to undo the new selection, and then release the right mouse button.

To create selections around complicated objects, it is usually best to use the Intelligent Scissors tool to select the general shape of the image. Once the general shape is selected, convert it to a Bezier curve for fine-tuning. A new feature in GIMP 1.2 is Paths. Paths give much greater control of Bezier curves.

If the object is quite complicated, and has a busy background, it will probably be necessary to zoom in very close. Then use the Freehand Select tool with the Shift and Ctrl key combinations to get every pixel right. If you do not need extreme precision, use the <Image>/Select/Feather to smooth the transition from the border to the background.

2.4.6 Invert

Invert is very useful when working with complicated selections. This option inverts the active selection so that anything that was not selected before is selected, and vice versa. Invert is found in <Image>/Select, and its hotkey is [Ctrl+I].

2.4.7 All and None

All and None are very straightforward. All ([Ctrl+A]) selects the entire current layer. None ([Shift+Ctrl+A]) cancels any active selection. Both of these operations are located in the <Image>/Select menu.

2.4.8 Float

Float creates a floating selection from an active selection. This option is used when you need a floating selection, but do not want to move the active selection that has been created. If there is an existing floating selection, it is canceled, and the active selection replaces it as the floating selection. Float is found in the <Image>/Select menu, and its hotkey is [Shift+Ctrl+L].

2.4.9 Sharpen

Sharpen removes the anti-aliasing from an active selection. When an elliptical selection is made, it is always slightly feathered, as seen in Figure 2.11. Sharpen removes this, resulting in an appearance such as that in Figure 2.12. This tool is useful if you have feathered a selection too much, and want to start over. Sharpen is found in <Image>/Select, and its hotkey is [Shift+Ctrl+H].

Figure 2.11 *A regular elliptical selection. Note the smooth edge.*

Figure 2.12 *The same selection after being sharpened. Note the jagged edge.*

2.4.10 Border

Border replaces the active selection's outer edges with a border. A window will pop up asking for the border's size. When you are using borders, you must remember that it takes the active selection's edges as the center of the border. If you make a border 10 pixels wide as in Figure 2.13, it will go inward 10 and outward 10 pixels. Note that this is a smooth transition. To get a sharp border, use <Image>/Select/Sharpen ([Shift+Ctrl+H]). Border is found in the <Image>/Select menu.

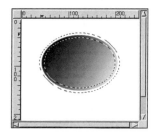

Figure 2.13 *A selection with a border size of 10.*

2.4.11 Feather

Feather does the opposite of sharpen. It gradually fades out a selection by a specific amount. This is very useful when editing scanned photographs to make pasted parts look more natural. It makes them fit into different backgrounds much more easily. Feather is found in <Image>/Select, and its hotkey is [Shift+Ctrl+F].

Figure 2.14 *A selection around a face in a photograph, feathered to look more natural, and less computer-generated.*

2.4.12 Grow and Shrink

Grow and Shrink change the size of active selections. They do this radially, so rectangular selections, or others with sharp corners, will lose the defined corners when Grow is used. Both Grow and Shrink are found in the <Image>/Select menu.

2.4.13   QuickMask

QuickMask is a new addition to the GIMP, and it makes working with selections much easier. The techniques here are very similar to the next section, Save to Channel, because that's how it was done in the days of yore. QuickMask mode is simply a shortcut to using channels.

To enter QuickMask mode, click on the red square at the bottom-left corner of the image window. This will place a red screen over the image that represents an unselected area. A selected area is chosen by using drawing tools. White paint represents the selected area; black paint indicates that it is not selected. Shades of gray represent partial selection. This mode gives very precise control over selections, since regular tools, filters, and scripts can be used to delicately feather selections.

To return to normal mode, simply click on the square with dotted line in the lower-left corner of the image window, and the QuickMask will be turned into a selection.

QuickMask is the most important part of this section on selections. It is an invaluable tool when creating images from scanned photographs. Look at Figures 2.15 and 2.16 to see QuickMask in action.

Figure 2.15   *The selection mask of a Porsche.*

Figure 2.16 *Viewing the selection mask of a Porsche in QuickMask mode. Note that the background seems very dull.*

2.4.14 Save to Channel and Channel to Selection

Save to Channel, and its counterpart, Channel to Selection, require some basic knowledge of channels. See "Channels Menu" on page 48 for more information.

Save to Channel takes the active selection and copies it to a channel for future use. In the Channels menu, it is displayed as a selection mask. Black appears on unselected portions. Where there is white paint, the selection is fully selected. Shades of gray represent partial selection. This selection mask can be edited with regular painting tools. The color of this selection mask can be changed by double-clicking on the channel name in the Layers and Channels menu, then clicking on the color box on the right.

When you are satisfied with the selection, right-click on the name of the selection mask in the Channels menu (see Figure 2.17) and choose Channel to Selection ([Ctrl+S]). This is one of the more advanced operations, but it becomes necessary when working with scanned photos. The regular selection tools do not have enough features to create complicated selections in order to work with photos.

Figure 2.17 *Using a selection mask allows for greater control with selections.*

2.4.15 Select by Color

Select by Color allows you to select regions based on their color. The interface to select by color is easy to learn:

■ The window that pops up shows a selection mask of the image.

■ Selected areas are white, unselected areas are black, and gray areas are partially selected.

■ Areas are selected by clicking on the colors in the image.

■ The fuzziness threshold slider at the bottom determines how much color change is required for the selection to end.

■ On the right hand side are the controls which determine how the selection acts:

   a. Replace

   b. Add (union)

   c. Subtract (difference)

   d. Intersect

Hold down the Shift and/or Ctrl key(s) while clicking to override these options.

2.4.16 Clear and Fill

Clear and Fill are simple tools for working with selections and entire layers. Clear ([Ctrl+K]) removes all paint from a selection or, if there is no selection, the entire active layer. If there are layers or Alpha channels, the selection becomes transparent. If there is no Alpha channel, the selection is set to the background color. The Fill ([Ctrl+.]) operation adds paint to the current selection. The selection is always the background color even if there are layers or an Alpha channel. Fill is therefore useless when working with a flat image without an Alpha channel because it has the same effect as Clear, but it has no hotkey. Clear and Fill are both found in the <Image>/Edit menu.

2.4.17 Stroke

Stroke is an interesting operation. It uses the current brush and foreground color to draw a line wherever there is a selection edge. This is useful for drawing simple rectangles, ellipses, and curves with the selection tools. Experiment with different brushes and tools, especially with different brushes and the spacing for them (see page 171). Interesting effects can be created using selection masks as well. Stroke is found in the <Image>/Edit menu.

2.5 Miscellaneous Operations

The following operations do not fit into any specific category, but they are all useful shortcuts. Shortcuts are abundant in the GIMP (you just need to learn how to use them to save time).

2.5.1 Printing from the GIMP

In the PC world, support for PostScript printers is rather poor, and most people do not have printers that support PostScript. There is a free PostScript interpreter, GhostScript, which has support for most printers. Most Linux distributions come with this interpreter installed. This section assumes you have a PostScript printer, GhostScript installed and configured properly, or a PCL printer.

Printing from the GIMP is fairly straightforward:

1. Click on <Image>/File/Print to get to the Print menu. There are several options presented in this menu. In the top-right corner is the destination for the image. There are normally two choices:

    a. File

    b. Lp (line printer)

    Detailed options for each of these are found in the Setup button to the right. If you have a printer supported in the Drivers section, definitely use it. You may be able to use additional features provided by the printer driver, such as resolution or media type. If you do not have a supported printer, you should use the generic PostScript Level 1 or 2 drivers.

1a. When using the PostScript drivers, an option is available to use a PPD (PostScript Printer Description) file. This allows you to include specific instructions for your printer. If you have a PostScript printer, you can obtain the PPD file in any of the following ways:

a. Your vendor may provide you with a PPD file.

b. They are available from Adobe by sending an email message to `ps-file-server@adobe.com` with the line "help".

c. You can check on their FTP server at `ftp://ftp.adobe.com/pub/adobe/printerdrivers`. There is a Linux-specific package found at `ftp://ftp.debian.org/debian/dists/stable/main/source/text/ppp-gs_1.1.orig.tar.gz`. This package is provided by Debian, but can be installed on any Linux system. The PPD files are found in the ppd/ directory when you decompress the package. There is no compilation needed, but you will have to run the install script to configure it for your system.

Note that there is relatively little support for PPD files; you may be stuck using the basic PostScript emulation provided by GhostScript.

2. After you have configured your printer, you will be presented with several options for the output of the image. Not all options will be available for each printer. If there are no choices presented for a certain option this does not indicate a problem.

a. **Media Size.** This option refers to the size of paper that the image is being printed on (Letter, Legal, A4, and so on).

b. **Media Type.** Media Type refers to the type of paper used (Plain, Premium, Glossy, or Transparency).

c. **Media Source.** If your printer supports this option, you can choose which tray of paper to use.

d. **Orientation.** This option determines the placement of the image on the paper. Auto will determine the best orientation for the image by comparing the size of the image to the size of the paper, or it can be set manually as Portrait or Landscape.

e. **Resolution.** Resolution determines the quality of the image being printed. Higher resolution results in slower printing, and possibly using more ink or toner. Output Type determines whether this is to be printed in black and white, or in color.

f. **Image Scaling.** Controlled by a slider bar, the scaling can be controlled by percentage or by ppi (pixels per inch). A monitor's resolution is usually about 72ppi. Higher ppi means better-quality images.

g. **Brightness.** Finding a satisfactory brightness value will require trial and error; there is no way of determining it before printing.

h. **Layout of the Image on the Paper.** This option is controlled by a point-and-click interface. The dark square represents the image, and the black line represents the paper size. There is no exact control over the position of the image.

2.5.2   Mailing Images from the GIMP

If you are not going to be printing your image from home, or you need to send it to a client, the Mail Image plug-in is very useful and easy to use. It assumes you have a working Internet connection and email setup on your system. The email address of the person is entered in the To: field. A subject can be entered as well. A brief comment can be entered if needed. The filename is important. The GIMP automatically converts the image depending on the filename. Be careful when you are using this feature: If the save fails, you will end up sending a blank email. Make sure the image type is correct for the format, and that you have flattened or merged the layers if needed. The last option is the format in which to send the attachment. MIME is the best, but if the recipient has an older email program, you may have to use uuencoding. This plug-in is found in <Image>/File/Mail Image.

2.5.3   Taking Screenshots

Screenshots can be very useful, especially if you are writing a book about an image manipulation program. It is entirely possible that there are other uses for it as well. The Screenshot tool is found in <Toolbox>/File/Acquire/Screenshot.

There are two main choices for taking a screenshot:

- Grab a window
- Grab the whole screen.

If you are taking a screenshot only of a specific window, you also have the option of not including decorations. Decorations are anything the window manager has added, such as a titlebar or handles for resizing the window. When taking full screenshots, it can be useful to show a menu's contents. The delay allows this to take place. It can be set to whatever time is needed.

To take a screenshot:

1. Select the options you need, then click Grab.
   a. If you are just grabbing a single window, click on the window you want.
   b. If you are taking a full screenshot, click on the Grab button, and the window will disappear. You now have time to adjust the screen as needed.
2. With all screenshots, it will beep twice before taking the screenshot, and then the new image will appear. Note that the mouse cursor is not shown when taking screenshots [3].

---

[3] *If you encounter any problems with colors distorting in screenshots, try running your X server at a different bit depth with this command:startx -- -bpp 16*

Some older distributions have problems with 24bpp screenshots.

Figure 2.18   *A screenshot of the screenshot window set to grab the full screen after four seconds.*

2.5.4 Tab Completion

The GIMP's Save and Open windows allows you to use tab completion similar to that found in the bash shell. If you type in partial filenames, as seen in Figure 2.19, and then press Tab, it will try to complete the filename. If there is more than one file that matches, it will only display the files that match. This is very useful if you are dealing with many different files in a directory.

Note that the window does not show hidden files. To view them, enter a period, then press Tab, and the hidden files will appear.

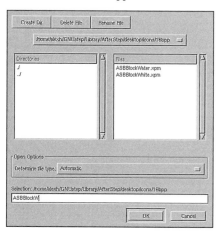

Figure 2.19   *The File Open window displaying only the matching filenames using tab completion.*

3
Layers and Channels

Layers and channels are very important in the GIMP for doing more advanced image processing. If you have worked with other graphics programs before, you may be familiar with the concepts of layers and channels. If you are not familiar with these simple concepts, by the end of this chapter you will be able to work with them easily.

Layers work like pieces of painted glass being laid on top of one another. They can contain transparent areas, opaque areas, and semi-transparent areas. With fully opaque areas, you will only see the top layer. With transparent areas, you will be able to see through to the next layers, until there is an opaque section you cannot see through. With semi-transparent layers, you will see a combination of the layers, like looking through colored glass.

Channels represent the color components of an image. They are 8-bit "layers." Because each channel is 8 bits, that means that there are 256 possible shades in each channel. The following list details the types of channels that the GIMP utilizes:

- **RGB.** These images all have Red, Green, and Blue channels. Therefore there are 16.8 million (256 × 256 × 256) possible color combinations.

- **Grayscale.** These images have only one channel. This means that there is a maximum of 256 shades of gray.

- **Indexed.** These images work slightly differently. They only have one channel, so there is a maximum of 256 colors, but they can be taken from any of the 16.8 million possible colors.

- **Selection Masks/QuickMask.** These are newer types of channels. Selection Masks are used to save complicated selections. They allow you to work with selections using the drawing tools found in the Toolbox.

3.1 The Layers Window and Channels Window

The first thing we'll cover in this chapter is the layout of the Layers Window and Channels window. If you have used Photoshop before, this will be very familiar to you.

3.1.1 Layout of the Layers Window

Location   <Image>/Layers menu

The layout of this menu (see Figure 3.1) is fairly simple. At the top, the name and thumbnail of the image are shown (1). These two double as a drop-down box for selecting images. The Auto button (2) will automatically display any changes made to a layer. If this is left off, the thumbnails will not be updated. Next, the mode of the layer is shown (3). More information about modes is provided on page 44.

There is a Keep Transparent button (4), and an Opacity slider bar (5). For more information about transparency, see page 46. In the middle of the window, all the layers are shown. The eyeball icons (6) mean that the layer is currently visible. Layer masks (see page 47) are shown to the right of the layers (7). The cross icons (8) mean that the layer is linked for moving (see page 41). Along the bottom of this window are the icons for editing layers (9). The currently selected layer is highlighted in blue (10).

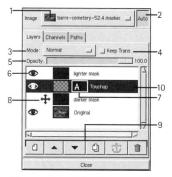

Figure 3.1   *The Layers window.*

3.1.2   Layout of the Channels Window

The Channels notebook page (see Figure 3.2) is accessed by clicking on the Channels tab (1) in the Layers and Channels window. If you are working on an RGB image, each color channel is shown here (2). Again, the eyeball icon (3) represents that the channel is being shown. Any additional channels that have been created are displayed here (4). The icons along the bottom (5) are for creating, deleting, or moving these channels.

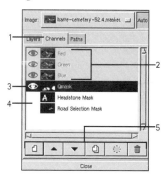

Figure 3.2   *The Channels window.*

3.2 Layer Operations

The operations found in this menu are extremely useful for working on any type of image. It is very helpful to know all the options in this menu. The layer to be edited is selected by clicking on the thumbnail of the image. It will then be highlighted in blue.

3.2.1 Viewing Individual Layers

A useful operation in the Layers menu (see Figure 3.3) is the ability to view certain layers and hide others. You do this by clicking on the eyeball icons. Any combinations of layers can be turned on and off. Note that changing a layer's visibility does not change which layer is currently selected. If you have many layers, and only want to view a specific one, hold down the Shift key while clicking the eyeball icon. All other layers will be hidden. To show them all again, just hold down the Shift key and click the eyeball again.

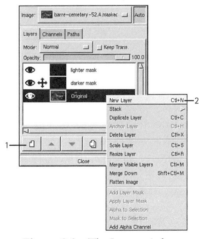

Figure 3.3 *The Layers window.*

3.2.2 Adding and Deleting Layers

Once you begin to get into more complicated image manipulation, you will want to add and delete layers as you work.

3.2.2.1 Adding Layers

There are several different methods you can use to add a layer:

- Click on the New Layer icon (1).
- Right-click on the layer name or thumbnail, and choose New Layer (2).
- Press the hotkey [Ctrl+N] when the Layers window is active.

When you have chosen one of the three preceding methods to add a layer, a new window similar to Figure 3.4 will pop up. This presents several options for the new layer:

- **Layer Name**
- **Layer Width**
- **Layer Height**
- **Units.** This is especially useful to use the percentage of the image size.
- **Layer Fill Type.** This determines what paint is used to fill the layer.

Figure 3.4   *The New Layer menu.*

3.2.2.2   Deleting Layers

Deleting layers is much simpler than adding layers. You can do either of the following:

- Right-click on the layer name or thumbnail, and choose Delete Layer.
- Press the hotkey [Ctrl+X] while the Layers window is active.

3.2.3   Moving Layers

When dealing with multiple layers, it is often necessary to move them. This is done via the Move tool (see page 158). You can move layers by simply clicking and dragging them. The outline of the layer is shown with a yellow and black dotted line. This operation is straightforward unless you are dealing with transparency.

When moving a layer with transparency, you must click on areas that contain paint. Paint on a specific area is indicated by the cursor becoming a cross like the Move tool's icon. If you do not click on an area with paint, the next layer down that contains paint will be selected and moved. When this is going to happen, the cursor turns into a hand icon. If there are no layers containing paint in that position, the cursor becomes an arrow. If you hold down the Shift key while clicking with the Move tool, it will force a move of the active layer, rather than choosing the next layer down with paint.

Guides can be used to precisely align layers. See page 21 for more information.

3.2.4 Resizing and Scaling Layers

The ability to resize and scale layers gives very precise control over the alignment of combinations of layers. These operations are very similar to resizing and scaling the entire image (see pages 65 and 66). *Resizing* a layer only operates on an image's borders. The contents do not change, so parts could be cut off. *Scaling* a layer actually changes the contents of the layer.

To resize a layer, follow these steps:

1. Right-click on the layer name or thumbnail.
2. Click on Resize Layer [Ctrl+R] when the Layers window is active.
3. Enter the new parameters for the layer:
   - New Width
   - New Height
   - Units
   - X ratio
   - Y ratio
   - X offset
   - Y offset

   The X and Y offset can also be controlled by clicking and dragging the box with the mouse.
4. Click OK.

To scale a layer, follow these steps:

1. Right-click on the layer name or thumbnail.
2. Click on Scale Layer [Ctrl+S] when the Layers window is active.
3. Enter the new parameters for the layer:
   - New Width
   - New Height
   - Units
   - X ratio
   - Y ratio
4. Click OK.

3.2.5 Merging Layers

Merging layers is useful when you are ready to put together your final product. Merge Visible Layers takes two or more layers that are visible (with the eye icon) and merges them into one. This technique is used when you have many layers that need to be consolidated, but you do not want to make a single-layer image because more work may be needed. This is the operation to use if you are making a GIF animation, or an image with transparency. When you choose to merge visible layers, a window pops up that determines the size of the new layer.

There are several ways to access the Merge Visible Layers operation:

- Right-click on the layer name or thumbnail, and choose Merge Visible Layers.
- Click on <Image>/Layers/Merge Visible Layers.
- Press the hotkey [Ctrl+M] when the image or the Layers window is active.

The following choices are available for merging:

- **Expanded as Necessary.** This option creates a layer just large enough to contain all of the merged layers.
- **Clipped to Image.** This creates a layer big enough to contain all parts of the layers, as long as they are inside the image borders.
- **Clipped to Bottom Layer.** This choice constrains the new layer size to the bottommost layer that is being merged.

3.2.5.1 Merge Down

A new feature in GIMP 1.2, Merge Down merges the active layer with the layer immediately below it.

There are several ways to access the Merge Down operation:

- Right-click on the layer name or thumbnail, and choose Merge Down.
- Press the hotkey [Shift+Ctrl+M] when the image or the Layers window is active.

3.2.6 Flattening Images

Flattening images will be one of the last steps of completing an image. This operation takes all of the image's layers and merges them into one final layer. It you want to get rid of Alpha in your image, this is the way to do it[1]. If you do not have an opaque background, the current background color will be used.

Flattening an image can be done in one of two ways:

- Right-click on the layer name or thumbnail, and click Flatten Image.
- Click on <Image>/Layers/Flatten Image.

---

[1] *Most file formats do not support layers or alpha, including JPEGs. Flattening the image is necessary to save images in these formats.*

3.2.7 Modes

Previously, when layers have been described, there has been no mention of *modes*.
Layers were simply described as slides stacking up on top of each other. This
definition was used because the layers were using the default setting, *Normal
mode*. There are many other modes as well, and they do not apply solely to layers.
Paint can work this way as well, as seen in the Brushes dialog box (see page 172).

There are many modes available:

- Normal
- Dissolve
- Behind
- Multiply
- Divide
- Screen
- Overlay
- Difference
- Addition
- Subtract
- Darken Only
- Lighten Only
- Hue
- Saturation
- Color
- Value

3.2.7.1 Normal

This is the default mode. As previously described, it acts as if each layer is a piece
of painted glass. If the paint is fully opaque, nothing below it is shown. If it is
partially opaque, the paint on the layers underneath are shown.

3.2.7.2 Dissolve

Dissolve mode uses transparency to create its effect. It acts similarly to normal
mode in fully opaque areas, but in semi-transparent areas, it uses a noise effect.
In fully opaque areas, pixels are fully opaque. In semi-transparent areas, pixels are
either fully transparent or fully opaque. This makes the layer look spotty and of
low quality.

3.2.7.3 Behind

Behind mode can only place paint on transparent areas, giving the illusion of
painting behind the existing paint on the layer. Semi-transparent areas combine
normally.

3.2.7.4 Multiply

In Multiply mode, the pixel color combines to decrease the brightness of the
paint below. This acts like two slides being projected through the same machine.
Any black pixels in Multiply mode become fully opaque, and white pixels
become fully transparent. Bright colors will affect pixels slightly, and dark colors
will affect pixels more. This attribute of the Multiply mode makes it perfect for
creating delicate shadows.

3.2.7.5 Divide

Divide mode works similarly to the Dodge tool. Mathematically speaking, each
color value in the bottom channel is multiplied by 256, then divided by the value
for the top layer. This means that black or very dark pixels in the top layer will set

the color to white. White or very light paint in the top layer will not effect the image. Grey pixels will lighten the color below.

3.2.7.6 Screen

Screen is the opposite of Multiply. It bleaches the image, and always makes it brighter than the original image. This is analogous to aiming two slide projectors at the same point. Any black pixels become fully transparent, and white pixels become fully opaque. This mode is well suited for creating reflection effects.

3.2.7.7 Overlay

Overlay emphasizes shadows and highlights in an image. Black pixels will affect shadow areas by making them darker. White pixels will affect highlight areas by making them brighter. Midtone areas are tinted with the paint color. Overlay works well for superimposing text on images.

3.2.7.8 Difference

Difference mode can produce some dramatic results. It compares the brightness of the pixels in the image. The resulting pixel is the absolute value of the difference between the two pixels. For example, if you have a pixel that is R:80 G:96 B:255 (light blue) on top of a R:255 G:100 B:100 (light red) pixel, the result would be $|(80\text{-}255)|=175$ $|(96\text{-}100)|=4$ $|(255\text{-}100)|=155$, or purple.

3.2.7.9 Addition

Addition adds the RGB values of the two layers together, to a maximum of 255 for each channel. This means that black pixels have no effect on the image (transparent), and white pixels are fully opaque. This is similar to Screen mode, but Addition depends more on the lower layer.

3.2.7.10 Subtract

Subtract is the opposite of Addition. It subtracts the RGB values of the upper layer from the lower layer. This means that black pixels behave as if they are transparent, but white pixels behave like they are black. Any colors on the upper layer tint the lower layer with their complementary color.

3.2.7.11 Darken Only

This mode will only affect the lower layer when the pixels in the upper layer are darker. This means that white pixels are normally transparent (very few images have perfectly white pixels), and black pixels are fully opaque. This effect is achieved by comparing the values in each RGB channel, and using the smaller values for the pixel.

3.2.7.12 Lighten Only

Lighten Only is the opposite of Darken Only. This only affects pixels on the lower layer that are lighter than those of the upper layer. This means that white pixels are opaque and black pixels are transparent. Darker colors won't affect the image unless it is very dark. Lighter colors will usually be opaque. This effect is achieved by comparing the values in each RGB channel, and using the larger values for the pixel.

3.2.7.13 Hue

Hue mode uses the upper layer's hue value to paint on the lower layer. This does not affect the saturation or value of the layer. This mode is perfect for tinting pictures.

3.2.7.14 Saturation

This mode affects only the saturation values of pixels. It generally affects the "purity" of the colors. Painting with higher saturation values enhances the base color of the layer. For instance, if you have an image with pastel colors and use a Saturation layer with high saturation values, this will make the colors more pure, or brighter. If you use low saturation values, it will remove the colors from the image, making it look more like a grayscale image.

3.2.7.15 Color

This mode affects both the hue and saturation of the lower layer. It is used to tint areas without affecting their brightness values.

3.2.7.16 Value

This mode affects only the value of pixels. It does not affect the color values at all. This mode is good for adjusting under-exposed or over-exposed areas in photographs.

3.2.8 Transparency and Alpha Channels

There are a few caveats when working with transparency and Alpha channels in layers. Consider the following:

- **The Opacity slider bar.** This controls the opacity for the entire layer. If there is semi-transparent paint on the layer, it becomes even more transparent. Opacity can range from 0 (fully transparent) to 100 (fully opaque).

- **Keep Transparent.** This toggles the transparent area between drawable and not drawable. If this option is turned on, you will not be able to draw on transparent areas. It is still possible to draw on semi-transparent areas with this option. Semi-transparent areas will retain their Alpha values; only the color will be changed. Any area may be erased as usual. This option is perfect for changing the color of a text layer, or using the Blend tool on a shape.

- **The background layer.** This layer is special because it cannot use transparency or layer masks until it has had an Alpha channel added to it. However, the overall transparency can be changed using the slider bar. Also, the background layer must be the *bottom* layer until the Alpha channel is added. If there is no Alpha channel, it cannot be raised or lowered.

3.2.9 Layer Masks

Layer masks provide greater control over opacity in an image. They control the opacity in a layer by representing it as a grayscale drawable. Black areas are fully transparent and white areas are fully opaque. Gray shades are semi-transparent. The advantage to using layer masks is that you can use tools, filters, and scripts to control the opacity rather than just using the eraser.

To create a layer mask, follow these steps:

1. Right-click on the layer name or thumbnail.
2. Click on Add Layer Mask.
3. Choose one of the following options to initialize the mask:
   a. White (Full Opacity)
   b. Black (Full Transparency)
   c. Layer's Alpha Channel

   Using the layer's Alpha channel is best so that there is no confusion between the transparency in the image layer and the transparency created by the layer mask.

Working with layer masks is straightforward. They are simple 8-bit channels that represent the Alpha channel in the image. By default, your image will still be shown when working with the layer mask. The part that is active for drawing is represented by a white border around its thumbnail. This way, you can easily alternate between editing the mask or the layer. To view the layer mask and not the layer, hold down the Alt key while clicking on the layer mask thumbnail. The layer mask will now become visible, and a green border will appear around its thumbnail. If you wish to hide the layer mask temporarily, hold down the Ctrl key while clicking on the layer mask thumbnail. A red border will appear around it. Note that these two modes can be on at the same time, but viewing the layer mask has higher priority, so that is the effect that is shown.

Anything that can be done to a grayscale image can be done to a layer mask. This includes applying filters and Script-Fu. Layer masks are well suited for editing scanned photographs where certain elements need to be cut and pasted. Make heavy use of the Airbrush and Convolver tools here. The Blur filters can also work well here.

Once you have a satisfactory layer mask, it can be applied. When a layer mask is applied, it adds the Alpha channel to the image and is then deleted. Any information outside the visible area is lost. If you are unhappy with the layer mask, it can be discarded.

To apply or discard a layer mask:

1. Right-click on the layer name or thumbnail.
2. Click on Apply Layer Mask.
3. Apply or discard the layer mask.
   a. To apply the layer mask, click on the Apply button.
   b. To discard the layer mask, click the Discard button.

3.3   The Channels Window

The Channels window is a part of the Layers and Channels window. It has two main uses:

- **Editing specific color channels.** This is used for working in certain color channels only. It is very useful for restoring scanned photographs or adding artistic effects to images.

- **Editing selection masks.** This is similar to layer masks, but these deal with selections instead of opacity. This is also very useful in working with scanned photographs.

3.3.1   Working in Specific Channels

The advantage to using channels is that you can edit and view them independently. To view individual channels, click on the eyeball icon beside the channel. Working in individual channels is also very easy to do. Selected channels are highlighted in blue. To select or deselect a channel, simply click on it near the thumbnail or channel name.

There are two modes for working with channels:

- **RGB Channels.** In this mode, any combination of the Red, Green, or Blue channels can be selected. Note that these control the channels in the active layer that is highlighted in the Layers menu.

- **Selection Mask.** In this mode, only one selection mask can be selected. There are no active layers in this mode. This is for working with selections.

3.3.2   Channel Operations

There are several operations available when working with channels. They are only available in the Selection Mask mode. The Channels window is pictured in Figure 3.2.

- **New Channel.** A new channel can be created by using any of the following methods:

  a. Right-clicking on the channel names or thumbnails and choosing New Channel

  b. Using the hotkey [Ctrl+N]

  c. Clicking on the New Channel button

  A window will appear prompting you for a name, opacity, and tint. It will be initialized with a 50% opacity value and tint of black by default. You can change the tint by clicking on the colored square.

- **Raise/Lower Channel.** Channels can be raised and lowered by using any of the following methods:

  a. Right-clicking on the channel name or thumbnail, and choosing Raise Layer or Lower Layer

  b. By using the hotkeys [Ctrl+F] and [Ctrl+B]

  c. The icons in the Channels window

- **Duplicate Channel.** Selection mask channels can be duplicated by using any of the following methods:

  a. Right-clicking a channel name or thumbnail, and clicking Duplicate Channel

  b. Using the hotkey [Ctrl+C]

  c. Clicking on the Duplicate Channel icon

- **Delete Channel.** Channels can be deleted by using any of the following methods:

  a. Right-clicking a channel name or thumbnail, and clicking Delete Channel

  b. Using the hotkey [Ctrl+X]

  c. Clicking on the Delete Channel icon

- **New Name/Opacity/Tint.** Double-click on the layer name to change its name, opacity, or tint. By default, new channels are initialized to 50% opacity, but you may want to change this. The tint is changed by clicking on the colored square (set to black by default).

3.3.3 Selection Masks

The main reason to use channels is to work with *selection masks*. These are 8-bit (grayscale) representations of a selection. A black pixel represents an unselected area. White pixels represent fully selected pixels. Shades of gray represent partial selections. The advantage to working with selection masks is that you can control the selections with a channel. Any tool, filter, or script that can affect grayscale images can be used on it.

If you have an existing selection, it can be converted to a channel with the Save to Channel operation (see page 30).

There are a few useful techniques to keep in mind when working with selection masks:

- Use fuzzy brushes and tools to create smooth selection lines.
- Try viewing the channel and changing its opacity for more control. Transparent areas are selected, black areas are unselected.

After you have edited the channel, there are two ways to convert it back to a selection:

- Right-click a channel name or thumbnail, and click Channel to Selection.
- Use the hotkey [Ctrl+S].

4
Image Operations

If you have a scanned image, or you have drawn an image that needs tweaking, the Image menu has many useful operations. These operations are performed on the active layer or selection. Some operations like RGB or Indexed are performed on the entire image.

4.1　Colors

The Colors menu involves operations that adjust the color balance in an image. These are very useful for improving the quality of scanned images. Operations in this menu are often the first used on photographs.

4.1.1　Equalize

Equalize fixes the color in an image if it is too bright or too dark. It will find the lightest color in an image and make it white, and it will find the darkest color and make it black. Equalize should not be used on images that are of good quality, but rather ones have a lot of light or dark areas. This operation may end up decreasing the quality of the picture, and additional adjustments are usually required. Figures 4.1 and 4.2 provide a (somewhat insufficient) grayscale example of Equalize.

Figure 4.1　*The original picture.*　　　**Figure 4.2**　*The image after it has been equalized.*

4.1.2 Invert

The *Invert* operation is very simple. It inverts the colors in the active layer or selection. The black pixels are changed to white and white pixels are changed to black. Colors become their opposite on the palette. Figures 4.3 and 4.4 give an example of the Invert operation.

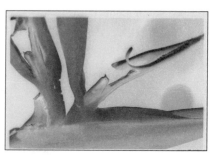

Figure 4.3 *The original picture.*   **Figure 4.4** *The inverted image.*

4.1.3 Posterize

Posterize changes the image to look like an indexed image, without changing the image type (see "Image Types," page 62). The number of levels entered in the dialog box determines the number of colors for each channel. Posterize affects grayscale and RGB images in several different ways:

- For grayscale images, the number of levels determines the number of shades of gray.
- For RGB images, the number of levels determines the number of shades in each channel (see "Channels," page 38). This means that for a level of 2, there are $2 \times 2 \times 2 = 8$ colors in an image.

This operation is not normally used to improve a scanned image because it does not produce accurate colors. It is usually used to add an interesting effect to an image. Figures 4.5 and 4.6 give an example of Posterize.

Figure 4.5 *The original picture.*   **Figure 4.6** *The picture after eight levels of posterization have been applied.*

4.1.4 Threshold

Threshold displays a histogram representing the brightness in an image, as shown in Figure 4.7. The greater the number of pixels with a certain intensity, the higher the bar at that position. Brightness is selected by dragging the mouse over the histogram (1), or entered with the keyboard. It is best to fine-tune the selection by entering values in the dialog boxes (2) above the graph. This creates a true/false image, in which each selected brightness is white, and each unselected one is black. (This operation can produce interesting images, but it is usually more useful to create a copy of the image layer and use Threshold on that.)

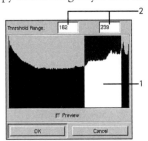

Figure 4.7 *An example of a threshold and the histogram.*

4.1.5 Color Balance

Color Balance is used for fine-tuning the color levels in your image. There are three sliders for each of the three brightness levels in the Color Balance menu:

- Cyan/Red
- Magenta/Green
- Yellow/Blue

You can adjust the fine-tuning by entering values in the dialog boxes above the sliders. Moving all three sliders towards the CMY (Cyan, Magenta, Yellow) colors will darken the image, whereas moving the sliders toward the RGB colors will lighten the image.

The option buttons at the bottom of the menu let you choose which pixels to adjust by their brightness:

- **Shadows.** Adjusts only the darkest pixels.
- **Midtones.** Adjusts the middle pixels.
- **Highlights.** Adjusts only the lightest pixels.

Preserve Luminosity keeps the intensity, or brightness, for each pixel fixed, which can produce some strange images when adjusting the color balance by large amounts.

4.1.6 Brightness and Contrast

Adjusting the brightness and contrast in a scanned image is very useful. The *Brightness* and *Contrast* sliders are centered at zero, and can be adjusted either way. Either can be fine-tuned by entering values with the keyboard. This operation is very straightforward. Figures 4.8 through 4.11 offer visual examples.

Figure 4.8 *The original picture.*

Figure 4.9 *The image after brightness and contrast have both been increased by 90.*

Figure 4.10 *The image after brightness is set to 90, and contrast to −90.*

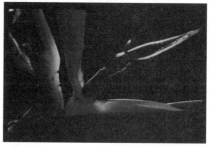

Figure 4.11 *The image after brightness is set to −90, and contrast to 90.*

4.1.7 Hue and Saturation

The Hue and Saturation operation works in the HSV model (see "Color Models," page 5). It adjusts the Hue, Saturation, and Lightness (Value) of an image. By default, the Master option button is checked, which means the operation is performed on all colors. Single colors can be adjusted by clicking on their option buttons. Note that adjustments to the Master option button and specific colors can be done at the same time.

The following options are available with this operation:

- **Hue.** A slider that rotates the color. It can be rotated from −180 to 180 degrees. 0 degrees is the default setting.

- **Lightness.** Changes the intensity of the colors in an image. It can change from -100 to 100.

- **Saturation.** Determines the purity of the image. It also ranges from −100 to 100. A setting of −100 creates a grayscale image. Anything less than 0 gives you a dull, washed-out image. Settings above 0 give you a bright, vibrant image.

4.1.8   Curves

The *Curves* menu, shown in Figure 4.12, is very useful. It allows you to adjust the color balance based on brightness using a graph. The operations can be done on the Red, Green, or Blue channels (1). In this operation, Value represents the intensity of the colors as in the HSV model, which means that it will adjust all of the color values at once. If this image has an Alpha channel, it can also adjust that. If left at the default values, the graph for each channel is a straight line. These lines can be moved by clicking and dragging with the mouse. By moving this line around, the color balance for specific intensities is changed. (This is very similar to Color Balance, but much more powerful.) To get rid of a point that you have created, just drag it off the grid.

The grid behind the line (2) in this menu represents the different intensity areas of the image. The first intersection (3) is the shadow part of the image. The center intersection (4) is the midpoint part of the image, and the top-right intersection (5) represents the highlights part of the image. The advantage of using the Curves menu rather than the Color Balance menu is that Curves gives you much more control over where the changes take place. You can adjust the line to affect only dull parts of highlights, or only bright parts of shadows, for example—something that the Color Balance can't do.

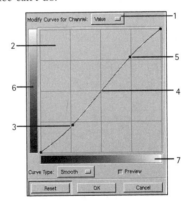

Figure 4.12   *The Curves menu with a good S-shaped curve.*

The idea behind the Curves menu is straightforward. Darker pixels are adjusted on the left side of the graph, and lighter pixels are adjusted on the right side. For reference, two grayscale gradients are placed at the bottom of the graph. The top gradient (6) is a representation of the actual image colors that are being changed. The lower gradient (7) is a reference gradient to show what a normal curve looks like. If you make a mistake in adjusting the curves, there is a reset button (8) at the bottom to return the graph to the original line.

For the best results in adjusting the curves of an image, gentle S-shaped curves are recommended, as seen in Figure 4.12. Changes to the curves should be minimal. To adjust the brightness in an image, drag the curve at the midpoint of the line. This adjusts the gamma of the image. Another useful operation is to drag a straight line along the top or bottom corners. This adjusts the contrast of the image. To understand the way the Curves menu works, it is helpful to view a histogram of before and after adjustments of curves (see Figures 4.13 and 4.14).

Figure 4.13   *The original picture.*   **Figure 4.14**   *The image after a gentle S-curve has been applied.*

4.1.9   Levels

Levels is another excellent graphical tool for adjusting color in an image. This menu has the same effect as the Curves menu, but its interface is different. In the Levels menu, a histogram of the image is shown, as seen in Figure 4.15.

There are two slider bars at the bottom:

- The top slider (1) represents the range of colors available.
- The bottom slider (2) represents the overall brightness of the image.

Levels can be used with all channels and value at once, or each channel separately. This tool also works on grayscale images, where only the black and white levels can be adjusted. Levels are adjusted by sliding the arrows or entering values with the keyboard (3). When modifying input levels for Value, you are adjusting the brightness of the image. Any pixels to the left of the black arrow (4) will be changed to black, and anything to the right of the white arrow (5) is changed to white. The gray arrow (6) represents the midrange of the colors. This gamma setting for the image can be altered in the same way as adjusting the midpoint of the curve in the Curves menu. Sliding it to the left makes the image lighter, and sliding to the right makes it darker.

When modifying input levels for specific Color channels, the slider works somewhat differently. The levels now work on the amount of color that is in the image. An area that is completely white has full amounts of all the colors, and will not be affected by adjusting levels. An area that is completely black has no color, and will not be affected by adjusting levels. The only areas that are affected are the ranges that are between black and white. Any pixel that is to the left of the black arrow (4), for example, will have its channel removed. Dragging the black arrow to the right has the effect of changing a gray image to the channel's complimentary color.

For example, when working on a gray image in the Red channel, dragging the black arrow (4) to the right will make it cyan. Any pixel that is to the right of the white arrow (5) will be given the full value of its channel. If you are working in the Green channel, this will give the image a green hue. The gray arrow represents the midrange of the color. Dragging to the left adds more of the channel's color to the pixels, and dragging to the right removes the channel's color from the pixels. The bottom slider represents the overall level of the channel. Dragging the black arrow to the right makes the image brighter, when using Value for the channel, or increases the amount of the color in the image for a specific color. Moving the white arrow to the left increases the amount of complimentary color in the image when working in a Color channel. When working in the Value channel, it makes the image darker. Unlike the input levels, the bottom slider does affect solid black and white areas.

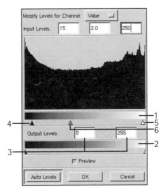

Figure 4.15 *The Levels menu with adjustments made to lighten the image.*

4.1.10   Desaturate

Desaturate removes all color values from the pixels in an image, turning it into a gray image. Note that this does not make it a grayscale image—it is still RGB.

4.1.11   Auto Stretch Contrast and HSV

The *Auto Stretch Contrast* and *HSV* tools automatically adjust the levels in an image. They stretch the color range in the image over the full range of colors. Whereas Contrast does this in RGB mode, HSV does it in HSV mode. These operations are both very useful for improving the quality of faded, overexposed, or poorly scanned pictures (see Figures 4.16 and 4.17).

Figure 4.16   *The original picture.*

Figure 4.17   *The image after being "auto stretched" with contrast.*

4.1.12   Normalize

Normalize works in much the same way as Auto Stretch Contrast. It is an excellent tool for improving the quality of scanned photos. The difference between Normalize and Auto Stretch Contrast is that Normalize adjusts the levels of each channel as a whole, whereas Contrast adjusts them independently (see Figures 4.18 and 4.19).

Figure 4.18   *The original picture.*

Figure 4.19   *The image after being normalized.*

4.2 Channel Operations

Channel operations don't fit into one specific category, but each one can be useful. Don't forget about these operations: They come in handy when working on scanned photos.

4.2.1 Duplicate   [Ctrl+D]

Duplicate creates a copy of the current image in another window. It keeps all properties like selections, layers, etc. This is very useful to do if you are going to change the image beyond the levels of undo.

4.2.2 Offset   [Shift+Ctrl+O]

Offset shifts the image in the x- and y-axis by a specified amount. By default, it will wrap the image. This can be turned off, and the empty space will be filled with the background color. By itself, this operation is not very useful, but it is used in other filters and scripts to create interesting effects.

There is a button that automatically sets the offset to half the height and width. This is useful for creating tileable images.

4.2.3 Compose and Decompose

Compose and *Decompose* are very useful for cleaning up scanned photos. These operations can also be used to create different artistic effects such as color swapping.

Decompose breaks an image down into its separate channels. Each channel is represented by a grayscale image.

There are several types of breakdowns in the Decompose menu:

- **RGB.** Separates the image into Red, Green, and Blue channels.
- **HSV.** Separates the image into Hue, Saturation, and Value channels.
- **CMY.** Separates the image into Cyan, Magenta, and Yellow channels.
- **CMYK.** Separates the image into Cyan, Magenta, Yellow, and Black channels.
- **Alpha.** Gives you a single window that represents the Alpha value of the image. Alpha works with RGBA only when composing, so always use RGB for decomposition if you have an Alpha channel. To use CMY or CMYK with Alpha, there are a few steps you must follow:

  1. Extract the Alpha channel.
  2. Decompose into CMY or CMYK.
  3. Edit the image as needed.
  4. Compose it into CMY or CMYK.

5. Decompose into RGB.

6. Compose (with the Alpha channel) into an RGBA.

Compose does the opposite of Decompose: It creates a color image from different grayscale images, as shown in Figure 4.20.

The options in this menu are similar:

- RGB creates a color image from three grayscale images that represent the Red, Green, and Blue channels.

- RGBA is similar; however, it allows you to add an Alpha for transparency.

- HSV composes an image based on Hue, Saturation, and Value.

- CMY and CMYK compose an image based on the complimentary colors of RGB: cyan, magenta, and yellow. CMYK adds a Black channel to CMY, which is essential if you are separating the image for printing.

Compose and Decompose can help you to adjust the Curves or Levels for a specific color. This is an advantage when manipulating scanned photos, as color problems are sometimes hard to fix when working in all colors at once. An excellent filter is Despeckle (see page 221). You will find that the blue channel looks very "noisy" on scanned photographs; running Despeckle improves it greatly.

Also, strange color effects can be created by composing an image. For example, the Green channel of an image can be used as the Red channel when composing.

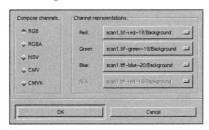

Figure 4.20   *The Compose menu creating an RGB image from three grayscale images.*

4.3 Alpha

This section of the Image menu deals with Alpha, or the transparency of an image.

4.3.1 Add Alpha Channel

Add Alpha Channel is the most commonly used operation. This creates an Alpha channel in the image to allow transparency in your background layer. Single-layer images cannot use transparency until this is done.

4.3.2 Threshold Alpha

Threshold Alpha is very similar to the Threshold operation. It is used to change an image with 255 "shades" of Alpha to a 1-bit Alpha layer. A 1-bit Alpha layer means that a pixel is either fully opaque, or fully transparent. This operation is used to change an RGB image with various levels of transparency to something suitable for the Web, such as GIF format. There is no histogram displayed, so you must guess as to the Alpha values for the image. Any pixel with an Alpha value that is less than the selected value will become fully transparent. Any pixel that has a higher Alpha value will become fully opaque.

4.4 Image Types

Image type is important in the Gimp. It determines how the Gimp deals with the color information in your image. What type you use depends on the application and the file format of the image. RGB is the preferred type to work in because it supports the greatest number of operations and filters. Chapter 5, "Choosing the Right File Format," discusses the different file formats and provides more information about which image type to use.

There are three different image types available[1]: RGB, Indexed, and Grayscale:

- **RGB.** Most common.
- **Indexed.** Popular because of the file formats that are indexed, the best known being GIF.
- **Grayscale.** Used the least because it doesn't support colors. If the image you are creating will be in black and white, however, it is much better to work in grayscale.

Changing the image type should be the first and/or last operation done on an image. Switching between different image types can cause you to lose information. RGB should be used whenever possible. Most plug-ins do not work with indexed images. If you load an indexed image, immediately change it to RGB.

---

[1]*People who do prepress work should note that the Gimp does not yet support CMYK. Anyone who adds CMYK support to the Gimp will earn their few minutes of net.fame.*

4.4.1 RGB

The method of representing colors in RGB is fairly straightforward. Each pixel can contain different amounts of red, green, and blue. The values can range from 0 (no color) to 255 (full color) for each channel. A white pixel has full amounts of all colors (R: 255, G: 255, B: 255). A black pixel has no color values at all (R: 0, G: 0, B: 0). This allows for many different color combinations. The Gimp also allows Alpha values that range from 0 (fully transparent) to 255 (fully opaque). The Color Selection menu is based on this color model. Most image formats such as JPEG, BMP, and PNG are able use the RGB color model.

4.4.2 Indexed

Indexed images work differently from RGB. Indexed images can use a maximum of 256 colors, which are chosen from a possible 16.7 million colors. The color table for each indexed image is stored in the image itself. This table might tell the program displaying the image to use color number 42 for pixel 25, for example.

The problem with this method is that not all programs have the same color for the value described in the image. This creates problems when viewing images in programs that don't have all of the colors available. There are huge problems when viewing indexed images on different platforms. Another disadvantage with indexed images is that they only have 1-bit Alpha support, so transparency doesn't work very well.

If there are so many problems associated with indexed images, why use them? There are a few advantages to using indexed images. If you are intend to display your images with the same program, on the same platform, indexed images can be very useful. Secondly, only the necessary colors are used, so the file sizes of indexed images are significantly smaller than those of another format. Indexed images also allow more colors to be used in other, more important, images and programs. Finally, indexed images are perfect for icons and other small images. The most common indexed file formats are GIFs and BMPs.

There are several options presented when converting an image to indexed form, as shown in Figure 4.21:

- **Number of colors.** Lowering the number of colors available will obviously degrade the image quality, but it will make the image size much smaller.
- **Custom palette.** This option lets you choose from one of the palettes included with the Gimp, or one you created yourself (see "Saving Palettes," page 65).
- **Use a 1-bit palette.** This option isn't very useful—you will rarely use it.

At the bottom of this menu is the option Floyd-Steinberg Dithering. This option will dither your image to appear to have a wider range of colors than you have. *Dithering* uses dots of color to create the illusion of different colors.

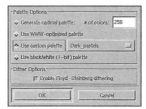

Figure 4.21   *The options available when converting to an indexed image.*

4.4.3   Grayscale

Grayscale images are similar to RGB images, but they only have one channel of color. This "color" is actually just shades of gray. Pixels in a grayscale image have a maximum of two values: Intensity and an optional Alpha. *Intensity* refers to how much white is in the pixel and can range from 0 (black) to 255 (white). Alpha can range from 0 (transparent) to 255 (opaque).

Grayscale images can be saved in most formats. It can easily be converted to Indexed, since indexed images support 256 colors. They don't care if these colors are just black and white.

4.5   Histograms

Histograms are very useful when working with scanned images and adjusting their curves and levels. A *histogram* displays a bar graph of the various levels of intensity in an image. Clicking and dragging on the bar graph shows specific information for that range.

The histogram for a scanned image can reveal some important information. If the right side of the histogram seems to be cut off, the picture was probably too dark, and the brightness on the scanner should have been adjusted. If the left side seems clipped, the picture was too light, and the scanner's brightness should be turned down. If there are many random spikes spread along the entire graph, the image is probably "noisy," and it could use some Despeckling (page 221). To get a good idea of what the Auto Stretch Contrast and HSV operations do, look at a histogram before and after it is applied, as in Figures 4.22 and 4.23.

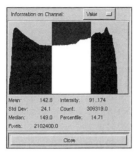

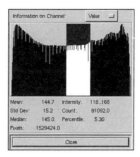

Figure 4.22 *A histogram of a scanned image before any adjustments are made.*

Figure 4.23 *A histogram of a scanned image after Normalize has been applied.*

4.6 Saving Palettes

Saving a palette is only possible when working on an Indexed image. This function is useful if you have created an image with the perfect color scheme, and want to use the same color scheme on other images. The GIMP will save your palette in your GIMP directory with all of the other palettes. To use it, you must refresh the Palette menu (see "Palettes," page 176).

4.7 Image Transforms

You will use these image transformations quite often when working on any image, so it is useful to become familiar with them. They all deal with layers as a whole rather than adjusting individual pixels. The most common transform is resizing an image.

4.7.1 Resizing Images

Resizing Images can be deceiving. This operation resizes the canvas of the image, not the layers in the image. With this operation, you can choose specific values to change, or adjust it by ratio. Units to measure by can be chosen in this menu. The menu is shown in Figure 4.24. By default, the ratios are constrained, but can be deselected and adjusted independently (1). The offset can also be chosen here (2). At the bottom of the Resize menu is a preview (3) of what the image will look like. It can be dragged to change the offset. The black box represents the new canvas size, and the movable gray box is the current image. Again, note that this does not adjust the size of any layers—just the canvas. Layer sizes must be adjusted in the Layers menu (see "Resizing Layers," page 42).

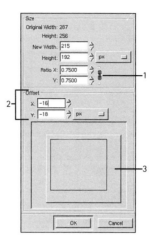

Figure 4.24   *The Image Resize menu.*

4.7.2   Scaling Images

This operation adjusts the image itself, not just the canvas size. Adjustments can be made to the actual size, or by ratio. Units used to scale can be chosen here. The height/width ratio can be constrained, or by clicking the "link," you can adjust them independently. In the second half of this menu, the image can be scaled based on real size and resolution.

4.7.3   Autocrop

Autocrop will automatically crop away large parts of single colors or transparency to leave the image in the center. Autocrop takes into account only the active layer, so you might lose parts of the image in other layers if you do this.

4.7.4   Zealous Crop

Zealous Crop is similar to Autocrop, but it will actually make changes to the active layer. It will attempt to move any objects in the image as close together as possible, and will crop away the outside edges. This effect is apparent only on simple images. On complex images it won't have much effect.

4.7.5   Image and Layer Rotations

These operations provide rotations without having to use the slow Transform tool. They can be applied to the active layer, or to the whole image. When applied to the active layer, they will not adjust the size of the layer. If needed, that must be done later. When they are applied to the entire image, there is no need to adjust the layer sizes. These rotations can only be done in 90-degree increments. They can only go clockwise, so if you want to rotate 90 degrees counterclockwise, choose 270 degrees.

5

Choosing the Right File Format

Page	Contents

In the world of computer graphics, paying attention to file format is essential. Different formats are used for different purposes, especially when designing images for the Web. In this chapter we will explore the various file formats the GIMP can use, and how you can make your images look the best. Tables 5.1 and 5.2 set the stage by outlining the various file formats we will be discussing, along with their respective capabilities.

Table 5.1   File Formats and Their Options Supported by the GIMP ("Y" = Yes, "N" = No)

Format	RGB	Grayscale	Indexed	Layers	Alpha	Compression
XCF	Y	Y	Y	Y	Y	N
TIFF	Y	Y	N	N	Y	Lossless
PostScript	Y	Y	Y	Y	N	N
JPEGY	Y	N	N	N	Lossy	
PNG	Y	Y	Y	Y	Y	Lossless
GIF	N	Y	N	N	1-bit	Lossless
XPMY	Y	N	N	1-bit	N	
XWDY	Y	N	N	N	N	
PSD[1]	Y	Y	N	Y	Y	N
HTML	Y	Y	Y	N	N	N

Table 5.2   Continuation of Table 5.1

Format	Interlacing	Channels	Selections	Layer Masks	Guides
XCF	N	Y	Y	Y	Y
TIFF	N	N	N	N	N
PostScript	N	N	N	N	N
JPEG	Y	N	N	N	N
PNG	Y	N	N	N	N
GIF	Y	N	N	N	N
XPM	N	N	N	N	N
XWD	N	N	N	N	N
PSD[1]	N	Y	Y	N	N
HTML	N	N	N	N	N

---

[1]*Due to the nature of this file format, some of these options may not be supported.*

5.1 The GIMP's Native File Formats

The GIMP has its own file formats for saving images, brushes, and so on. A knowledge of these formats is very helpful. As you begin to use the GIMP, get in the habit of saving often in the XCF format—it supports all of the options in the GIMP.

5.1.1 Loading and Saving Files

Loading and saving files are simple operations. The interface is standard with all GTK+ applications, so this menu will probably be familiar to you.

5.1.1.1 Loading Files

There are three ways of loading files:

- Click on <Image>/File/Open.
- Click on <Toolbox>/File/Open.
- Press the hotkey [Ctrl+O].

This will bring up the Load Image window, as shown in Figure 5.1. At the top of this window are three buttons:

- **Create Dir (1).** This creates a directory inside your current one.
- **Delete File (2).** This button deletes the currently selected file.
- **Rename File (3).** This brings up a dialog box to rename the currently selected file.

Next, there are controls for the file to be loaded:

- **Location bar (4).** This displays the current location of the file browser. It is also a drop-down menu to access the parent directories.
- **Directories (5).** This shows the directory structure. This works similarly to other programs in which double-clicking accesses the directory.
- **Files (6).** In this section, the files in the directory are displayed. The currently selected file is highlighted in blue. If you double-click on a file here it will be loaded.
- **Determine File Type (7).** This drop-down menu allows you to select the file format. If you use Automatic, it determines the file type for you.
- **Selection (8).** The filename is entered here. Tab line completion similar to the bash shell can be used to filter files and directories.
- **Preview window (9).** This new addition to the GIMP loads a thumbnail of the image when it is clicked.

After you have selected a file, click the OK button at the bottom and the file will be loaded.

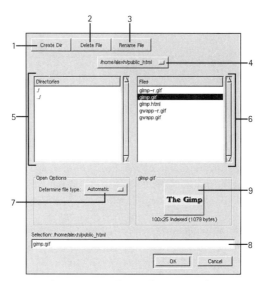

Figure 5.1 *The Load Image window.*

5.1.1.2   Saving Files

There are two ways to save a file: *Save* and *Save As*. If you are saving an untitled image, you will automatically be prompted with the Save As menu. If the image already has a filename, you have a choice between Save and Save As.

There are two steps in using Save:

1.   Click on <Image>/File/Save ([Ctrl+S]).

2.   Enter any relevant options for the file format. If there are no options for this file format, it will simply overwrite the old file.

There are three steps in using Save As (Figure 5.2):

1.   Click on <Image>/File/Save As.

2.   Enter the filename in the dialog box (1). This menu works the same as the Load Image menu. Click OK once you have chosen a location and filename.

3.   Enter any relevant options in the window that pops up, then click OK.

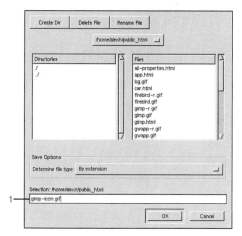

Figure 5.2   *The Save As menu.*

5.1.2   XCF: The GIMP's Native Format

XCF[2] is the GIMP's main file format. It can do everything. If you are working on an image, and would like to save it to work on later, this is what you use. This is because the XCF format supports everything the GIMP does. Layers, selections, Alpha channels, and so on, are all saved in the image when you use XCF.

There are disadvantages to XCF, however. The first, and most apparent, is the lack of support for this format in other programs. No other programs can read or write this format. If you are sending an image to another GIMP user, this is what you use. Don't send an XCF to the printer, however; they will have no idea what to do with it. The second disadvantage is the size of the image. Because every minute piece of information is saved in this image, the file size can grow quite quickly. You may want to use gzip or bzip2 compression on these files (see "gzip and bzip2," page 79).

---

[2] *It is often rumored that XCF stands for Xtra Cool Format, but it more likely comes from the eXperimental Computing Facility where the GIMP was first developed.*

The XCF format supports the following options:

- RGB
- Grayscale
- Indexed
- Layers
- Channels
- Layer masks
- 8-bit Alpha
- Selections
- Guides
- Paths

5.1.3 PAT: The GIMP's Pattern Format

Patterns are useful in the GIMP, and this format is used for reading and writing them. You will find patterns installed in <Gimp Directory>/share/gimp/patterns. If you have created your own patterns, or have downloaded them off the Internet, put them in your own GIMP directory: ~/.gimp/patterns. Patterns can be saved in any format, although Indexed images will not always produce correct results. RGB is the best to use. You can find a more thorough discussion of patterns on page 175.

5.1.4 GBR: The GIMP's Brush Format

The GIMP's brush format is an important one if you need custom brush shapes to get your image looking just right. Brushes are found in <GIMP Directory>/share/gimp/brushes. If you created your own brushes, they are found in your own GIMP directory: ~/.gimp/brushes. Brushes are saved in grayscale format. To learn about creating your own brushes, see page 174.

5.2 Other Image Formats

In this section, image formats that you will encounter on a day-to-day basis are discussed. Obscure formats are not covered.

One fundamental mistake that many people make when saving images is not flattening and removing Alpha channels. Most image formats do not support transparency, and files do not turn out properly if they have transparency in them when saved. See "Flattening Images" on page 43 for more information.

5.2.1 Image Compression

Image compression is very important for the Web, and even for pre-press work when you don't want to take up huge amounts of disk space. To learn what type of compression to use in a given situation, it is useful to know the basic theory behind the different types of compression.

5.2.1.1 Lossy Compression

Lossy compression means that information in the image will be lost during the compression. This form of compression is achieved by throwing away unnecessary details that the eye will not see. This works by tricking the human brain into thinking that the detail is still there, even though it is not; the brain conveniently fills in the missing portions of the picture. Lossy compression will be apparent when the image is enlarged, however, even by a small amount. Because of the way this compression loses important information, it should only be used for Web graphics where size is essential. Also, never use it for saving an intermediate file. Only use formats with lossy compression as the final format.

5.2.1.2 Lossless Compression

Lossless compression will compress the image, but will not lose any information in the image. File formats with lossless compression do this by looking for rows of solid color. In computer language, this would be represented by a line of 0's or 1's. For example, it would take a line like 1111111111 00000 and store it as 10 1's and 5 0's. More advanced types of lossless compression can find complicated patterns and compress them, giving them an even smaller size. See Figures 5.3 and 5.4 for a demonstration. The advantage to lossless compression is that you will not lose any information in the image.

Figure 5.3 *Using lossless compression, an image like this compresses quite well. Saved as a GIF, its file size is 2.5KB.*

Figure 5.4 *The same image rotated 90 degrees does not compress as well due to the GIF's method of using lossless compression. Saved as a GIF, its file size is a whopping 7.3KB, even though it is the same image as Figure 5.3!*

5.2.1.3 Interlacing

Another option available that provides the "illusion" of smaller size is the *progressive* JPEG, or the *interlaced* GIF. This is extremely useful for Web graphics. As the file is downloaded, a very poor resolution is shown first, and it gradually improves as more of the file is downloaded. When using this option, the files are saved differently, but they still look the same when fully loaded.

Normally, the files are saved in one horizontal line at a time, in numerical order. Line 1 is first, line 2 is second, and so on. This makes sense when you are loading images off a hard drive. When an interlaced file is saved, every other line is saved first, then the rest of the lines are saved at the end of the file. When a user views an image on the Web, line 1 is downloaded first, then line 3, until it reaches the bottom of the image. This gives rough detail of the image. As the file continues to download, it goes back to the top and fills in line 2, then line 4, and so on. When the interlaced file is fully downloaded it looks *exactly* the same, but it may be more entertaining to the user viewing the image because there is something to view while the image is downloading.

5.2.1.4 Dithering

Yet another part of image formats to be aware of is dithering. *Dithering* occurs when there are not enough colors available to the computer's video card or the file format itself. When there are not enough colors available, the computer will try to approximate the color by creating many dots of different colors that are available. Dithering does not look good for images with large areas of solid color that become dithered (such as GIFs), but it is hardly noticeable on photographs (such as JPEGs). This is why the Web palette is so important (see "The Web Palette," page 80). An example of dithering is shown in Figures 5.5 and 5.6.

Figure 5.5 *A 24-bit (mostly) solid color image with no dithering.*

Figure 5.6   *The same image made with six colors. Note the dithering around the area near the bottom.*

5.2.2 TIFF

The *TIFF*, or *Tagged Image File Format*, is an industry standard. It was developed by Aldus, which was purchased by Adobe. This is the format to use when dealing with people who aren't using the GIMP. Viewers and editors on every platform support this format. It does not compress as well as the JPEG format, but it will retain image quality because of its lossless compression.

TIFF images support the following options:

- RGB
- Grayscale
- 8-bit Alpha
- Lossless compression

TIFF images also support CMYK, but the GIMP does not. If you are having problems reading TIFF files, make sure the file is in RGB, and the PC version.

5.2.3 PostScript

PostScript is another widely recognized file format, although it is not common in the DOS world. If you have a PostScript-compatible printer, it would be advantageous to use this format. PostScript images are made to be printed, so you are prompted for the dimensions of the image when you save. Another option is to use Encapsulated PostScript and to include a preview with the image. Unless space is an issue, use previews. It helps when you are going to load the image in other programs. Layers are treated as separate pages in PostScript format.

This plug-in supports reading, but not writing, Adobe PDF files.

PostScript images support the following options:

- RGB
- Grayscale
- Indexed
- Layers

5.2.4 JPEG

The *JPEG* format is perfectly suited for the Web. All graphical browsers support it. It achieves the best compression for scanned photos rather than computer-generated ones. Never save an image in JPEG format until you have the final copy. Too much information is lost in its lossy compression.

There are a few options when saving JPEG images. The first is *compression*. The more the image is compressed, the more you lose in quality. The second is *smoothing*. This will help in the compression, but it will make the image seem blurry. The last option is to *optimize* the image. This is only useful for larger images like photographs. Small images that are under 10KB may actually increase in size.

JPEG images support the following options:

- RGB
- Grayscale
- Lossy compression
- Huffman optimization

5.2.5 PNG

PNG, or the *Portable Network Graphic* format, is gaining popularity, partially from the backlash against GIFs. They are more sophisticated than GIFs, but do not have the market share that GIFs do. This format is perfect for the Internet; it can contain color management support for different monitors. The latest versions of graphical browsers support PNGs; however, not many people use PNGs yet. The compression in PNGs is lossless. Higher levels of compression will just take longer to load than uncompressed images. PNGs are best suited for computer-generated images. Scanned photos do not compress very well with PNG compression.

PNG images support the following options:

- RGB
- Grayscale
- Indexed
- 8-bit Alpha

- Interlacing (see "Image Compression," page 73)
- Lossless compression
- Support for gamma correction

5.2.6 GIF

GIF, the *Graphics Interchange Format*, is owned by UniSys[3]. They were created for use in CompuServe, but soon spread because they are so useful for computer graphics. They are perfect for creating small icons and images, and are now the industry standard for Internet images. They can also handle animations.

Animations are created with each different layer as a frame. The timing between each frame is set in the name of the layer. The time for the layer to display is just written in the name of the layer, so a 100 millisecond display time is written as (100ms). Another option is how the frames are displayed. A frame can either combine with the frame before it or replace it. This is done by adding (combine) or (replace) in the layer name. Note that some programs do not support replacing—they will always combine—while others do not support combining.

GIF images support the following options:

- Indexed
- Grayscale
- 1-bit Alpha
- Lossless compression
- Interlacing
- Animations

5.2.7 XPM

XPM, or the *X PixMap* format, is used for creating small pictures, especially icons for Unix/Linux systems. There is 1-bit Alpha support, and when saving, it will ask for an Alpha Threshold. It is better to do this before saving so that you can see what the image looks like (see "Threshold Alpha," page 62).

XPM images support the following options:

- RGB
- Grayscale
- 1-bit Alpha

---

[3] *Problems arose when UniSys demanded that developers pay them royalties to use GIF support in their programs. This shocked the programming community, but UniSys has not done much to enforce the royalties. Some Linux distributions—Debian, for example—do not include GIF support because of this.*

5.2.8 XWD

XWD, or *X Window Dump*, is the file format for screenshots taken in the X Windowing System. It should be used only for a temporary file format. TIFF is much better.

XWD images support the following options:

- RGB
- Grayscale

5.2.9 PSD

PSD images are Adobe Photoshop's native file format. This plug-in allows you to read, but not write, these images. In theory, PSDs should support the same number of options that XCF files do. In practice, they do not because the Photoshop file format is proprietary. If you have a PSD that loads correctly— great! If it doesn't work, you should submit a bug report with an example image that doesn't work.

PSD images are *supposed* to support the following options:

- RGB
- Grayscale
- 8-bit Alpha
- Layers
- Selections
- Channels

The PSD format also supports CMYK, but the GIMP does not. Make sure PSD files are in RGB format.

5.2.10 BMP

The *BMP* format is quite common because it is used as the native image format for Microsoft Windows. Most graphics programs will support this format. The disadvantage is that it does not support Alpha or layers.

BMP images support the following options:

- RGB
- Grayscale
- Lossless compression (RLE)

5.2.11 HTML

This plug-in lets you save an image as an HTML table, with each pixel being a cell. This could be used to design tables quickly, or create huge tables with a low-resolution graphic. There aren't many applications for this, but it is worth mentioning.

The HTML plug-in supports the following options:

- RGB
- Grayscale
- Indexed

5.2.12 gzip and bzip2

Many image formats have image compression built in, but some do not. The most obvious one is the XCF format. A useful plug-in that is built in to the GIMP is the ability to read and write images compressed with gzip or bzip2. All you need to do is add .gz or .bz2 to the filename (while still including the format's proper extension). It will automatically compress and decompress. Images that have built-in compression, such as JPEGs, will not benefit from this— the file sizes may actually increase in some cases.

5.3 Graphics for the Web

The GIMP is *the* program for creating graphics for the Web. There are many different plug-ins related to Web graphics for the GIMP, including ImageMaps, GIF animations, and image optimization. There is no need for external programs to optimize or animate your graphics—it can all be done within the GIMP.

There are two important concepts to be aware of when designing Web graphics. The first is that people from all over the world are going to be viewing them with all kinds of computers, from high-end Sun workstations, to Palm Pilots. Colors display differently on these different platforms, so be aware. The second thing to remember is that some people are still using 14.4Kbps modems to connect to the Internet, so graphics should be as small as possible. Choose a format that will give you the best compression.

5.3.1 Choosing File Formats

There are basically two image formats used on the Web: GIF and JPEG. PNG has acheived some popularity, but it is far from mainstream. Certain version 4 browsers still don't support PNG, so this chapter discusses only GIF and JPEG.

One of the biggest dilemmas facing Web designers is the choice of file format for their images. The quick and dirty solution is simple:

- If it is a scanned picture, use a JPEG.
- If it is a computer-generated image with areas of solid color, use GIFs.

JPEGs are best suited for scanned photos. JPEG compression is controlled by a slider bar when saving. Generally, you will start to lose quality when compressing more than 85%. The image will become unrecognizable at 30% quality. JPEGs will dither large areas of solid color found in cartoonish images, causing them to look spotty and of low quality.

GIFs are well suited to display images with areas of solid color. This is because their method of compression works differently than JPEGs. With GIFs, you have several options when saving. When creating images for the Web, always try to use the fewest number of colors possible without changing the image.

The best bet, if you have an image with many colors, is to use the Web Palette (see the section "The Web Palette"). If you have an image with colors blending, use Floyd-Steinburg dithering to make it appear more smooth. This will increase the file size slightly but reduces "banding" in gradients. If you have an image with areas of solid color, do not use dithering or you will have a spotty image. Also, Web browsers will dither images if there are not enough colors available, and it will look even worse.

Another option to be aware of is interlacing. This saves every second line in the GIF first, and then saves the remaining lines. This has the effect of displaying a rough, pixelated image that gradually comes into focus. This does not affect the file size, but it does make the images seem like they are downloading faster. Your choice becomes very simple when you need animation or transparency: JPEGs don't support them. Use GIFs.

5.3.2   The Web Palette

The Web Palette has come to be because PCs and Macintoshes display the colors in Indexed images differently. Only the first 216 colors are the same—the last 40 are different. This can have the effect of making an image look entirely different when viewed on different platforms. When creating GIF images, always try this palette first. If the image isn't affected by this, try using fewer than 216 colors to save some space. If it distorts the image, you are stuck with the colors it gives you. Using any more colors will cause it to display improperly on different platforms. Lynda Weinman, author of several Web design books, has a palette with these colors. It can be found at `http://www.lynda.com/hex.html`. Note that paying attention to this is only necessary with GIFs, because JPEGs will dither the colors in photographs quite well.

5.3.3 GIF Animations

GIFs are very useful because they allow you to create simple animations for the Web. The GIMP has a very simple and intuitive way of working with animations. You do not need any third-party software to create cool GIF animations—the GIMP does it all by treating each layer as a frame of the animation. In the layer name, the timing and mode of displaying the layer is described. One must remember that GIF animations are very primitive—the computer equivalent of a flip book. This means that timing is not exact, faster computers will play them more quickly, and different programs will play them at different speeds. One way to save space in animations is to use a main background. All the other layers combine with it using transparency. See page 77 for more information on GIF animations.

5.3.4 ImageMap Plug-In

Menu Location   <Image>/Filters/Misc/ImageMap

There is new plug-in called *ImageMap*, which is still in active development as of this writing, but has been proven to be very useful. It creates and saves ImageMaps through a very simple point and click interface. As a stand-alone program, it would be very useful. It is not in the current distribution of the GIMP, so you must download it off the Internet. It can be found at `http://registy`
`.gimp.org/`. A link to the plug-in's homepage is provided at the GIMP Plug-In Registry. To use this program, you will need GTK+ 1.2.0 and GIMP 1.0.4 or 1.1.x.

ImageMap's interface is very easy to learn. In the center, the current layer is displayed, with the list of HTML links to the right. Along the top of the window are the controls for the plug-in, such as saving, loading existing maps, and so on. On the left edge are the buttons for creating clickable areas on the image.

This description assumes you have basic knowledge of ImageMaps. For more information on creating ImageMaps and using them in Web pages, see
`http://home-2.consunet.nl/~cb007736/imagemap.html`.

To create a clickable area, follow these steps:

1. Choose the shape of the area first. Shapes available are circles, rectangles, or polygons.

2. Click and release the mouse button on the area you wish to create.

3. Drag the mouse to the endpoint of the area and click the mouse button again.

Now that you have created an area, a new window pops up where the HTML link information is described. The first tab in the window is for HTML related information: addresses, frame targets, and comments. The second tab is for adjusting the placement of the area, and the third tab is for JavaScipt. When the link has been created, it will appear in the list on the right side.

Existing areas can be editing by clicking on the pencil icon. This brings up the window with all of the options on it for the selected shape. If you wish to delete a selected area, click on the red X.

The Preferences menu provides options on the toolbar that allow the user to choose which type of ImageMap to use:

- NCSA
- CERN
- CSIA

It also provides options for changing the look of the interface.

The Information menu is where the map's general information is entered. The author's name, the title of the map, and most importantly, the default URL can be entered here.

6
Writing Your Own Script-Fu

The GIMP comes with an extremely powerful scripting system called Script-Fu. Script-Fu is based on SIOD—Scheme In One Defun[1]. By way of comparison, it is worth noting that this is more advanced than anything that Adobe Photoshop has. (The only thing that is similar to Script-Fu in Photoshop is macro recording.) Learning how to use Script-Fu is a good idea because it will save you a lot of time doing menial, repetitive tasks. For a Web designer, Script-Fu can very useful because it allows you to create a theme to design all of your icons and headers quickly.

6.1   Introduction to Scheme

Scheme is a programming language based on Lisp, an advanced scripting language. As a GIMP user, you don't really need to know the background to this, but if you have any experience with Lisp you will be familiar with the syntax. Additionally, if you are the proud owner of a Hewlett Packard 48-series calculator, or any other that uses Reverse Polish Notation, the syntax should also be familiar to you.

6.1.1   Basic Scheme Operations

Some basic operations with Scheme are described here. A full listing of the operations in Scheme can be found at `http://people.delphi.com/gjc/siod.html`.

The first thing to learn about Scheme is that it is a language based on *parentheses*. The basic syntax to Scheme functions is as follows:

```
(function parameters)
```

In each set of parentheses, the first item is the function. The rest of the items are the parameters passed to the function. Comments are created with semicolons. They are similar to C++ style comments—preceded by two forward slashes.

For example, consider the following:

```
; Declare Width and Height variables and assign a dummy value

(imgWidth 1)
(imgHeight 1)
```

The GIMP includes an interactive Scheme interpreter that allows you to enter Scheme commands (see Figure 6.1). The results of any commands you have run are shown here (1). The commands are entered in the Current Command section (2). To view the DB Browser, click the Browse button (3).

---

[1] *The home page for SIOD is located at* `http://people.delphi.com/gjc/siod.html`.

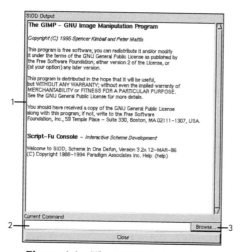

Figure 6.1 *The SIOD Output window.*

It is a good idea to keep this window open as you experiment with the various functions described in Table 6.1. The following simple example of a mathematical function would return 13:

```
(+ 5 8)
```

Other operations are just as easy to use. Table 6.1 outlines some other common mathematical functions.

Table 6.1 Basic Mathematical Functions in SIOD

Function	Description
(+ x1 x2 ...)	Returns the sum of its arguments.
(- x1 x2 ...)	With one argument, it returns the negation. With multiple arguments, it returns the difference of the first argument and the sum of the rest.
(/ x1 x2 ...)	With one argument, this returns the inverse; otherwise, it returns the quotient of the first argument and the product of the rest.
(< x y)	Returns true if x is less than y.
(<= x y)	Returns true if x is less than or equal to y.
(= x y)	Returns true if x is equal to y.
(> x y)	Returns true if x is greater than y.
(>= x y)	Returns true if x is greater than or equal to y.

Expanding on our simple example, more than two parameters can be passed to functions. The following example would return 17:

```
(+ 4 6 7)
```

Functions can also be nested. This is where Scheme can get somewhat confusing. Consider the equation (3×5)+12=?. You would type the following, which would return 27:

```
(+ 12 (* 3 5))
```

Because there can be so many nested brackets, try using a text editor that utilizes syntax highlighting.

6.1.2 Variables

After you know the basics of Scheme, you will want to move on to declaring variables. This is used when passing parameters to your script from a dialog box, or another script. The most common method of declaring local variables is through the let or let* statement. It uses the following form:

```
(let (variable1 variable2 ...) expression1 expression2 ...)
```

Any number of variables and expressions can be created within a let statement. Here's an example:

```
(let ((a 2) (b 4) (c 6)) (+ a b c))
```

This statement initializes three variables (a, b, and c) and returns their sum, which is 12. If you now try the following statement, however, an error is returned:

```
(+ a b)
```

This is because there were only *local* variables inside the parentheses. To create variables that work *outside* their statement, use the set! statement. Its syntax is as follows:

```
(set! variable value)
```

For example, executing these two statements would return 14:

```
(set! Xpos 10)
(+ Xpos 4)
```

6.1.3 Lists

Lists are slightly more complicated and powerful than variables. They allow you to define a group of variables that can be processed by Scheme. These are very important for defining colors, since they are defined as a list with Red, Green, and Blue values. It is very easy to declare a list. The syntax is as follows:

```
'(variable1 variable2 ...)
```

For example, a list to declare the variable lightGray would look like this and would return (200 200 200):

```
(let ( lightGray '(200 200 200)) lightGray)
```

Lists can contain strings, other lists, and variables. Strings are defined using quotation marks. For example, a list could be defined as follows:

```
'("The GIMP" "Essential" "Reference" (1 2 4))
```

6.1.3.1   List Creation Functions

List processing is very powerful. There are several functions for dealing with lists. The first function to learn is cons. It concatenates variables into a list. The syntax is as follows:

```
(cons variable1 variable2)
```

The problem is that only two variables can be passed to the cons function at a time. If you want to create a new list with four parameters, you must nest the function like this:

```
(cons 1 (cons 2 (cons 3 (cons 4))))
```

cons does work with existing lists, however. You can take an existing list with two parameters and append a new parameter to it. For example, the following function would return (1 2 3):

```
(let ((smallList (cons 1 '(2 3)))) smallList)
```

append is another function for dealing with lists. It appends one or more lists onto another. Its syntax is as follows:

```
(append list1 list2 ...)
```

6.1.4   List Processing Functions

Now that you have created a list, you should take a look at several functions for dealing with getting parameters out of lists. The first function to use is car. This returns the first parameter, or *head*, of the list. It does not affect the list at all. For example, if you have a list called textString that is set to '("The GIMP" "Script-Fu" "Scheme"), the following function would return The GIMP:

```
(car textString)
```

Another function is cdr. This returns the *tail* of the list. The following example would return ("Script-Fu" "Scheme"):

```
(cdr textString)
```

Note that car returns a single parameter, whereas cdr returns a list. If there is only one parameter in a list, cdr will return ()—an empty list.

6.1.4.1   Advanced List Processing

Now that you know the basics of car and cdr, it gets more complicated. Different combinations of car and cdr can be used to return specific parts of lists. For example, (cdddr x) is equivalent to (cdr (cdr (cdr x))).

Any combination of a's and d's can be used, to a maximum of three letters. These functions can be nested as well. Here's an extreme example: (caddr (cdddr x)) is equivalent to (car (cdr (cdr (cdr (cdr (cdr x)))))).

6.1.5   Functions

The next step in learning Scheme is to define functions. This is the most flexible part of working with Scheme. The syntax for defining functions is simple:

```
(define (function variable1 variable2 ...) (operations))
```

For example, the following would create a function that calculates the area of a circle with a certain radius:

```
(define (circleArea radius) (* *pi* radius radius))
```

It could then be called later with a radius value of 2:

```
(circleArea 2)
```

The `circlearea` function would then return `12.5664`.

Like lists, functions can be nested inside one another.

6.2 Scheme Function Reference

The following table is a list of the Scheme functions available to the GIMP.

Table 6.2   Scheme Functions Available to the GIMP

Function	Description
`(abs x)`	Returns the absolute value of x.
`(acos x)`	Returns the inverse cosine of x.
`(append l1 l2 l3 l4 ...)`	Returns a list that is the result of appending all of its arguments. Example: `(append '(a b) '(c d)) => (a b c d)`
`(asin x)`	Returns the inverse sine of x.
`(atan x)`	Returns the inverse tangent of x.
`(atan2 x y)`	Returns the inverse tangent of x/y.
`(butlast x)`	Returns a new list that has all the elements of the argument x except for the last element.
`(cons x y)`	Allocates a list object with x as the `car` and y as the `cdr`. For example: `(cons 1 (cons 2 (cons 3 ())))` becomes (1 2 3).
`(cos x)`	Returns the cosine where x is in units of radians.
`(eq? x y)`	Returns `true` if x and y are the same object.
`(equal? x y)`	Returns `true` if x and y are equal objects.
`(eqv? x y)`	Returns `true` if x and y are the same object or numerically equal.
`(exp x)`	Computes the exponential function of x.
`(list item1 item2 ...)`	Uses the `cons` function to merge its arguments into a list.
`(log x)`	Computes the natural logarithm of x.

Function	Description
(max x1 x2 ...)	Returns the maximum of x1, x2, and so on.
(min x1 x2 ...)	Returns the minimum of its arguments.
(null? x)	Returns true if x is the empty list.
(number->string x base width precision)	Formats the number according to the *base*, which may be 8, 10, 16, or the symbol e or f. The *width* and *precision* are both optional.
(number? x)	Returns true if x is a number.
(parse-number str)	Converts a string to a number.
(pow x y)	Computes the result of x raised to the y power.
(reverse x)	Returns a new list that has elements in the reverse order of the list x.
(sin x)	Computes the sine of the angle x in radians.
(sqrt x)	Computes the square root of x.
(string-append str1 str2 str3 ...)	Returns a new string that contains the concatenation of all its string arguments.
(string-downcase str)	Returns a new string converting all the characters of *str* to lowercase.
(string-trim str)	Returns a new string made by trimming whitespace from the left and right of the specified string.
(string-trim-left str)	Like string-trim but only the left side.
(string-trim-right str)	Like string-trim but only the right side.
(string-upcase str)	Returns a new string with all the lowercase characters converted to uppercase.
(string? x)	Returns true if x is a string.
(tan x)	Computes the tangent of the angle *x* specified in radians.
(while pred-form form1 form2 ...)	If pred-form is true, it will evaluate all the other forms and then loop.

6.3 Script-Fu

After you have become familiar with the basics of Scheme, you can move on to creating Script-Fu for the GIMP. This section outlines the creation of a fairly simple script. Incidentally, it is the script I used to create the logos on my homepage (http://www.dowco.com/~alexh)[2]. Script-Fu is perfect for this type of job.

---

[2]*I have also made the two examples in this chapter available on my home page.*

6.3.1 Writing a Basic Script

The first part of any Script-Fu is to define the function. Our example script is defined as:

```
(define (script-fu-alexh-logo textStuff fontType fontSize bgColor))
```

This means there is a function called `script-fu-alexh-logo`. It does not actually do anything, but it is a good start. It takes the following variables as input:

- `textStuff`. This is the actual text that is created.
- `fontType`. This determines the type of font. By default it will be Agate.
- `fontSize`. This is the size of the font.
- `bgColor`. This variable allows you to set the background color manually.

6.3.1.1   Registering the Script

The second part of the script registers itself with the GIMP, and defines what parameters are passed to it. This is done through the function `script-fu-register`. These parameters can be passed manually, or through another script that calls it.

Here is the example of a `script-fu-register` function:

```
(script-fu-register "script-fu-alexh-logo"
"<Toolbox>/Xtns/Script-Fu/Web page themes/AlexH/Basic Logo"
"Makes a basic logo in the theme used in Alex Harford's Webpage"
"Alex Harford "
"Copyright 1999 Alex Harford "
"July 21,1999 "
""
SF-STRING "Text:" "Home"
SF-FONT "Font:" "-freefont-agate-normal-r-normal-*-24-*-*-*-p-*-*-*"
SF-VALUE "Font size:" "25"
SF-COLOR "Background Color:" '(222 234 234)

)
```

Note that the `script-fu-register` function takes seven parameters plus the number of parameters passed to it. In this case, it is a total of 12. The first seven parameters are used in registering the script with the GIMP:

- **Name.** Determines the script's function name for calling it within the GIMP, and also how it appears in the DB Browser.
- **Location.** Determines where this script appears. It can be placed anywhere in the GIMP. It will always begin with <Toolbox> or <Image>, depending on where you want to put it. The GIMP will automatically create menus and submenus. Spaces are allowed in the location as well.
- **Description.** A simple description of the script.
- **Author name.**
- **Copyright.**
- **Date.** Usually the date of last revision.

- **Image type.** Determines the type of the image that can use the script. Some plug-ins cannot use certain image types, so this is used to avoid errors. The following types are available:

  a. RGB

  b. RGBA

  c. GRAY

  d. GRAYA

  e. INDEXED

  f. INDEXEDA

  g. Asterisks can be used as wildcards here (such as in RGB*)

The rest of the parameters in the script-fu-register function determine the default values for the script. The following types are available:

- SF-IMAGE. Used in the form of SF-IMAGE "Image Name" 0.

- SF-DRAWABLE. Used in the form of SF-DRAWABLE "Drawable" 0.

- SF-VALUE. An older, generic way of assigning variables. GIMP 1.1 introduced better methods to do this. Avoid using SF-VALUE.

- SF-COLOR. Used in the form of SF-COLOR "Color Name" '(R G B), where R, G, and B are values from 0 to 255.

- SF-TOGGLE. Used as a Boolean type in form of SF-TOGGLE "Toggle?" FALSE.

- SF-ADJUSTMENT. Used in interactive mode to enter a value. This should be used instead of SF-VALUE. The format of the SF-ADJUSTMENT variable is SF-ADJUSTMENT "label" '(value, lower boundary, upper boundary, step increment, page increment, digits, type). The *type* is either a slider (0) or arrows (1).

- SF-FONT. Used to choose a font name. This should be used instead of SF-VALUE. The form is SF-FONT "label" "fontname". Note that this will ignore font size.

- SF-PATTERN. Used in interactive mode to select a pattern. The form of this variable is SF-PATTERN "Prompt" "Pattern Name".

- SF-BRUSH. Used to interactively select a brush. The form is SF_BRUSH "Brush" '("Name (radius)" X Y Z), where X is the opacity (ranging from 0.0 to 1.0), Y is the spacing, and Z is the mode. The following modes are available:

  a. NORMAL (0)

  b. DISSOLVE (1)

  c. BEHIND (2)

  d. MULTIPLY (3)

    e. SCREEN (4)

    f. OVERLAY (5)

    g. DIFFERENCE (6)

    h. ADDITION (7)

    i. SUBTRACT (8)

    j. DARKEN-ONLY (9)

    k. LIGHTEN-ONLY (10)

    l. HUE (11)

    m. SATURATION (12)

    n. COLOR (13)

    o. VALUE (14)

- SF-GRADIENT. Used in interactive mode to choose a gradient. The form for this variable is SF-Gradient *"Prompt"* *"Gradient Name"*.

- SF-FILENAME. Used in interactive mode to specify a filename. The form for this variable is SF-FILENAME *"Environment Map"* *"filename"*.

- SF-STRING. Used in interactive mode for string entry, without having to use multiple quotation marks. The form for this variable is SF-STRING *"Prompt"* *"Text goes here"*.

- SF-LAYER. Used in interactive mode to choose a specific layer to apply the script. The form for this variable is SF-LAYER *"Prompt"* *X*, where *X* is a number referring to the position of the layer. 0 is the background layer.

- SF-CHANNEL. Used in interactive mode to select a channel. The form for this variable is SF-CHANNEL *"Prompt"* *X*, where *X* is a number referring to the position of the channel. Note that the channels referred to here are the channels used for selection masks, not the three color channels.

6.3.1.2 Saving Script-Fu

This example has been saved in the ~/.gimp/scripts directory. This is where all custom scripts are placed. To get a feel for things, type in this script and save it as alexh-logo.scm. Then, refresh the scripts by clicking on <Toolbox>/Xtns/ Script-Fu/Refresh. The script will now appear in <Toolbox>/Xtns/Script-Fu/ Web page themes/AlexH/AlexH Logo.

The DB Browser (see Figure 6.2) should now show the script in its window. Open up the DB Browser by clicking on <Toolbox>/Xtns/DB Browser. All plug-ins are listed here alphabetically (1). You can search for scripts by typing in the text box and clicking on Search by Name or Search by Blurb (2). The name of the plug-in will then be displayed (3). The information about the parameters passed to the plug-in are also listed here (4).

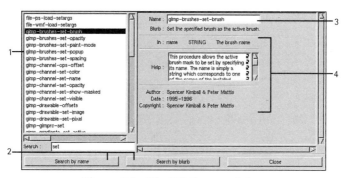

Figure 6.2 *The DB Browser window.*

6.3.2 Adding Functionality to the GIMP

Now it is time to make the script actually do something. For now, we will just have a simple script that creates a layered image that fits around some example text. It will follow these steps:

1. Declare all variables.
2. Create the new image.
3. Create the new layers.
4. Clear the background layer so that it has the correct background color.
5. Add alpha to the layer.
6. Clear the layer.
7. Set the foreground color.
8. Place the text on this new layer.
9. Resize the image so that it fits precisely around the text layer.

All of this will be done inside the `define` function.

6.3.2.1 Declaring Variables

First, we must use a `let*` function to declare all the variables we need:

- *imgWidth.* The width of the image. Used to determine size of layers.
- *imgHeight.* The height of the image. Used to determine size of layers.
- *img.* The actual image.
- *bgLayer.* The layer called Background.
- *baseLayer.* The layer called Text Layer.

It will look something like this:

```
(let*
(

; Declare Width and Height variables and assign a dummy value

(imgWidth 1)
(imgHeight 1)

; Declare and create the new image

(img
   (car (gimp-image-new imgWidth imgHeight RGB))
)

; Declare and create the layers in the image:

(bgLayer
(car
(gimp-layer-new img imgWidth imgHeight RGB_IMAGE "Background" 100 NORMAL))
)

(baseLayer
(car
(gimp-layer-new img imgWidth imgHeight RGB_IMAGE "Text Layer" 100 NORMAL))
)

)

; Rest of script goes here.

)
```

6.3.2.2   Create the New Image

Inside the variable declaration, we have created the new image with the
gimp-image-new function. As shown in the DB Browser, it takes three parameters:

- Width
- Height
- Type

The output of this function is a list, so we need to use the car function to get the
proper image name.

6.3.2.3   Adding the New Layers

We also need to create two new layers—bgLayer and baseLayer—with the
gimp-layer-new function. According to the DB Browser, it takes seven
parameters to achieve this:

- **Image.** The name of the layer.
- **Width.**
- **Height.**
- **Type.** The layer type, not the image type.
- **Name.** The name of the layer in quotation marks.

- **Opacity.** The opacity of the layer (from 0 to 100).

- **Mode.** The combination mode of the layer. (See "Modes," page 44, for more information.)

The output of this function is, once again, a list, so we need to use the car function to get the proper names.

The next step is to add the layers we created to the image. This is done through the gimp-image-add-layer function. We need to add both bgLayer and baseLayer to the image:

```
(gimp-image-add-layer img bgLayer 1)
(gimp-image-add-layer img baseLayer 0)
```

The numbers at the end of the function represent the position of the layers. 0 is the highest layer, 1 is next, and so on.

6.3.2.4   Setting Colors

We now set the foreground and background colors. These are set with lists that contain three numerical values. Note that the background color is a variable, and the foreground color is a constant. The colors are set with the gimp-palette-set functions:

```
(gimp-palette-set-background bgColor)
(gimp-palette-set-foreground '(0 0 100))
```

6.3.2.5   Clearing the Background Layer

Now that the colors are set, we need to clear the bgLayer to set its color. (If we did not include this step, it would just be random colors.) This is done with the gimp-edit-clear function:

```
(gimp-edit-clear bgLayer)
```

6.3.2.6   Editing the Base Layer

Next, we need to deal with the baseLayer. This must be cleared to transparency, but there is no alpha channel in this layer. We use the gimp-layer-add-alpha function to do this:

```
(gimp-layer-add-alpha baseLayer)
(gimp-edit-clear baseLayer)
```

6.3.2.7   Adding Text

Now we must create the text used in the script. This is done with another let* function. If looks like this:

```
(let*
(
(floatText
(car
(gimp-text-fontname img baseLayer 0 0 textStuff 5 TRUE fontSize PIXELS
fontType)
```

continues

```
        )
        )
        )

      ; Resize the Image to proper size

      (set! imgWidth  (car (gimp-drawable-width  floatText) ) )
      (set! imgHeight (car (gimp-drawable-height floatText) ) )

      (gimp-image-resize img imgWidth imgHeight 0 0)
      (gimp-layer-resize bgLayer imgWidth imgHeight 0 0)
      (gimp-layer-resize baseLayer imgWidth imgHeight 0 0)

      (gimp-floating-sel-anchor floatText)
      )
```

This function does several things, which can be thought of as several sub-steps:

1. Creating the `floatText` drawable
2. Writing text on the `floatText` drawable
3. Resizing the image and the layers
4. Anchoring the `floatText`

The `floatText` drawable is created with the following function:

```
      (
      (floatText
      (car
      (gimp-text-fontname img baseLayer 0 0 textStuff 5 TRUE fontSize PIXELS
      fontType)
      )
      )
      )
```

This creates the `floatText` drawable, and draws the text with the `gimp-text-fontname` function. It draws on the `baseLayer`, but is still a floating selection. We do not anchor the floating selection yet because we still need some information from it.

6.3.2.8   Resizing the Image

The next step is to change the values of the `imgWidth` and `imgHeight` variables to the width and height of the `floatText` variable. This ensures that the image is big enough for the text. We then resize the image and all layers to be this size:

```
      (gimp-image-resize img imgWidth imgHeight 0 0)
      (gimp-layer-resize bgLayer imgWidth imgHeight 0 0)
      (gimp-layer-resize baseLayer imgWidth imgHeight 0 0)
```

Finally we can anchor the `floatText` drawable with the `gimp-floating-sel-anchor` function:

```
      (gimp-floating-sel-anchor floatText)
```

At this point, the second `let*` function ends, and we return to the first. The script is almost finished. We must now tell the GIMP to flatten the layers and display this new image with the `gimp-display-new` function:

```
(set! bgLayer (car (gimp-image-flatten img)))

(gimp-display-new img)

)
)
```

The two parentheses close the `let*` statement. This completes the script. The finished script looks like this:

```
;

(define (script-fu-alexh-logo textStuff fontType fontSize bgColor)

; Begin Script

(let*
(

; Declare Width and Height variables and assign a dummy value

(imgWidth 1)
(imgHeight 1)

; Declare and create the new image

(img
    (car (gimp-image-new imgWidth imgHeight RGB) )
)

; Declare and create the layers in the image:

(bgLayer
(car
(gimp-layer-new img imgWidth imgHeight
     RGB_IMAGE "Background" 100 NORMAL)
)
)

(baseLayer
(car
(gimp-layer-new img imgWidth imgHeight
     RGB_IMAGE "Text Layer" 100 NORMAL)
)
)

; Add the layers to the image

(gimp-image-add-layer img bgLayer 0)
(gimp-image-add-layer img baseLayer 0)

; Set the foreground and background colors

(gimp-palette-set-background bgColor)
(gimp-palette-set-foreground '(0 0 100))

; Clear the background layer

(gimp-edit-clear bgLayer)

; Add alpha and clear the text layer
```

continues

```
(gimp-layer-add-alpha baseLayer)
(gimp-edit-clear baseLayer)

; Create the new text layer

(let*
(
(floatText
(car
(gimp-text-fontname img baseLayer 0 0 textStuff 5 TRUE fontSize PIXELS
fontType)
)
)
)

; Resize the Image to proper size)

(set! imgWidth  (car (gimp-drawable-width  floatText) ) )
(set! imgHeight (car (gimp-drawable-height floatText) ) )

(gimp-image-resize img imgWidth imgHeight 0 0)
(gimp-layer-resize bgLayer imgWidth imgHeight 0 0)
(gimp-layer-resize baseLayer imgWidth imgHeight 0 0)

(gimp-floating-sel-anchor floatText)
)

; Flatten the Image

(set! bgLayer (car (gimp-image-flatten img)))

; Display the new image

(gimp-display-new img)
)
)

; Register script with the GIMP

(script-fu-register "script-fu-alexh-logo"
"<Toolbox>/Xtns/Script-Fu/Web page themes/AlexH/AlexH Logo"
"Makes a basic logo in the theme used in Alex Harford's Webpage"
"Alex Harford"
"Copyright 1999 Alex Harford"
"July 21,1999"
""
SF-STRING "Text:" "Home"
SF-FONT "Font:" "-freefont-agate-normal-r-normal-*-24-*-*-*-p-*-*-*"
SF-VALUE "Font size:" "25"
SF-COLOR "Background Color:" '(222 234 234)

)
```

6.3.3 Enhancing the Script

Now that we have a basic script, let's add some additional effects to it. The first will be to add a 3D effect to the text. Follow these steps:

1. Duplicate the baseLayer twice.

2. Change the first new layer's color to black.

3. Change the second layer's color to white.

4. Offset the first new layer down and to the right.

5. Offset the second new layer up and to the left.

These steps are discussed in the following sections.

6.3.3.1 Duplicating the baseLayer

Duplicating the baseLayer is done with the gimp-layer-copy function. First of all, we must declare the variables in the let* statement. Then we copy the layers, as follows:

```
(set! blackLayer (car (gimp-layer-copy baseLayer TRUE)))
(set! whiteLayer (car (gimp-layer-copy baseLayer TRUE)))
```

These layers must then be added to the image:

```
(gimp-image-add-layer img blackLayer 2)
(gimp-image-add-layer img whiteLayer 1)
```

6.3.3.2 Adjusting the Color

We will now use the Bucket tool to adjust the color. There are several steps to follow:

1. Set the preserve transparency bit to TRUE:

```
(gimp-layer-set-preserve-trans blackLayer TRUE)
(gimp-layer-set-preserve-trans whiteLayer TRUE)
```

2. Select the entire image:

```
(gimp-selection-all img)
```

3. Set the foreground color to black:

```
(gimp-palette-set-foreground '(0 0 0))
```

4. Fill the blackLayer:

```
(gimp-bucket-fill blackLayer 0 0 100 15 FALSE 0 0)
```

5. Set the foreground color to white:

```
(gimp-palette-set-foreground '(255 255 255))
```

6. Fill the whiteLayer:

```
(gimp-bucket-fill whiteLayer 0 0 100 15 FALSE 0 0)
```

7. Deselect the entire image:

```
(gimp-selection-none img)
```

6.3.3.3 Offsetting the Layers

Next, each layer is offset slightly. This is done with the gimp-layer-set-offsets function:

```
(gimp-layer-set-offsets blackLayer 1 1)
(gimp-layer-set-offsets whiteLayer -1 -1)
```

6.3.3.4 Further Improvement of the Script

The script now runs, but a better drop shadow effect is required. Two more layers are created that are duplicates of blackLayer and whiteLayer:

```
(set! blackblurLayer (car (gimp-layer-copy baseLayer TRUE)))
(set! whiteblurLayer (car (gimp-layer-copy baseLayer TRUE)))
```

They are bucket–filled and offset the same as the other layers. The preserve transparency bit is set to FALSE, then the layers have the plug-in-gauss-iir function applied to give a better shadow:

```
(gimp-layer-set-preserve-trans blackblurLayer FALSE)
(gimp-layer-set-preserve-trans whiteblurLayer FALSE)
(plug-in-gauss-iir TRUE img blackblurLayer 2 TRUE TRUE)
(plug-in-gauss-iir TRUE img whiteblurLayer 2 TRUE TRUE)
```

6.3.3.5   Cleanup

The script is now basically in working order. However, there is some additional cleanup required. We will disable undo recording with the following function:

```
(gimp-image-disable-undo img)
```

Now enable it again at the end of the script with the following:

```
(gimp-image-enable-undo img)
```

We will also autocrop the image to save space:

```
(plug-in-autocrop TRUE img bgLayer)
```

Also, clear the dirty count so the image can be closed without any prompting:

```
(gimp-image-clean-all img)
```

Another trick is to make sure the foreground and background colors are not changed. Add these lines to the first let* function:

```
(old-fg (car (gimp-palette-get-foreground)))
(old-bg (car (gimp-palette-get-background)))
```

Add these lines to the end of the script:

```
(gimp-palette-set-foreground old-fg)
(gimp-palette-set-background old-bg)
```

Now let's add some other variables that make the script more configurable:

- SF-COLOR "Font Color:" '(0 0 100)
- SF-COLOR "Dark Offset Color:" '(0 0 0)
- SF-COLOR "Light Offset Color:" '(255 255 255)
- SF-ADJUSTMENT "Blur Radius:" '(2 1 50 1 10 0 0)
- SF-ADJUSTMENT "Dark Offset:" '(1 -100 100 1 10 0 1)
- SF-ADJUSTMENT "Light Offset:" '(-1 -100 100 1 10 0 1)

6.3.3.6   The Completed Script

The appropriate variables have been added to the define function, and the variable names have replaced the hardcoded variables. Our completed script looks like this:

```
;
(define
(script-fu-alexh-logo textStuff fontType fontSize fontColor
     bgColour darkOffset lightOffset
     blurRadius posoffset negoffset )
```

```
; Begin Script

(let*
(

; Declare Width and Height variables and assign a dummy value

(imgWidth 1)
(imgHeight 1)

; Declare and create the new image

(img
(car
(gimp-image-new imgWidth imgHeight RGB)
)
)

; Declare and create the layers in the image:

(bgLayer
(car
(gimp-layer-new img imgWidth imgHeight
    RGB_IMAGE "Background" 100 NORMAL)
)
)

(baseLayer
(car
(gimp-layer-new img imgWidth imgHeight
    RGB_IMAGE "Text Layer" 100 NORMAL)
)
)


; Keep the background colors

(old-fg (car (gimp-palette-get-foreground)))
(old-bg (car (gimp-palette-get-background)))
)

; Disable undo recording

(gimp-image-disable-undo img)

; Add the layers to the image

(gimp-image-add-layer img bgLayer 0)
(gimp-image-add-layer img baseLayer 0)

; Set the foreground and background colors

(gimp-palette-set-background bgColor)
(gimp-palette-set-foreground fontColor)

; Clear the background layer

(gimp-edit-clear img bgLayer)

; Add alpha and clear the text layer

(gimp-layer-add-alpha baseLayer)
(gimp-edit-clear baseLayer)

; Create the new text layer
```

continues

```
(let*
 (
  (floatText
   (car
    (gimp-text-fontname img baseLayer 0 0 textStuff 5 TRUE fontSize PIXELS
fontType)
   )
  )
  (blackblurLayer)
  (whiteblurLayer)
 )
)

; Resize the Image to proper size

(set! imgWidth  (car (gimp-drawable-width  floatText) ) )
(set! imgHeight (car (gimp-drawable-height floatText) ) )

(gimp-image-resize img imgWidth imgHeight 0 0)
(gimp-layer-resize bgLayer imgWidth imgHeight 0 0)
(gimp-layer-resize baseLayer imgWidth imgHeight 0 0)
(gimp-floating-sel-anchor floatText)

; Duplicate the layers

(set! blackLayer (car (gimp-layer-copy baseLayer TRUE)))
(set! whiteLayer (car (gimp-layer-copy baseLayer TRUE)))
(set! blackblurLayer (car (gimp-layer-copy baseLayer TRUE)))
(set! whiteblurLayer (car (gimp-layer-copy baseLayer TRUE)))

(gimp-image-add-layer img blackLayer 1)
(gimp-image-add-layer img whiteLayer 1)
(gimp-image-add-layer img blackblurLayer 3)
(gimp-image-add-layer img whiteblurLayer 2)

; Set the preserve transparency bit

(gimp-layer-set-preserve-trans blackLayer TRUE)
(gimp-layer-set-preserve-trans whiteLayer TRUE)
(gimp-layer-set-preserve-trans blackblurLayer TRUE)
(gimp-layer-set-preserve-trans whiteblurLayer TRUE)

; Use the bucket fill tool

(gimp-selection-all img)
(gimp-palette-set-foreground darkOffset)
(gimp-bucket-fill blackLayer 0 0 100 15 FALSE 0 0)
(gimp-bucket-fill blackblurLayer 0 0 100 15 FALSE 0 0)
(gimp-palette-set-foreground lightOffset)
(gimp-bucket-fill whiteLayer 0 0 100 15 FALSE 0 0)
(gimp-bucket-fill whiteblurLayer 0 0 100 15 FALSE 0 0)
(gimp-selection-none img)

; Offset the layers

(gimp-layer-set-offsets blackLayer posoffset posoffset)
(gimp-layer-set-offsets whiteLayer negoffset negoffset)
(gimp-layer-set-offsets blackblurLayer posoffset posoffset)
(gimp-layer-set-offsets whiteblurLayer negoffset negoffset)

; Blur the blur layers

(gimp-layer-set-preserve-trans blackblurLayer FALSE)
(gimp-layer-set-preserve-trans whiteblurLayer FALSE)
(plug-in-gauss-iir TRUE img blackblurLayer blurRadius TRUE TRUE)
(plug-in-gauss-iir TRUE img whiteblurLayer blurRadius TRUE TRUE)
)
```

```
; Flatten the image

(set! bgLayer (car (gimp-image-flatten img)))

; Autocrop

(plug-in-autocrop FALSE img bgLayer)

; Clear the dirty count.

(gimp-image-clean-all img)

; Display the new image

(gimp-display-new img)

; Add undo support again

(gimp-image-enable-undo img)

; Reset the colors

(gimp-palette-set-foreground old-fg)
(gimp-palette-set-background old-bg)

)
)

; Register script with the GIMP

(script-fu-register "script-fu-alexh-logo"
"<Toolbox>/Xtns/Script-Fu/Web page themes/AlexH/AlexH Logo"
"Makes a basic logo in the theme used in Alex Harford's Webpage"
"Alex Harford"
"Copyright 1999 Alex Harford"
"July 21,1999"
""
SF-STRING "Text:" "Home"
SF-FONT "Font:" "-freefont-agate-normal-r-normal-*-24-*-*-*-p-*-*-*"
SF-VALUE "Font size:" "25"
SF-COLOR "Font Color:" '(0 0 100)
SF-COLOR "Background Color:" '(222 234 234)
SF-COLOR "Dark Offset Color:" '(0 0 0)
SF-COLOR "Light Offset Color:" '(255 255 255)
SF-ADJUSTMENT "Blur Radius:" '(2 1 50 1 10 0 0)
SF-ADJUSTMENT "Dark Offset:" '(1 -100 100 1 10 0 1)
SF-ADJUSTMENT "Light Offset:" '(-1 -100 100 1 10 0 1)
)
```

6.3.4 Using Script-Fu on an Image or Drawable

In the previous section, creating a new image was described. In this next example, we will learn about a simple script that works on an existing layer. It will create a new image and turn it into an animation. This animation will gradually fade an image from a pixel width of 1 to a maximum pixel width defined in the script. It is similar to the effect used in some of the Super Mario fadeouts[3].

---

[3]This script is loosely based on Sven Neumann's waves-anim.scm script. However, his wacky frame numbering method was changed.

We will do this in several steps:

1. Copy the image to a new one.
2. While the number of frames left is greater than one, loop:
   a. Copy the base layer.
   b. Rename it to the number of frames left.
   c. Pixelize it a certain amount.
   d. Decrease the number of frames and the pixelization amount.
3. Rename the base layer as `Frame 1`.
4. Clean up.

It will take only two variables:

■ Maximum Pixelization
■ Number of Frames

6.3.4.1 Defining the Function

The first step in writing the script is to create the `define` function and the `script-fu-register` function:

```
(define (script-fu-pixel-anim img drawable maxPixel totalFrames)

)

(script-fu-register "script-fu-pixel-anim"
                    "<Image>/Script-Fu/Animators/Pixelate"
                    "Pixelize an image Super Mario Style"
                    "Alex Harford (alexh@dowco.com)"
                    "Copyright 1999 Alex Harford"
                    "July 21, 1999"
                    "RGB RGBA GRAY GRAYA"
                    SF-IMAGE "Image" 0
                    SF-DRAWABLE "Drawable" 0
                    SF-ADJUSTMENT "Max Pixelization" '(10 1 100 1 10 0 0)
                    SF-ADJUSTMENT "Number of Frames" '(10 1 100 1 10 0 1)
)
```

Note that there are two extra variables here: `img` and `drawable`. These are automatically passed to the script by the GIMP because they are applied to a specific drawable on a specific image. This is always used when writing a script that affects an existing image. Also note the location of this filter: <Image>/Script-Fu/Animators/Pixelate. Generally, scripts that work on existing images are placed in the <Image>/Script-Fu section.

6.3.4.2 Assigning Variables

Now that there is a skeleton in place for the script, we can begin creating the script. It begins with a `let*` function:

```
(let*
    (

    ; Declare variables and assign values
```

```
          (maxPixel (max 1 maxPixel))
          (totalFrames (max 1 totalFrames))
          (delta ( / maxPixel totalFrames))
          (framesLeft totalFrames)
          (image (car (gimp-channel-ops-duplicate img)))
          (base-layer (car (gimp-image-get-active-layer image)))
          )
    )
```

This function accomplishes several things:

- Makes sure maxPixel and totalFrames are greater than 1.
- Declares the variable delta and initializes it to maxPixel divided by totalFrames.
- Declares the variable framesLeft and initializes it to totalFrames.
- Declares a new variable image and sets it to be a duplicate of the active image passed to the script by the GIMP.
- Declares the variable base-layer and initializes it to be the active layer in image.

6.3.4.3 Pixelization

Now we must decide on how we will deal with the actual pixelization. This is done with a while loop and a let* function:

```
(while ( > framesLeft 1)
(let*
(

(pixel-layer (car (gimp-layer-copy base-layer TRUE)))
(layer-name (string-append "Frame " (number->string framesLeft)))
)

(gimp-image-add-layer image pixel-layer (- totalFrames framesLeft))
(gimp-layer-set-name pixel-layer layer-name)

(plug-in-pixelize
        TRUE
        image
        pixel-layer
        maxPixel
    )
    (set! framesLeft (- framesLeft 1))
    (set! maxPixel (- maxPixel delta))
    )
)
```

The while loop runs if the number of frames left is greater than 1. If it is, it goes into the let* function. This function declares two new variables:

- pixel-layer. This is a copy of the base layer.
- layer-name. This simply sets the variable to its corresponding frame number.

The function then adds the new layer to the image and puts it in the correct position by subtracting the total number of frames by the frames left. It then renames the layer to layer-name.

The next step is the actual pixelization. `plug-in-pixelize` is called to pixelize the layer with an amount of `maxPixel`. The number of frames left is then decremented by 1, and `maxPixel` is decremented by `delta`. This finishes the `let*` and `while` statements.

Finally, the base layer is renamed to `Frame 1`, and the new image is displayed:

```
(gimp-layer-set-name base-layer "Frame 1")

(gimp-display-new image)
```

6.3.4.4 Cleanup

We will also add some additional cleanup by disabling undo recording. Our final script looks like this:

```
(define (script-fu-pixel-anim img drawable maxPixel totalFrames)

(let*
   (
   ; Declare variables and assign values

   (maxPixel (max 1 maxPixel))
   (totalFrames (max 1 totalFrames))
   (delta ( / maxPixel totalFrames))
   (framesLeft totalFrames)
   (image (car (gimp-channel-ops-duplicate img)))
   (base-layer (car (gimp-image-get-active-layer image)))
   )

   ; Disable undo recording

   (gimp-image-disable-undo img)

   ; Set loop condition

   (while ( > framesLeft 1)
      (let*
      (

   ; Copy layer

      (pixel-layer (car (gimp-layer-copy base-layer TRUE)))
      (layer-name (string-append "Frame "
      (number->string framesLeft)))
      )

      (gimp-image-add-layer image pixel-layer
      (- totalFrames framesLeft))
       (gimp-layer-set-name pixel-layer layer-name)

   ; Pixelize it by the maximum - % frames elapsed

      (plug-in-pixelize
         TRUE
         image
         pixel-layer
         maxPixel
      )

   ; Decrement framesLeft and maxPixel

      (set! framesLeft (- framesLeft 1))
```

```
      (set! maxPixel (- maxPixel delta))
      ))

  ; Set base layer as Frame 1

  (gimp-layer-set-name base-layer "Frame 1")

  ;Cleanup

  (gimp-image-enable-undo img)
  (gimp-display-new image)



  )
  )

(script-fu-register "script-fu-pixel-anim"
    "<Image>/Script-Fu/Animators/Pixelate"
    "Pixelize an image Super Mario Style"
    "Alex Harford (alexh@dowco.com)"
    "Copyright 1999 Alex Harford"
    "July 21, 1999"
    "RGB RGBA GRAY GRAYA"
    SF-IMAGE "Image" 0
    SF-DRAWABLE "Drawable" 0
    SF-ADJUSTMENT "Max Pixelization" '(10 1 100 1 10 0 0)
    SF-ADJUSTMENT "Number of Frames" '(10 1 100 1 10 0 1)
)
```

Extending the GIMP

7

If you were able to listen to the developers of the GIMP describe its advantages, you would hear that it is *modular* and as *independent* as possible. For you and me, this means that it is very easy to customize and streamline the GIMP as much as we please. Almost every aspect of the GIMP can be changed if you know how. For instance, the look of the GIMP is easily changed through GTK+, plug-ins can be downloaded off the Internet and installed easily, and scripts can be downloaded and used instantly. This chapter will look at these extensions, and more like them, so you can get the most out of the GIMP.

7.1 Fonts

The first thing you will want to do if you are going to be using the GIMP seriously is to ensure that you have all the necessary fonts installed. Fonts are controlled by your X server, so this procedure may require you to dig through your documentation. In this book, configuration specific to the XFree86 system is used. This is because it is the most common and portable. If you are not using XFree86, consult your vendor for assistance on adding fonts.

7.1.1 The Freefont Package

The Freefont package is very useful for using the Script-Fu. The fonts used by default on most Script-Fu scripts are ones from the Freefont package. If you can use fonts like Blippo or Roostheavy, then you have the Freefont package. Linux distributions these days will usually come with the Freefont package installed. If you have an older distribution of Linux, you may have to install Freefont. It can be downloaded from `ftp://metalab.unc.edu/pub/Linux/X11/fonts/freefonts-0.10.tar.gz`. RedHat and Debian users may be able to download the appropriate package files. Check their respective Web sites for more information.

To manually install the fonts, follow these steps:

1. Log in as root, or use the `su` - command to become root.
2. Change into the `/usr/X11/lib/fonts` directory.
3. Type `tar zxvf <path to file>`.
4. Start your X server if it is not already running.
5. Type `xset fp+ /usr/X11/lib/fonts/freefont && xset fp rehash` to make your X server aware of these new fonts.
6. Check whether the fonts have been installed properly by using the xfontsel program. If you see fonts like Roostheavy and Dragonwick, the installation worked.

This will set the fonts up for the current X session only. To make these fonts available to all users, you must edit the /etc/XF86Config file. Look for the line that contains the word FontPath. There will be a listing of directories here pointing to the location of various fonts. They are all separated by commas. Add the directory /usr/X11/lib/fonts/freefont to this list. Remember to separate the new entry with a comma. Once these changes have been made, you will need to restart your X server to read the changes.

Now this program will be run whenever you start your X Window System, and the fonts will be available. This process should work for any set of fonts for Unix that you download off the Internet. Just replace the Freefont name with the name of the font package you downloaded. One exception is TrueType fonts, which need a lot of additional setup.

7.1.2 TrueType Fonts

TrueType font support can be added to your X server, which then allows the GIMP to use them. TrueType fonts provide better detail in the various sizes, and are widely used in the computing environment, not just the Unix community. There are two ways of adding TrueType support:

- **Patch the server.** The patches for TrueType fonts are found at http://www.dcs.ed.ac.uk/home/jec/programs/xfsft/. These patches use a rendering program found at http://www.physiol.med.tu-muenchen.de/~robert/freetype.html. This is a very large undertaking even for someone who is experienced in using Linux, as it requires rebuilding your X server, a process that is beyond the scope of this book.

- **Use the Xfstt server.** This is an external font server that can be run separately from your X server. This server can be found in the ftp://ftp.metalab.unc.edu/pub/Linux/X11/fonts/ directory. It will have the name xfstt-<version number>.tar.gz. This program is also complicated to install, and is beyond the scope of this book.

7.2 Plug-Ins

Plug-ins are essential to the GIMP. Almost every function performed in the GIMP is done through a plug-in. *Plug-ins* are programs that are run by the GIMP to perform some sort of operation. This makes it very easy to add new features. There is a registry for plug-ins on the GIMP's Web site, located at http://registry.gimp.org/. There you can find the latest version for every plug-in ever used in the GIMP. You may find old plug-ins that will be useful for you, or new plug-ins that are still under development. Subsequently, they are not included in the stock GIMP distribution. The two plug-ins to download if you are using the stable version of the GIMP are the GIMP Animation Plug-In (GAP), and

ImageMap. ImageMap is an extremely useful and well-designed plug-in that will make your life much easier if you need to do complicated HTML ImageMaps (refer to the ImageMap Plug-In, page 113). GAP has a better interface for creating complicated animations.

7.2.1 Adding Plug-Ins

Now that you've checked out the plug-in registry and have a pile of neat new plug-ins to try, you need to install them. This is done with a small program called gimptool. Gimptool is located in the same directory as the GIMP binary. After you have downloaded a plug-in from the registry, you will probably need to uncompress it. If it is a single file, it is very straightforward to build and install. If it consists of a number of files, it most likely includes a makefile, which will try to make your life easier.

If you encounter difficulties with installation, it may be that you have downloaded a plug-in for the wrong version of the GIMP. Always read the README and INSTALL files that are (hopefully) included with a plug-in before installing it. Check the homepage of the plug-in author for any additional instructions.

7.2.1.1 Building a Single File

When building a single file, type the following:

```
gimptool --install <plug-in.c>
```

This will compile and install the plug-in into your `.gimp/plug-ins` directory. If you are concerned about keeping the binary as small as possible, type the following:

```
gimptool --install -strip <plug-in.c>
```

This will strip the debugging information from the binary and make it run slightly faster.

When gimptool is used this way, the plug-in is installed into your personal directory only. If you want other users to be able to use it, use **--install-admin** instead of **--install**.

7.2.1.2 Installing with a Makefile

If you have a plug-in that comes with a makefile, you should be able to type the following to install the new plug-in:

```
make && make install
```

7.2.1.3 Installing Scripts

If you downloaded a script, gimptool is again used to install it. Just type the following:

```
gimptool --install-script <script.scm>
```

There is very little that can go wrong with scripts. There will be no errors when installing scripts, but you may have problems when trying to run them. If you do have problems running scripts, make sure you have reasonable values for the script, and ensure that the font you are trying to use is installed on your system.

If you cannot find the new script you installed, open it in a text editor and look for the following line:

```
script-fu-register "script-name"
```

Below that line, the location of the script is shown.

7.2.2 The ImageMap Plug-In

Location   <Image>/Filters/Misc/ImageMap

A new plug-in called ImageMap is still in active development, but has been proven to be very useful. It creates and saves image maps for Web pages through a very simple point-and-click interface. As a stand-alone program, it would be very useful. It is not in the current distribution of the GIMP, so you must download it off the Internet. This is a good example for the first plug-in to install. It can be found at `http://registy.gimp.org/`. A link to the plug-in's homepage is provided at the GIMP Plug-In Registry. To use this program, you will need GTK+ 1.2.x and GIMP 1.0.4 or 1.1.x.

7.2.2.1 Installing the ImageMap Plug-In

Follow these steps to install the plug-in:

1. Download the latest version from the Plug-In Registry (discussed previously).

2. Unpack the package in your home directory. This will be available to only one user.

3. Change into the ImageMap plug-in directory.

4. Type `make && make install`. This will install the plug-in into your `~/.gimp` directory. You do not need to use gimptool because the ImageMap plug-in includes a makefile.

5. Restart the GIMP. The plug-in will be found in `<Image>/Filters/Misc/ImageMap`.

7.2.2.2 Using the ImageMap Plug-In

ImageMap[1] has a very easy-to-learn interface, shown in Figure 7.1:

- In the center, the current layer is displayed (1).
- A list of html links to the right (2).

---

[1] *This description assumes that you have basic knowledge of ImageMaps. For more information on creating ImageMaps and using them in Web pages, see* `http://home-2.consunet.nl/~cb007736/ ImageMap.html`.

- Along the top of the window are the controls for the plug-in, like saving, loading existing maps, and so on (3).
- On the left edge are the buttons for creating clickable areas on the image (4).

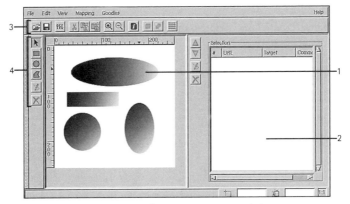

Figure 7.1   *The main ImageMap window.*

To create a clickable area, follow these steps:

1. Choose the shape of the area. The shapes that are available include circles, rectangles, and polygons.
2. Click and release the mouse button on the area you wish to create.
3. Drag the mouse to the endpoint of the area and click the mouse button again.

Now that you have created an area, a new window pops up in which the HTML link information is described:

- The first tab in the window is for HTML-related information: addresses, frame targets, and comments.
- The second tab is for adjusting the placement of the area.
- The third tab is for JavaScript.

When the link has been created, it will appear in the list on the right side. You can edit existing areas by clicking on the pencil icon. This brings up the window with all of the options on it for the selected shape. If you want to delete a selected area, click on the red X.

The Preferences menu provides options on the toolbar that allow the user to choose which type of ImageMap to use:

- NCSA
- CERN
- CSIA

This menu also provides options for changing the look of the interface.

The Information menu is where the map's general information is entered. The author's name, the title of the map, and, most importantly, the default URL can be entered here.

When the map is finished and saved, it can be inserted into an HTML file.

7.3   Customizing the GIMP

The GIMP uses the GIMP ToolKit as its widget set. A widget set simply controls the look of an application, including scrollbars, buttons, etc. The advantage to using the GIMP ToolKit is that it is highly customizable. There are two ways of changing the look of your GTK+ applications: by editing the gtkrc file manually, or by downloading themes off the Internet.

7.3.1   Basics of the gtkrc File

The gtkrc file contains all the information telling a GTK application what to look like. You can find a default gtkrc in your ~/.gimp directory. It looks similar to the following:

```
 1  # style <name> [= <name>]
 2  # {
 3  #    <option>
 4  # }
 5  #
 6  # widget <widget_set> style <style_name>
 7  # widget_class <widget_class_set> style <style_name>
 8
 9  style "ruler"
10  {
11    font = "-adobe-helvetica-medium-r-normal—*-80-*-*-*-*-*-*"
12  }
13
14  style "default"
15  {
16    font = "-adobe-helvetica-medium-r-normal—*-100-*-*-*-*-*-*"
17  }
18
19  widget_class "*Ruler*" style "ruler"
20  widget_class "*" style "default"
```

Another gtkrc file[2] is included in the GIMP source directory. The filename is called gtkrc.forest2. It looks similar to the following:

```
 1  # style <name> [= <name>]
 2  # {
 3  #    <option>
 4  # }
 5  #
 6  # widget <widget_set> style <style_name>
 7  # widget_class <widget_class_set> style <style_name>
 8
 9  pixmap_path "/home/tigert/.gnome/textures"
10
```

continues

---

[2] gtkrc.forest2 *was created by the famous Gimp'er, tigert.*

continued

```
11 style "default"
12 {
13 # font = "-schumacher-clean-medium-r-normal—8-80-75-75-c-50-iso8859-1"
14  font = "-*-lucida-medium-r-normal-*-10-*-*-*-*-*-iso8859-1"
15
16 # base, text, bg, fg are possible
17 bg[NORMAL] = { 0.70, 0.75, 0.67 }
18 bg[SELECTED] = { 0.31, 0.35, 0.35 }
19 bg[INSENSITIVE] = { 0.70, 0.75, 0.67 }
20 bg[ACTIVE] = { 0.61, 0.65, 0.58 }
21 bg[PRELIGHT] = { 0.84, 0.89, 0.81 }
22
23 fg[NORMAL] = { 0.0, 0.0, 0.0 }
24 fg[SELECTED] = { 0.9, 0.9, 0.9 }
25 fg[ACTIVE] = { 0.33, 0.2, 0.0 }
26 fg[PRELIGHT] = { 0.5, 0.1, 0.0 }
27
28 text[INSENSITIVE] = { 0.60, 0.65, 0.57 }
29
30 }
31
32 style "ruler" = "default"
33 {
34   font = "-adobe-helvetica-medium-r-normal—*-80-*-*-*-*-*-*"
35 }
36
37
38 widget_class "*Ruler*" style "ruler"
39 widget_class "*" style "default"
```

If you want to use tigert's gtkrc, just copy it to your `.gimp/gtkrc` file, and when
you restart the GIMP, it will be in that style.

The look is controlled by creating various "styles" in the gtkrc file. These styles
follow this form:

```
style "name"
{
# Configuration information
}
```

Inside the style section, there are several different options that can be changed.
The font is chosen with a line similar to this:

```
font = "-adobe-helvetica-medium-r-normal—*-80-*-*-*-*-*-*"
```

This example uses the Adobe Helvetica font. Specific font information can be
selected through the program xfontsel.

The next set of options that can be affected involve the color. Color is chosen
using percentage values such as this:

```
Attribute[STATE] = { Red, Green, Blue }
```

There are three different attributes for the color:

- fg. The foreground color.
- bg. The background color.
- text. The text color.

Within each of these, there are five different states in which these attributes can exist:

- NORMAL. The normal color of the attribute.
- PRELIGHT. The color of the attribute when the cursor is placed over it.
- ACTIVE. The color of the attribute when the mouse button is clicked.
- INSENSTITIVE. The color of the attribute when it cannot be clicked on.
- SELECTED. The color of the attribute when it is selected.

The style must then be applied to a set of widgets. Wildcards can be used to specify multiple widgets. To use the style "default" on all widgets, it would look similar to this:

```
widget_class "*" style "default"
```

Learning everything within the gtkrc file is beyond the scope of this book. The best thing to do would be to experiment with tigert's gtkrc file and see what you can do. For more information on the gtkrc file, look in your GTK directory in docs/. An HTML version of the tutorial can be found in docs/html/gtk_tut-21.html.

7.3.2 Themes

Themes can now be downloaded off the Internet. The best place to look is at http://gtk.themes.org/.

There are three different types of themes available:

- **gtkrc files.** These simply replace the gtkrc file in your .gimp directory. They just change the colors of the various attributes.
- **Pixmap themes.** Themes of this type use pixmaps to create a theme. In general, these are the best-looking themes. They use pixmaps installed in your home directory, and referred to in the .gtkrc file.
- **Theme engines.** These themes are the most difficult to install. They require the GTK theme engine program, which is still being developed. As a result, these themes are not very stable.

7.4 Hotkeys

Hotkeys are very useful, and can save you a lot of time. It is very simple to assign hotkeys to specific tasks, and changes are effective immediately. All you need to do is place the cursor over the operation you want to assign a hotkey to, hold down the keystroke you want to use, and the hotkey will appear. It is saved when you exit the GIMP in the .gimp/menurc file. An example menurc file looks like the following:

```
(menu-path "<Image>/Filters/Misc/ImageMap" "<Shift><Control>i")
(menu-path "<Image>/AnimFrames/Goto Next" "")
(menu-path "<Toolbox>/Xtns/Script-Fu/Make Brush/Rectangular"
"<Shift><Control>b")
(menu-path "<Image>/Image/Colors/Normalize" "<Control><Alt>n")
(menu-path "<Image>/View/Toggle Statusbar" "")
(menu-path "<Image>/Filters/Enhance/Sharpen" "<Shift><Control>s")
(menu-path "<Image>/Select/Border" "")
(menu-path "<Toolbox>/Xtns/Script-Fu/Make Brush/Rectangular,
Feathered" "<Shift><Control>f")
(menu-path "<Image>/Layers/Layers & Channels..."
"<Control><Alt>c")
(menu-path "<Toolbox>/File/Dialogs/Input Devices..."
"<Shift><Control><Alt>q")
(menu-path "<Toolbox>/File/Dialogs/Brushes..." "")
(menu-path "<Image>/View/Window Info..." "")
(menu-path "<Image>/Layers/Layer to Image Size" "<Alt>l")
```

Note that some of these hotkeys seem to assign nothing to an operation. This is because a different operation has taken its default hotkey.

If you are a Photoshop user and use its hotkeys often, you may want to replace your menurc file with the ps-menurc file found in the GIMP source directory. It replicates some of the hotkeys used in Photoshop.

8
Performance

Page	Contents

There is a lot of discussion about getting the most out of your computer. In this chapter, instead of focusing on your computer, we'll cover various methods of improving the performance of the GIMP. The techniques described here are not for the faint of heart. If you are new to Linux/Unix, or you do not have superuser access, be very careful.

8.1   Compiling with Optimization

Most people are content with the basic version of the GIMP they get in their distribution. What they don't realize is that these packages are made to run on almost any computer. For instance, there are no optimizations for these packages to run on their Pentium computer. Not having optimizations on packages like the GIMP is a waste, because not many people run the GIMP on a 386. Some distributions, like Stampede, are starting to optimize for Pentiums and higher. The following sections outline some steps you can take to optimize the GIMP for your machine.

8.1.1   The egcs Compiler

The first step to making the GIMP run faster is to use the latest and greatest compiler. It is available from `http://egcs.cygnus.com`. Additional information is provided at `http://egcs.cygnus.com/faq.html`. These compilers can be very difficult to install, so it is recommended that you download the appropriate package for your distribution. The egcs compiler is soon to become the official GNU compiler, so it will become the standard compiler on newer distributions.

In Appendix A, "Installing the GIMP," the compilation of the GIMP is described. When you compile the GIMP, you add in optimizations through the `configure` command.

When you type the `configure` command, put a `CFLAGS` entry with the additional options in front of it:

```
CFLAGS="-O3" ./configure  —< Additional Option added here. >
```

The following compiler options are available. Note that these options are available to every CPU:

- **-O1.** This option adds some optimizations to the code. It will not sacrifice any debugging information. This is not needed unless you are debugging the GIMP.

- **-O2.** This is probably the best option to use with the GIMP. It performs various optimizations to the code, and may increase the file size somewhat.

- **-O3.** This option performs the greatest number of optimizations. It performs the same optimizations as -O2, plus some additional ones. Try using this optimization level on the GIMP. If you notice that the GIMP begins to crash after this option is used, recompile with -O2.

The following sections are paraphrased from the EGCS site at `http://egcs.cygnus.com/onlinedocs/gcc_2.html`. There are many different processor architectures available to users, and using code that is specific to your machine will give you a noticeable increase in performance. Note which CPU you have and optimize for it.

8.1.2   Sparc Options

The following option is available if you are using a Sparc machine.

`-mcpu=cpu_type`

This option sets the instruction set, register set, and instruction scheduling parameters for a specific machine type.

Supported values for *cpu_type* are as follows:

- `v7`
- `cypress`
- `v8`
- `supersparc`
- `sparclite`
- `hypersparc`
- `sparclite86x`
- `f930`
- `f934`
- `sparclet`
- `tsc701`
- `v9`
- `ultrasparc`

Some cpu types are subsets of others:

- `v7`: `cypress`
- `v8`: `supersparc`, `hypersparc`
- `sparclite`: `f930`, `f934`, `sparclite86x`
- `sparclet`: `tsc701`
- `v9`: `ultrasparc`

8.1.3   IBM RS/6000 and PowerPC Options

Although these processors are different, they share many instructions, so they are in the same section for compiler options.

The processor type is set with -mcpu=*cpu_type* and the following lists the different processor types available:

- rs6000—RS 6000 chips
- rios1
- rios2
- rsc
- 601—PowerPC chip
- 602—PowerPC chip
- 603—PowerPC chip
- 603e—PowerPC chip
- 604—PowerPC chip
- 604e—PowerPC chip
- 620
- 740—G3
- 750—G3
- power—IBM PowerPC
- power2—IBM PowerPC
- powerpc—General PowerPC optimizations
- 403
- 505
- 801
- 821
- 823
- 860
- common—General IBM/Mac optimizations

common generates code used by all processors.

Use the -mthreads option to generate code that supports AIX Threads.

Use -mcall-solaris to compile code for the Solaris operating system.

Use -mcall-linux to compile code for the Linux-based GNU system.

8.1.4 Intel 386 Options

Use -mcpu=*cpu_type* to specify the type of processor to optimize for.

The choices for *cpu_type* are as follows:

- i386
- i486

- i586
- i686
- pentium
- pentiumpro
- k6

If you use the -mcpu option, it will produce code that is optimized for the specific processor, but it will still run on other processors. If you use -march=cpu type, it generates cpu-specific code, and will not run on other processors. The options are the same for the -march option as the -mcpu option.

Using -malign-double will produce code that runs somewhat faster on a Pentium at the expense of more memory.

8.1.5   DEC Alpha Options

The following options are available when compiling on a DEC Alpha machine.

Use -mcpu=cpu_type to produce code that is optimized for the cpu_type.

Supported values for cpu_type are:

- ev4
- 21064
- ev5
- 21164
- ev56
- 21164a
- pca56
- 21164pc
- 21164PC
- ev6
- 21264

8.2   Memory and Swap Space

The GIMP is a memory-intensive program. Working with high-resolution images can take up a lot of memory, especially when there are multiple layers. Having swap space on your system allows you to use the hard drive as virtual memory, which is cheaper than standard memory, although slower.

There are several conventions dealing with memory for the GIMP:

- Use at least 64MB of RAM if possible. Anything less will lead to constant swapping while using the GIMP.

- Older kernels could only handle up to 127MB of swap space. Kernels 2.2 or newer can handle higher amounts, so take advantage of this.

- Swap space should be at least as big as the physical RAM in your system. Problems will arise when working with large images if there is too little swap space.

- The GIMP also uses your `~/.gimp` directory for swap files. If you find that you are running out of memory, make sure you are not running out of space on that partition.

- The GIMP's Tile Cache Size can be increased to keep it from using memory saved for other applications. This is found in the Preferences menu.)

8.3 X Optimizations

The X Windowing System is probably the most resource-intensive program that will run on a system. There are many different ways of improving the performance of X[1]. The following suggestions should help X performance:

- **Run the appropriate X server.** There are many X servers available, so make sure you are running the correct one.

- **Run at the minimum bit-depth needed.** Most people will not notice a difference between 24 and 32 bits per pixel (bpp). For even faster performance, run at 16bpp.

- **Use a lighter-weight window manager.** Blackbox and icewm are two good window managers that are very fast. Fvwm and twm are also small, but are somewhat older. If you are having performance problems, don't run KDE, Gnome, or Enlightenment with complicated themes—they are resource hogs.

- **Disable background images.** Or use small tileable ones with a small amount of colors.

---

[1]*Additional information can be found in the monthly FAQs posted in the comp.windows.x newsgroup.*

9

Using Peripherals

In this chapter, the installation, configuration, and usage of scanners and pen tablets are discussed[1]. These are useful tools to have when working in the GIMP. Scanners are especially useful, and they are becoming less expensive. Pen tablets are not as common, but they too are useful tools. The mouse is not the best tool to use for touching up images.

9.1 Sane

Sane stands for *Scanner Access Now Easy*. It is an open source project aimed at supporting as many types of scanner hardware as possible. You will need this program if you want to use your scanner under Linux/Unix. Currently, SCSI scanners have the most support, although parallel port scanners are starting to be supported. There are many front-ends and plug-ins available with this package. Sane's homepage is located at `http://www.mostang.com/sane`. There is also a program called XSane found at `http://www.wolfsburg.de/~rauch/sane/sanexsane.html`. It can be run stand-alone, or as a GIMP plug-in.

The following scanner models are supported[2]:

Table 9.1 Supported Scanner Models

Backend	Version	Status	Manufacturer	Model	Comment	Manual Page
abaton	0.1	alpha	Abaton	Scan 300/GS	All known modes and functions supported	sane-abaton
				Scan 300/S	Untested, use with caution	
agfafocus	0.2	alpha	AGFA	Focus GS Scanner	6-bit gray	sane-agfafocus
				Focus Lineart Scanner	Lineart only? Untested	
				Focus II	Gray only	
				Focus Color		
				Focus Color Plus	3-pass	
			Siemens	S9036	Gray only	

---

[1] *Much of the information in this chapter is subject to change and should be used with caution. My expectation is that some elements will be out of date soon after this book goes to print.*

[2] *This table is found at* `http://www.mostang.com/sane/sane-backends.html`. *Please note that this information changes frequently and may be obsolete as you are viewing it.*

Backend	Version	Status	Manufacturer	Model	Comment	Manual Page
apple	0.31	alpha	Apple	Apple Scanner	4-bit, 16 shades of gray	sane-apple
				OneScanner	8-bit, 256 shades of gray. The backend needs work, especially in the quantization code but it may work.	
				ColorOne-Scanner	Truecolor (needs much work) but it scans in non-color modes.	
artec	0.4	alpha	Artec/Ultima	AT3	It works	?
				A6000C	Very alpha	
				A6000C PLUS		
				AT6		
				AT12		
			BlackWidow	BW4800SP	Rebadged Artec AT3	
canon	0.1	alpha	Canon	CanoScan 300	1-pass flatbed scanner	?
				CanoScan 600	1-pass flatbed scanner	
				CanoScan 2700F	1-pass film scanner	
coolscan	0.3	beta	Nikon	LS-20	The LS-20 has been replaced by the LS-30	?
				LS-1000	Doesn't support gamma correction	
dc210	0.0	alpha	Kodak	DC210		sane-dc210
dc25	1.1	alpha	Kodak	DC25		sane-dc25
				DC20	DC-20 is untested	
dll	0.73	beta	Dynamic loading. of shared-library backends.			sane-dll
dmc	1.0	stable	Polaroid	DMC		sane-dmc
epson	?	?	Epson	GT-5500	OK	sane-epson
			Epson	GT-7000	OK	

continues

Table 9.1   Continued.

Backend	Version	Status	Manufacturer	Model	Comment	Manual Page
hp	0.80	alpha	HP	HP ScanJet Plus		sane-hp
				HP ScanJet Iic		
				HP ScanJet Iip		
				HP ScanJet Iicx		
				HP ScanJet 3c		
				HP ScanJet 4c		
				HP ScanJet 6100C		
				HP ScanJet 3p		
				HP ScanJet 4p		
				HP ScanJet 5p		
				HP ScanJet 6200C		
				HP ScanJet 6250C		
				HP PhotoSmart PhotoScanner		
microtek	0.10	beta	Microtek	Scanmaker E6		sane-microtek
				Scanmaker E3		
				Scanmaker E2	3-pass	
				Scanmaker 35t+		Slide-scanner
				Scanmaker III		
				Scanmaker IISP		
				Scanmaker IIHR		3-pass
				Scanmaker IIG	Gray only	
				Scanmaker II	3-pass	
				Scanmaker 600Z(S)	Untested (color?)	
				Scanmaker 600G(S)	Gray only (see manpage)	
			Agfa	Arcus II	Arcus *II*, not Arcus	
				StudioScan II	Not quite functional yet	
				StudioScan IIsi	Not quite functional yet	
microtek2	0.6	alpha	Microtek	parallel models unsupported		sane-microtek2
				ScanMaker V300		
				ScanMaker V310		
				ScanMaker V600		
				ScanMaker E3plus		

Backend	Version	Status	Manufacturer	Model	Comment	Manual Page
				ScanMaker X6		
				ScanMaker X6EL		
				ScanMaker 330		
				ScanMaker 630		
				ScanMaker 636		
				ScanMaker 9600XL	Only flatbed mode	?
				Phantom 636		
			Vobis	HighScan	Only E3plus-based models	
mustek	0.73	beta	Mustek	MFC-600S	1 pass; (f/w >= 1.01 scsi id MFC-06000CZ)	sane-mustek
				MFC-600CD	1 pass; (f/w >= 2.03 scsi id MFC-06000CZ)	
				MFS-6000CX	3 pass; (f/w >= 2.71 scsi id MSF-06000CX)	
				MSF-6000SP	1 pass; (f/w >= 3.12 scsi id MSF-06000SP)	
				MFS-8000SP	1 pass; (f/w >= 2.05 scsi id MSF-08000SP); Lineart drops lines?	
				MFC-800S	1 pass; (f/w == 1.06 scsi id MFC-08000CZ): Color fails?	
				MFS-1200SP	1 pass; (f/w == 1.00 scsi id MSF-12000SP)	
				MFS-1200SP	1 pass; (f/w == 1.07 scsi id MFS-12000SP)	

continues

Table 9.1   Continued.

Backend	Version	Status	Manufacturer	Model	Comment	Manual Page
				MFS-1200SP	1 pass; (f/w == 1.02 scsi id MFS-12000SP); Color fails?	
				MFS-12000 CX	3 pass; (f/w == 2.71 scsi id MFS-12000CX)	
				SE-6000SP	1 pass; (f/w == ? scsi id C03 S10IDW)	
				SE-12000SP	1 pass; (f/w == 1.01 scsi id C06 S12IDW)	
net	0.73	beta	Network access to saned servers		sane-net	
pint	?	?	?			sane-pint
plustek	0.11	beta	Plustek	Plustek 4830	OK	?
				Plustek 9630	Doesn't work	
				Plustek OpticPro 600	Doesn't work	
pnm	?	beta	Reads PNM files		Used for debugging frontends	sane-pnm
qcam	?	?	?			sane-qcam
s9036	?	?	?		?	?
sagitta	0.3	alpha	Qtronix	Sagitta Gray	No monocrome-mode at the moment	?
				Sagitta Color	Not supported at the moment	
sharp	0.15	new	SHARP	JX-610	Preview/Color Lineart/Lineart/ Threshold does not work (JX-610)	?
				JX-250	Color Lineart does not give useful output	
				JX-330	Backend is not yet tested with a JX 330	

Backend	Version	Status	Manufacturer	Model	Comment	Manual Page
SnapScan	0.5	alpha	AGFA	SnapScan 300	Only 8 bits/sample at present	?
				SnapScan 310	Only 8 bits/sample at present	?
				SnapScan 600	Only 8 bits/sample at present	?
				SnapScan 1236s	Only 8 bits/sample at present	?
			Vuego	310S	Close SnapScan 310 compatible	
st400	?	alpha	Siemens	ST400	6-bit gray	sane-st400
tamarack	0.5	beta	Tamarack	Artiscan 6000C	3 pass, 300 DPI	?
				Artiscan 8000C	3 pass, 400 DPI	
				Artiscan 12000C	3 pass, 600 DPI	
umax	1.01-build-3	stable	UMAX	parallel scanners	Not supported	sane-umax
				Vista S6	OK	
				Vista S6E	OK	
				UMAX S-6E	OK	
				UMAX S-6EG	OK	
				Vista-S8	Not tested	
				Supervista S-12	OK	
				UMAX S-12	OK	
				UMAX S-12G	OK	
				Astra 600S	OK	
				Astra 610S	OK	
				Astra 1200S	OK	
				Astra 1220S	OK	
				UC 630	Version 1.6 OK, others only lineart; OK	
				UG 630	OK	
				UG 80	OK	
				UC 840	Version 1.6 OK, others only lineart; OK	
				UC 1200S	Does not work. (firmware version?)	

continues

Table 9.1   Continued.

Backend	Version	Status	Manufacturer	Model	Comment	Manual Page
				UC 1200SE	?	
				UC 1260	Version 1.6 OK, others unknown	
				Mirage	Not tested	
				Mirage II	Not tested	
				Mirage IIse	Not tested	
				Vista-T630	OK for some firmware versions; on others only lineart OK	
				PSD	OK	
				PowerLook	Not tested	
				PL-II	Only works with some scanners (unknown why)	
				PowerLook III	Not tested	
				PowerLook 2000	Not tested	
				PowerLook 3000	Not tested	
				Gemini D-16	OK	
			Linotype Hell	Jade	OK, SCSI-ID =LinoHell Office	
				Jade2	OK, SCSI-ID =LinoHell Office2	
				Saphir	Not tested	
				Saphir2	OK, SCSI-ID =LinoHell SAPHIR2	
				Saphir Ultra	Not tested	
				Saphir Ultra II	Not tested	
				Saphir HiRes	Not tested	
				Opal	Not tested	
				Opal Ultra	Not tested	
			Vobis/ Highscreen	Scanboostar Premium	OK, SCSI- ID =LinoHell Office2	
			Escom	Image Scanner 256	OK, SCSI-ID =UMAX UG 80	
			Nikon	AX-210	OK	

9.1.1 Installation of Sane

To install Sane and XSane, follow these steps:

1. Download the latest version of Sane from their Web site
   (`http://www.mostang.com/sane`).

2. Unpack the package into your `/usr/local/src` directory.

3. Enter the Sane directory and type `./configure`.

4. Type **make**.

5. If the previous step ran without any problems[3], change to root and type
   make install. This will install the files into your `/usr/local/bin` and
   `/usr/local/lib` directories. Configuration files are installed into
   `/usr/local/etc/sane.d/`.

6. Edit your `/etc/ld.so.conf` to include the line `/usr/local/lib/sane`.
   Then type **ldconfig**.

7. Create a symbolic from your scanner device to the scanner device[4]:
   ```
   cd /dev && ln -s sg0 scanner
   ```

8. Download the XSane package from
   `http://www.wolfsburg.de/~rauch/sane/sane-xsane.html`.

9. As a non-root user, unpack the package into your `/usr/local/src` directory.

10. Type `./configure && make`.

11. If the previous step was successful[5], change to root and type **make install**.

12. Copy the XSane binary to your `~/.gimp/plug-ins` directory.

13. Restart the GIMP.

9.1.2 Using Sane

The best way to use Sane is through the XSane front-end. It is found in the
<Toolbox>/Xtns/XSane. A listing of the devices will be displayed here. When the
device is clicked on, the screen similar to figure 9.1 appears. Depending on the
device you are using, not all options will be available to you.

---

[3] *This program is fairly straightforward. It can be built on almost any Unix system. If the configure script does not detect GTK+, you will need to fix this, since the xscanimage program is required. This is usually caused by GTK+ being installed in a non-standard location. You may need to add* `--with-gtk-prefix=<Path to GTK+>`.

[4] *In this description, it is assumed that you have the appropriate device connected to your system, and support for it is compiled in the kernel. If not, recompile the kernel or load the appropriate module. Replace* `/dev/sg0` *with the correct device file for your scanner.*

[5] *Like the Sane package, this program can be built on almost any Unix system. If the configure script does not detect GTK+, you will need to fix this. This is usually caused by GTK+ being installed in a non-standard location. You may need to add* `--with-gtk-prefix=<Path to GTK+>`. *If the program still refuses to compile and you are sure that GTK+ is installed correctly, add* `--disable-gtktest` *to force compilation.*

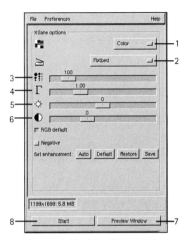

Figure 9.1   *The XSane Menu.*

When using XSane within the GIMP, usage is fairly simple:

1. Choose the color mode (1).

2. Choose the scanner type (2).

3. Choose the resolution (3). See "Resolution," page 6.

4. Choose the gamma correction (4).

5. Choose the amount of brightness adjustment (5). See "Brightness and Contrast," page 59.

6. Choose the amount of contrast adjustment (6). See "Brightness and Contrast," page 55.

7. Click on the preview window (7) to select the area you wish to scan.

8. When you are ready to scan, click the Start button (8). The image will automatically be transferred to the GIMP.

XSane is a new program that is still under development, so options may change between different versions. There is additional documentation found in your /usr/local/share/sane directory describing use of XSane without the GIMP.

9.2   Pen Tablets[6]

Pen tablets are great pieces of hardware that can replace the mouse as the pointing device. They are perfect when using the GIMP for drawing and doing touch-ups. If you already have a pen tablet for your computer, chances are it is supported in the GIMP. Not all functions may be available, but the basics, like pressure and tilt, should be. This is a basic overview of how to use pen tablets with the GIMP. For more detailed information, see Owen Taylor's page at `http://www.gtk.org/ ~otaylor/xinput/howto/`.

9.2.1   Supported Hardware

The first step is to make sure your pen tablet is supported. The following devices are supported:

- AceCad ADVANCEDigitizer tablets
- Elographics touchscreens
- Joysticks
- MicroTouch TouchPen touchscreens
- SGI dial boxes
- Summagraphics tablets
- Wacom tablets:
  a. ArtZ II series[7]
  b. ArtPad II
  c. Pen Partner
  d. PL300
  e. Intuos series[8]

9.2.2   Configuring XFree86 for XInput

XFree86 must now be configured to recognize the pen tablet. Make sure that the version of XFree86 installed on your system is at least 3.3.4. If you have an older version, please upgrade. It is easiest to do this through your distribution's package manager.

---

[6] *Much of the information here is paraphrased from the XInput HOWTO by Owen Taylor.* `http://www.gtk.org/~otaylor/xinput/howto/`. *Copyright (c) 1997–1999 Owen Taylor.*

[7] *This is called the UltraPad series in Europe.*

[8] *XFree86 3.3.3.1 includes a early version of an Intuos driver with a number of bugs. For updated beta versions see* `http://www.levien.com/free/linux_intuos.html`.

It is necessary to edit your /etc/XF86Config file. This must be done as root. To be safe, make a backup of the file before you start to edit.

The following changes must be made to the file:

1. In the Section "Module," add the line Load "*module.so*". It should look like this:

   ```
   #Section "Module"
   #
   # This loads the module for the Joystick driver
   #
   Load "xf86Wacom.so"
   #
   #EndSection
   ```

   The following modules are available:

   - xf86Dial.so—SGI Dial boxes driver
   - xf86Jstk.so—Joystick driver
   - xf86Summa.so—Summagraphics tablet driver
   - xf86AceCad.so—AceCad ADVANCEDigitizer tablets driver
   - xf86Elo.so—Elographics touchscreens driver
   - xf86MuTouch.so—MicroTouch TouchPen touchscreens driver
   - xf86Wacom.so—Wacom pen tablet driver

2. Now you must add the XInput entry to the file. Find the section "XInput" and add a new subsection for your hardware. It should look similar to this entry for a Wacom Stylus:

   ```
   Section "Xinput"
       SubSection "WacomStylus"
           Port "/dev/ttyS1"
           DeviceName "Wacom"
           Mode Absolute
           Suppress 6
       EndSubSection
       SubSection "WacomEraser"
           Port "/dev/ttyS1"
           Mode Absolute
           Suppress 6
       EndSubSection
   EndSection
   ```

Read the manpage XF86Config (type **man XF86Config**) for information about your specific hardware.

9.2.3 Configuring GTK+ for XInput

Now that XFree86 recognizes the hardware, GTK+ must be configured to recognize XInput. This is done by recompiling GTK+. (See Appendix A for more information on compiling GTK+.) Note that you do not need to recompile glib.

To recompile GTK+:

1. Run the `./configure` command, add the statement `--with-xinput=xfree` to any other options you need to compile GTK+.

2. Type **make**.

3. If the previous command completed without any errors, type **make install && ldconfig**.

You should now be able to restart the GIMP and try out your device. Follow these steps:

1. Re-start the GIMP.

2. Create a new image.

3. Choose <Image>/Dialogs/Input Devices.

4. Change the device mode from Disabled to Screen.

5. Test the tablet by drawing some example lines.

6. To check the settings of the available tools, click on <Image>/Dialogs/Device Status.

10
Drawing Tools

Depending on what you are doing, you may find that you never use the drawing tools at all. If you are touching up photographs, you may only use the airbrush tool with a very soft brush. If you are creating interesting logos and computer graphics, you may need to use the Text tool many times. It is useful, however, to know how to use each tool to its full potential to get the most out of the GIMP.

10.1   The Pencil   [Shift+P]

Description   The Pencil tool draws sharp lines that are the exact size of the current brush. It is useful for creating images with defined edges, or where it will be smoothed later. It ignores opacity information in brushes, making it either fully transparent, or fully opaque.

Options
Straight Line   Hold down the Shift key while clicking to draw a straight line from the last Pencil position to the current one.

Color Picker   Holding down the Ctrl key while clicking changes the tool to the Color Picker (page 166).

Usage   The Pencil tool works very much like a pencil would in real life. It has a hard edge, exactly the size of the brush. This is very useful for touching up images when using the 1×1 size brush. (It edits just one pixel at a time.) It ignores transparency information provided by the brush, and will either make it opaque or transparent. This tool is most useful with computer-generated images. An example of lines drawn by the Pencil tool is shown in Figure 10.1. Figure 10.2 is an enlarged area of the same picture to demonstrate the jaggedness.

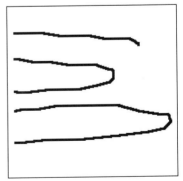

Figure 10.1   *Some example lines drawn with the pencil. Notice how they seem very rough around the edges.*

Figure 10.2   *A portion of the image, enlarged so the jagged edges are apparent.*

▸**See Also** Brushes (172)

10.2 The Paintbrush   [P]

Description   The Paintbrush tool creates lines with smooth edges, and acts very similarly to a paintbrush in real life.

Options

Incremental   When this option is set, the brush strokes will add to one another. This option works only when the brush is set to an opacity less than 100.

Fade Out   This option makes the brush act as if there is a finite amount paint on it. When the mouse is used without releasing the button, the line will gradually become more transparent. This setting also depends on the size of the brush. The distance it travels before it begins to fade is the product of the brush size and the fade-out distance. When the brush begins to fade, it will always act as incremental, up to its maximum opacity. A setting of 0 turns the fade-out effect off.

Gradient   This option uses the active gradient as the paint color. The distance the gradient travels is the length multiplied by the current brush's radius. There are four types of gradient drawing methods:

- Once Forward. Draws the gradient only once, starting at the first color.

- Once Backward. Draws the gradient once, starting with the last color and working backward.

- Loop Sawtooth. Repeats the gradient, starting with the first color, going to the last, then starting over with the first color.

- Loop Triangle. Repeats the gradient, starting with the first color, going to the last, then drawing the gradient backward. This makes a much smoother transition for most gradients.

Straight Line   Hold down the Shift key while clicking to draw a straight line from the last Paintbrush position to the current one.

Usage   The Paintbrush works very much like a paintbrush would in real life. It creates lines with smooth edges through anti-aliasing, like paint spreading out on the paper. The Fade Out option is especially useful. It makes the brush seem as if it has paint on it, and it fades as you make brush strokes. Every time you release the mouse button, it is as if you are adding more paint to the brush. The most effective brushes to use are the larger solid brushes. Feathered brushes will seem much smaller than solid ones of the same size. Some example lines drawn with the brush are shown in Figure 10.3. Note the much smoother lines, as shown in the enlarged portion in Figure 10.4.

Figure 10.3 *Lines drawn with the Paintbrush tool. Note that the edges seem much smoother (than the pencil tool, for instance) and the paint fades out to transparency on some of the strokes.*

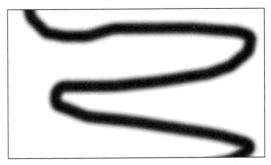

Figure 10.4 *A zoomed area from Figure 10.3, showing the smooth edges.*

▸**See Also** Brushes (172)

✎ 10.3 The Airbrush   [A]

Description   The Airbrush tool works like an airbrush or spray paint in
real life. It creates very smooth lines.

Options

Rate   This option is related to the movement of the cursor. A
low setting will create a uniform line, and is not affected
by movement as much. A higher rate setting means that the
"paint" in the airbrush leaves faster, and will leave darker
patches when the cursor slows down.

Pressure   This setting controls how much "paint" is sprayed out of the
airbrush. Higher pressure settings make darker, more uniform
lines. Low pressure settings are very uneven.

Straight Line   Hold down the Shift key while clicking to draw a straight
line from the last Airbrush position to the current one.

Usage   The Airbrush works like a can of spray paint. You can vary
the rate of "paint" coming out of the nozzle, and the pressure
of the paint. For dark, uniform lines with soft edges, use a
high pressure, but a low rate. To create a line that looks like it
was created with a spray can, use a higher rate, but a lower
pressure. This will make the line darker where the cursor is
moved more slowly. The best brushes to use with this tool are
the feathered ones. Feathered brushes appear much smoother
and realistic than the solid ones. Some example lines drawn
with the Airbrush tool are shown in Figure 10.5.

Figure 10.5   *Lines drawn with the Airbrush tool. Notice how some lines are uneven, and others are more uniform.*

▶**See Also** Brushes (172)

10.4   The Bucket Fill Tool   [Shift+B]

Description   The Bucket Fill tool fills areas of similar color with the foreground color.

Options

Fill Threshold   (1) (see Figure 10.6 for all options). This setting determines how much the Bucket Fill will "spill over." This is detected by changes in color or transparency. A higher setting will spread further over different colors.

Fill Type   (2) The fill type is chosen here with an option button. FG Color Fill will fill with the active foreground color. BG Color Fill will fill with the active background color. Pattern Fill will fill with the current pattern.

Sample Merged (3). This option takes into account all of the layers for the threshold, but paints only on the active layer.

Background Color   Hold down the Shift key while clicking to use the background color to fill.

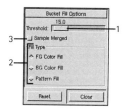

Figure 10.6 *Options menu for the Bucket Fill tool.*

Usage

The Bucket Fill tool fills large areas of similar color or a selection with a solid color or pattern. This tool is most often used to fill in backgrounds or flat areas in computer-generated images. The Bucket Fill tool does not work well with photographs because of their subtle variations in color. The tool determines how much area it fills by detecting color changes. To stop after only a slight change in color, use a small threshold. To fill large areas, even after a significant color change, use a high threshold. A value of 255 for the threshold fills everything. If you have an active selection, using the Bucket Fill tool will fill the entire selected area, regardless of color.

▶**See Also** Modes (44)

10.5   The Blend Tool   [L]

Description

The Blend tool creates a gradient between where the mouse button is clicked and where it is released.

Options

Offset (1)

Offset determines where the foreground color begins to fade into the background color (see Figure 10.7 for all options). A higher offset value makes the foreground color more prominent. This is not used for linear, shapeburst, or spiral gradients.

Blend (2)

Blend determines how the colors in the gradient change.

- **RGB** is the standard color blend.
- **HSV** travels the full spectrum of colors for the blend.
- **FG to Transparent** gradually fades the foreground to transparency.
- **Custom from Editor** allows users to use a gradient from the gradient editor, or to make their own.

Gradient (3)

Determines the shape of the gradient.

- **Linear** spreads from the foreground color to the background, following the mouse click.

- **Bi-Linear** fades from the background color, to the foreground, and to the background again. This is useful in creating 3D pipes and other objects.

- **Radial** creates a circular gradient, with the mouse click as the center, and the release as the edge.

- **Square** creates a square gradient, with the mouse click as the center, and the release as the far edge.

- **Conical** creates a gradient that is similar to looking at a 3D cone from above. Symmetric continues completely around the cone, and Asymmetric creates a distinct border between the foreground and background.

- **Shapeburst** is used to create a gradient inside a selection. It gives the selection a 3D feel. Angular emphasizes the foreground color, Spherical creates a rounder gradient, and Dimpled creates a sharper gradient.

- **Spiral** (**Clockwise/Anticlockwise**) creates a spiral pattern using the foreground and background colors.

Repeat (4)

Repeat determines whether the gradient should repeat. Sawtooth repeats the pattern, without blending the two. Triangular repeats, blending continuously between the foreground and background. Sawtooth and Triangular do not work with the Shapeburst gradient. Repeat is also ineffective with the Conical gradient.

Adaptive Super-sampling (5)

This option uses more intermediate colors for the gradient. It creates a smoother blend, but takes longer to render. Increasing the maximum depth and threshold improves the quality of the blend, but also increases rendering time.

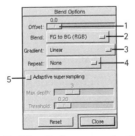

Figure 10.7 *The Options menu for the Blend tool.*

Usage   The Blend tool creates gradients on layers or selected areas. There are no brush options—everything is controlled in the Blend tool's Options window (refer to Figure 10.7). Blend will be most useful when creating logos, cartoons, or other computer-generated images.

As an example, let's create a simple text logo with a gradient in it.

1. Create a new RGB image, approximately 350×100.

2. Select the Text tool (page 148).

3. Click on the image to place the text. The Text tool window will come up. Choose a good, thick font like Blippo, and set the size to 72.

4. Type a simple phrase, like "The Gimp" into the preview area, as shown in Figure 10.8, and click OK.

Figure 10.8   *The Text Entry window.*

5. The text will now be a floating selection, shown in Figure 10.9, and the current tool is automatically the Move tool. Use it to position the text precisely.

Figure 10.9   *The new text placed on the image.*

6. Open the Layers and Channels menu, shown in Figure 10.10 (<Image>/Layers/Layers and Channels). You will see the text in the floating selection (1). Click on the New Layer button (2) to create a new layer.

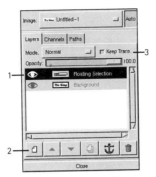

Figure 10.10   *The Layers and Channels menu.*

7. Make sure the Keep Transparent toggle (3) is turned on.

8. Switch to the Blend tool ([L]).

9. Set the foreground and background colors. The colors in the figures will just appear black and white here.

10. Click and drag with the Blend tool to apply a simple blend to the text layer. This step can be repeated as many times as necessary.

Figure 10.11   *The finished image.*

▶**See Also** Gradient Editor (179), Color Selection (12), Modes (44)

T 10.6   The Text Tool   [T]

Description   The Text tool draws text on the active layer.

Options
Anti-Aliasing   Toggles anti-aliasing on and off. It makes fonts look smoother by using transparency to round edges.

Border   Specifies how much border is placed around the text if a new layer is created.

Use Dynamic   This toggle uses the Dynamic Text plug-in to place the text.
Text

You will see three different tabs when you click on the area to place text (see Figure 10.12).

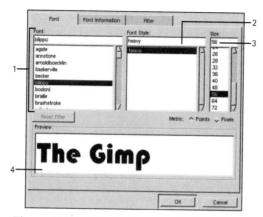

Figure 10.12   *The Options menu for the Text tool.*

| **Font** | This is the most important part of the window. It controls the actual font to be placed. |

- **Font** (1). Lists the fonts available on your system.
- **Font Style** (2). Select a specific style (for example, Italic or Bold) if available to a font.
- **Size** (3). Choose the size of the font to use. Can be set to pixels or points.
- **Text entry box** (4). Enter text in this box. The preview is updated automatically whenever a change is made to the font.

Font Information   All of the information about the specific font is displayed here. Values cannot be changed.

Filter   This menu allows you to filter out different types of fonts depending on their properties:

- **Font Types.** There are three choices here: Bitmap, Scalable, and Scaled Bitmap.
- **Foundry.** The manufacturer of the font.
- **Weight.** Determines the boldness of the font.
- **Charset.** The character set of the font: English, Greek, and so on.
- **Slant.** Determines the slant of the font: Italic, Roman, or Oblique.
- **Set Width.** Determines the horizontal width of the font.

- **Spacing.** Determines the spacing between letters. C and M options stand for character cell and monospaced, respectively. These produce spacing similar to computer terminals, in which each character occupies the same amount of space. P stands for proportional, which allows letters to occupy different amounts of space.

Usage

The ability to use text is somewhat lacking in the GIMP, as it is for many image-manipulation programs. If you are going to be doing large amounts of text processing, you may want to use TeX[1] or another typesetting program first, then import it as a PostScript file into the GIMP.

If you are only inserting small amounts of text, the Text tool should be adequate. To get the best results, use anti-aliasing for your fonts. Also, choose fonts that are scalable—for example Blippo or RoostHeavy—so that your text doesn't look chunky.

▶**See Also** Fonts (110), Resizing Layers (42)

10.7 The Ink Tool [K]

Description

The Ink tool simulates painting with a calligraphic pen. It changes its width depending on the speed at which the cursor is moving. If you have a pen tablet that includes pressure and tilt support, the width of the pen depends on the pressure and the tilt.

Options

Size

Determines the maximum radius of the nib (brush shape). Note that the brush size and shape are irrelevant.

Sensitivity

Determines how sensitive the tool is to change. A higher sensitivity will produce less uniform lines.

Tilt Sensitivity

Determines how sensitive the tool is to the tilt of a pen tablet. This option is not used if the pointing tool is a mouse.

Speed Sensitivity

This option determines how sensitive the paint applied is to speed changes. Low sensitivity means that the width of the ink changes very little. Higher sensitivity will give a more realistic ink tool.

Angle

Determines the angle offset for the nib. This option is only used if you have a pen tablet.

---

[1] *Another method is to use a new Perl script to render TeX. It is found at* `http://imagic.weizmann. ac.il/~dov/gimp/tex-to-float/`.

Nibs

There are three different nibs, or brush shapes, that can be used with this tool:

- **Round**
- **Square**
- **Diamond**

Usage

The Ink tool was originally designed to help with the development of pen tablet drivers for X servers. This small program has grown into an excellent tool that simulates real ink very well. It produces the best results when using a pen tablet, but it is still useful when using a mouse. To use this tool, simply draw lines on your image, and move the mouse at varying speeds. The faster the cursor is moved, the thinner the line becomes. Figure 10.13 shows some example lines drawn this way.

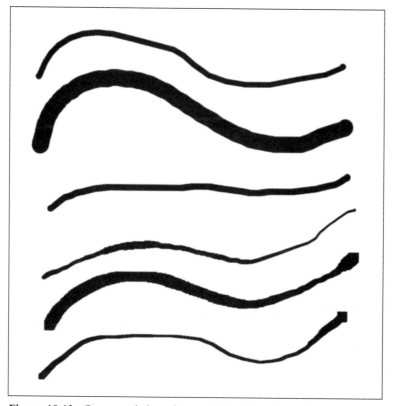

Figure 10.13 *Some sample lines drawn with the Ink tool at various sensitivities.*

11
Selection Tools

Page	Contents

Now that you have drawn on your image, it is useful to move these drawings around on the canvas to get them to look just right. The selection tools provide many different ways of doing this. They allow you to work in very specific areas to draw and apply filters. After you have mastered these selection tools, you will be able to work very efficiently in the GIMP. The controls for these tools can be very complicated, and it is recommended that you read the "Advanced Selections" section (page 24) very carefully.

11.1 Rectangular Select   [R]

Description	This tool makes rectangular selections on the active layer.
Options	
Feather	This option makes the border of the selection fuzzy. It will make the part of the image near the edge of the selection gradually fade to full transparency.
Fixed Size/ Aspect Ratio	This toggle allows you to constrain the size of the selection to a certain size or ratio. The most useful units to use are pixels, which give an absolute value. Percentage is also useful; it creates a selection that is a certain percentage of the image size.
Union	Hold the Shift key, then click to add the selection to an existing one.
Force Square	Hold the Shift key while dragging to force the selection into a square.
Difference	Hold the Ctrl key, then click to subtract the selection from an existing one.
Center Selection	Hold the Ctrl key while dragging to center the selection from where the mouse was clicked.
Intersection	Hold the Ctrl and Shift keys, then click. This selects only where the original selection and the new section overlap.

▶**See Also** Advanced Selections (24)

11.2 Elliptical Select   [E]

Description	This tool makes elliptical selections on the active layer.
Options	
Anti-Aliasing	This makes curves look smoother by using transparency.
Feather	This option makes the border of the selection fuzzy. It will make the part of the image near the edge of the selection gradually fade out to transparency.

Fixed Size/ Aspect Ratio	This toggle allows you to constrain the size of the selection to a certain size or ratio. The most useful units to use are pixels, which give an absolute value. Percentage is also useful; it creates a selection that is a certain percentage of the image size.
Union	Hold the Shift key, then click to add the selection to an existing one.
Force Circle	Hold the Shift key while dragging to force the selection into a circle.
Difference	Hold the Ctrl key, then click to subtract the selection from an existing one.
Center Selection	Hold the Ctrl key while dragging to center the selection from where the mouse was clicked.
Intersection	Hold the Ctrl and Shift keys, then click. This selects only where the original selection and the new section overlap.

▶**See Also** Advanced Selections (24)

11.3   Freehand Select   [F]

Description	The Freehand Select tool allows you to create freely drawn selections. It is very useful for touching up selections for photo editing.
Options	
Anti-Aliasing	This makes curves look smoother by using transparency.
Feather	This option makes the border of the selection fuzzy. It will make the part of the image near the edge of the selection gradually fade to full transparency.
Union	Hold the Shift key, then click to add the selection to an existing one.
Difference	Hold the Ctrl key, then click to subtract the selection from an existing one.
Intersection	Hold the Ctrl and Shift keys, then click. This selects only where the original selection and the new section overlap.

11.4   Fuzzy Select   [Z]

Description   The Fuzzy Select tool allows you to take selections based on color. It will select anything near the mouse click and spread until the color becomes too different. Dragging the cursor as you click changes the selection threshold. Dragging to the left will decrease the threshold; dragging to the right will increase the threshold.

Options

Sample Merged   This option determines the threshold from the image formed by all the layers, not just the active one. It creates the selection only on the active layer.

Anti-Aliasing   This option makes curves look smoother by using transparency.

Feather   This option makes the border of the selection fuzzy. It will make the part of the image near the edge of the selection gradually fade out to transparency.

Threshold   This slider controls the base threshold used when clicking, but can be increased or decreased by clicking and dragging the mouse to the right or left.

Union   Hold the Shift key, then click to add the selection to an existing one.

Difference   Hold the Ctrl key, then click to subtract the selection from an existing one.

Intersection   Hold the Ctrl and Shift keys, then click. This selects only where the original selection and the new section overlap.

11.5   Bezier Select   [B]

Description   This tool is excellent for cutting out complicated shapes from photographs. It is a complicated tool, so its Options menu is shown in Figure 11.1.

Options

Anti-Aliasing   This makes curves look smoother by using transparency.

Feather   This option makes the border of the selection fuzzy. It will make the part of the image near the edge of the selection gradually fade out to transparency.

Union   Hold the Shift key, then click to add the selection to an existing one.

Move Handle   Hold the Shift key and click while in Editor mode to move a single handle on an anchor point.

Difference   Hold the Ctrl key, then click to subtract the selection from an existing one.

Move Anchor   Hold the Ctrl key and click while in Editor mode to move the anchor point.

Intersection   Hold the Ctrl and Shift keys, then click. This selects only where the original selection and the new section overlap.

Figure 11.1   *Options menu for the Bezier Select tool.*

Usage   The Bezier Select tool is the most complicated and powerful selection tool. To make a selection, outline the object needed by clicking the mouse button wherever there is a curve or sharp corner. This will create a series of anchor points around the object. When the object is completely encircled, click on the original anchor point. This will bring you into editing mode. To create curves, click and drag an anchor point. This will turn the anchor point into a curve. Hold down the Shift key while clicking and dragging to move a single handle. To move an anchor point, hold down the Ctrl key while clicking and dragging. After you have a satisfactory curve, click inside the selection. If you are doing a union, difference, or intersection, hold down the appropriate key while clicking. This will give you the selection. Once the selection is made, the Bezier curve is converted to a "path."

▶**See Also** Intelligent Scissors (157)

11.6   Intelligent Scissors   [I]

Description   The Intelligent Scissors tool is an excellent tool for quickly making selections from complicated images. It has some fairly complicated options, so the menu is shown in Figure 11.2. Note that this tool does not always work properly, so it may be removed from future versions until it is fixed.

Options

AntiAliasing (1)   This makes curves look smoother by using transparency.

Feather (2)   This option makes the border of the selection fuzzy. It will make the part of the image near the edge of the selection gradually fade out to transparency.

Curve Resolution (3)   This determines how detailed the curves in the Intelligent Scissors are. A lower resolution value makes the curves look more jagged.

Edge Detect Threshold (4)   This option determines how sensitive the tool is to a change in color. This can range from 1 to 255. A threshold of 15 is generally a good value to use.

Elasticity (5)   Elasticity determines how much the tool will bend away from the drawn curve to snap to the image. This can range from 0 to 1.0. Higher values in this setting do not always produce correct results.

Convert to Bezier Curve (6)   A very useful option, Convert to Bezier Curve changes the curve drawn by the scissors into a Bezier curve for further tweaking.

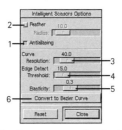

Figure 11.2   *The Options menu for the Intelligent Scissors.*

►**See Also** Bezier Select (156)

⊹ 11.7 Move   [M]

Description   With the Move tool, you can move a selection or layer by clicking and dragging it.

Cursor Keys   This option moves the selection in very small increments. Hold down Shift while using the cursor keys to move the selection with slightly larger increments.

Move Layer   Hold the Shift key, and click and drag to move the entire active layer.

Move Border   Hold the Alt key, and click and drag to move the selection border, but not the selection contents.

Usage   Care must be taken when moving layers with transparency.
            To move a layer with transparency, you must click on a part
            of the image that has paint on it; otherwise, the Move tool
            will move the layer below it. This can lead to confusion
            when dealing with many layers. If, however, you are using
            the Shift key to drag the layer, it will always move the active
            layer.

11.8   Crop   [Shift+C]

Description   The Crop tool resizes an image.

Options

**Current Layer   This toggles betweencropping the current layer or the entire
Only**   image.

Allow Enlarging This option allows you to toggle the ability to enlarge the
                    image. This is not always useful, so it is best left turned off.

Crop/Resize   This allows you to select which type of cropping occurs. If
                    you choose crop, the information outside of the border is
                    thrown away. When resize is used, the information is not lost,
                    and can be resized again.

Usage   After choosing the crop area, a dialog box will appear. It
                    contains the coordinates of the cropping. Click the Crop
                    button to crop the image to the chosen area. Clicking inside
                    the chosen area will crop as well. Clicking on the selection
                    button will shrink the crop area to an area you have selected.
                    To resize the area, click and drag the upper-left or lower-
                    right corner of the crop. To move the area, click and drag
                    the lower-left or upper-right corner. Precision adjustments
                    can be made with the cursor keys. In the dialog box, the
                    coordinates can also be entered with the keyboard.

12
Image Transformation Tools

Image transformation tools perform operations on images, but do not actually draw on the images. These tools are used after the basic image has been created, or on scanned images after the color has been corrected. Generally speaking, the most useful of the bunch is the Clone tool (page 165). Some new tools added in GIMP 1.2 are also useful: Dodge and Burn, and Smudge. Dodge and Burn lets you work with brightness values in pixels; it can be applied with a brush. Smudge turns an image into finger paint, and allows you to drag the paint with a brush.

As always, the Options menu for each tool is accessed by double-clicking on the tool's icon in the Toolbox.

12.1   The Magnify Tool   [Z]

Description   The Magnify tool enlarges or shrinks the image for viewing more or less precise areas, respectively.

Options
Allow Window Resizing   This option automatically resizes the window to the image size upon zooming. This option is useful for working on images that fit on the monitor, but should be turned off when working on very large images.

Zoom Out   Hold down the Shift key while clicking to zoom out.

Zoom Box   Click and drag the mouse to zoom in to a specific area.

Usage   Clicking on the image zooms in. Shift+clicking zooms out. To zoom in on a specific area, click and drag a box over the area. Note that Undo and Redo do not affect zooming— all zooming (or un-zooming) must always be done with the Zoom tool.

▶**See Also** "Preferences" (page 16), "Window Operations" (page 20), and "Undo/Redo" (16)

12.2   The Transform Tool   [Shift+M]

Description   The Transform tool performs several different operations on an image: rotation, scaling, shearing, and perspective.

Options
Rotation   Rotates the layer inside the canvas. Holding down the Ctrl key constrains it to 15-degree intervals. Specific information about using this tool is found in the following "Usage" section.

Scaling	Scales the image inside the canvas. This is similar to Scale in the Image menu, except it only acts on the active layer. Holding down the Shift key while dragging keeps the height constant, whereas holding down the Ctrl key keeps the width constant. Holding down both keys at the same time keeps the height/width ratio constant. Specific information about using this tool is found in the following "Usage" section.
Shearing	Distorts the image in the X or Y axis. This transform is analogous to folding a cardboard box flat, only the length of the sides can change. This can only be done to one axis at a time. The chosen axis is determined by the direction in which the mouse is first moved. Specific information about using this tool is found in the following "Usage" section.
Perspective	Adjusts the perspective of the current layer. Each corner can be adjusted independently, allowing for very interesting and potentially unrealistic perspectives to be created. Specific information about using this tool is found in the following "Usage" section.
Tool Paradigm	This determines how the movement of the border affects the image. There are two options here:

- **Traditional** This option is straightforward. It transforms the image to fit the border to which it has been dragged. Rotation and Shearing almost always use this mode. Scaling and Perspective usually use this option as well.

- **Corrective** This option is used to correct an image that needs fixing. It does the reverse of Traditional mode by transforming the new border to fit in the old border. For example, if there is a scanned photograph that is crooked, it can be fixed in this mode. Simply drag the border in Perspective mode to the correct shape. When the Transform button is clicked, it will stretch this new border into the old one, making the photo perfectly straight. This mode is usually only used in Perspective mode, but it can be used in others.

Smoothing	This option works like anti-aliasing: It makes jagged edges smoother. It works on all types of transformations.
Show Path	This option shows the last path created during the transformation.
Show Grid	This option turns on the grid inside the transform border.

Grid Density	This option defines the grid density if the grid is turned on. For larger images, use a lower grid density. This value ranges from 0 to 5.
Clip Result	This option, when selected, will keep the layer the same size, and lose any information outside the layer. If it is not selected, the layer will be as large as needed.
Usage	Each part of the Transform tool has similar usage. When the tool is chosen, the layer must first be clicked on. Small boxes will appear in the corners of the active layer. Clicking and dragging the corners will adjust the image. All four corners can be used for these transformations.
	GIMP 1.2 comes with an improved interface for this tool. For each mode, there is an Information window that pops up. This gives the necessary information for the tool. Keyboard and mouse input can be used in this menu, making it much more precise. When the information has been input, clicking on the Rotate, Scale, Shear, or Transform button will start the transformation. To discard the changes, click on the Reset button.

▶ **See Also** "Resizing and Scaling" (page 42)

12.3   The Flip Tool   [Shift+F]

Description	The Flip tool mirrors the active layer either horizontally or vertically.
Options	
Horizontal	Flips images horizontally. The arrow will turn into a double-headed arrow aligned horizontally.
Vertical	Flips images vertically. The arrow will turn into a double-headed arrow aligned vertically.

12.4   The Eraser   [Shift+E]

Description	The Eraser tool removes paint from the image.
Options	
Straight Line	Hold down the Shift key while clicking to draw a straight line from the last Eraser position to the current one.
Hard Edge	When selected from the Options menu, the brush for the eraser will not have any transparency (it will look very rough around the edges).

Incremental   This option makes eraser strokes cumulative, so it will erase more paint when the mouse is moved over a specific area several times. This is only useful when the brush transparency is less than 100 percent.

Usage   The Eraser tool is very similar to the Pencil tool. It uses the brush selected in the Brushes menu. Using a solid brush with the eraser will give you a fuzzy line, making it look smoother. To get a completely solid shape, select the Hard Edge option. Using a fuzzy brush will give you a very fuzzy line. The color that the eraser will reveal is the background color, unless there is an Alpha channel. If there is an Alpha channel in the image, it will erase to transparency.

▶**See Also** "Adding Alpha Channels" (page 61) and "Brushes" (page 172)

12.5   The Clone Tool   [C]

Description   The Clone tool copies a selected image or pattern, and paints with it like a brush. It is perfect for doing photo editing.

Options

Source   Lets you choose the source for the paint in the Clone tool. Image uses a selected image layer to paint with. Pattern uses the current pattern.

Aligned   This option keeps the source aligned with the mouse click. When it is not selected, the brush will always start to paint from the starting point.

Straight Line   Hold down the Shift key while clicking to draw a straight line from the last Paintbrush position to the current one.

Select Source   Hold down the Ctrl key while clicking to select the source point for the Clone tool when using the image for the source.

Usage   The Clone tool is excellent for touching up areas of skin, grass, or other complicated textures found in scanned images. The best brush to use is one with fuzzy edges. Holding down the Ctrl key while clicking chooses the point to use as the source for painting. This is a good tool for removing blemishes, because it is very hard to draw skin, but it is easy to copy other similar areas of skin[1].

---

[1] *Another more comical use is to switch peoples' heads in a scanned photograph.*

12.6　The Convolve Tool　　　　　　　[V]

Description　　　The Convolve tool manually blurs or sharpens areas of an image.

Options

Pressure　　　Determines the amount of blurring or sharpening that will occur. This is similar to the Pressure option for the Airbrush tool.

Blur　　　Causes the area to become blurred.

Sharpen　　　Sharpens the area.

Straight Line　　　Hold down the Shift key when clicking to blur or sharpen from the last point drawn to the new position.

Usage　　　The Convolve tool is used to manually blur or sharpen specific areas of the image. Sharpening does not always work properly; it can produce spotty images with poor colors. It is often better to use the Sharpen filter in the Enhance menu.

▶**See Also** "Sharpen" (page 224) and "Blur Filters" (page 193)

12.7　The Color Picker　　　　　　　[O]

Description　　　The Color Picker selects selected colors from the image for the foreground or background color.

Options

Sample Merge　　　This takes the averaged color from all layers instead of just the active one.

Usage　　　The Color Picker replaces the foreground or background color with one from the image. Selecting the foreground or background color is done by clicking on the desired color. A window appears when a color is chosen, which displays the RGB values, the Alpha value, and the Hex triplet of the color. The Hex triplet is used for colors in Web pages.

▶**See Also** "Color Selection" (page 12)

12.8 Dodge and Burn   [Shift+D]

Description	This tool adjusts the intensity values using a brush.
Options	
Exposure	This is a percentage amount that controls the amount of intensity change.
Dodge	This toggle increases the intensity of the affected pixels, making them seem brighter.
Burn	This toggle decreases the intensity of the affected pixels, making them seem darker.
Highlights	This toggle selects pixels with high intensity values only.
Midtones	This toggle selects pixels with medium intensity values.
Shadows	This toggle selects pixels with low intensity values.
Straight Line	Hold down the Shift key while clicking to dodge or burn a straight line from the last drawn position.
Invert Tool	Uses the other method for drawing. For example, if Dodge is selected in the Options menu, Burn will be used when the Shift key is held down.
Usage	The Dodge and Burn tool is used for touching up images where the intensity in certain areas needs to be changed. The area affected is determined by the active brush. The best brushes to use are ones with soft edges. This tool is very useful for emphasizing or hiding elements in scanned photographs, like faces, or chrome on cars. Note that these tools are not incremental, so an area can be drawn over multiple times, but it will only be affected once.

The Burn tool is perfect for removing the "red-eye" effect in scanned photographs. To remove red-eye from a picture, follow these steps:

1.   Open the picture in the GIMP. An example is shown in Figure 12.1.

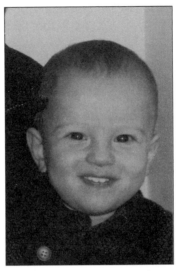

Figure 12.1   *An example picture to remove red-eye. This picture needs a lot of work.*

2.   Open the Layers and Channels menu.

3.   Click on the Channels tab.

4.   Click on the Blue and Green channels to deselect them. Only the Red channel should be highlighted.

5.   Choose the Dodge and Burn tool ([Shift+D]).

6.   Double-click on the Dodge and Burn tool to open the Options menu.

7.   Choose Burn as the type.

8.   Lower the exposure to 20.0.

9.   Depending on the brightness of the red eye, choose the appropriate mode. Shadows is usually the best to use.

10. Zoom in on the area to be edited. Figure 12.2 shows the zoomed area.

Figure 12.2   *The zoomed-in area around the eye.*

11. Select a brush that is small enough to work on the eye. Use a feathered brush that is small enough to edit the red perimeter, without affecting the light center.

12. Using small strokes, use the Burn tool to darken the red area. Avoid darkening the light center. The fixed area is shown in Figure 12.3.

Figure 12.3   *The fixed area after the red-eye has been removed. Note that in the grayscale version, it just looks darker. In a color print, all of the red has been removed.*

13. Zoom back out to view the changes.

▸**See Also** "Curves" (page 56)

🖉 12.9 Smudge   [Shift+S]

Description   The Smudge tool smudges the paint in a layer with the current brush. The effect is similar to smearing oil paint on a canvas. This effect resembles the IWarp filter (page 210).

Options

Pressure   This percentage value determines the amount of smudging that occurs. The higher the percentage, the further the paint travels, which gives it a greater smudging effect. Using a pressure of 100 percent will cause the initial area to be smudged forever.

Straight line   Hold down the Shift key while clicking to smudge in a straight line from the last drawn position.

Usage   The Smudge tool is useful for creating artistic effects in an image. It is useful to smear background areas in order to bring them out of focus as an alternative to blurring. This tool is generally not used to enhance photographs, but to add an artistic flair.

▸**See Also** "Iwarp" (page 210)

13
Brushes, Patterns, Palettes, and Gradients

The information in this chapter will be familiar to the experienced graphic artist. People new to graphics programs will need to read this chapter to be able to use the GIMP to its full potential.

13.1 Brushes

The first part of this chapter is the most important: Brushes. You will be using brushes on every image in the GIMP.

Brushes are used for the following tools:

- Pencil
- Paintbrush
- Airbrush
- Eraser
- Clone
- Convolver
- Stroke
- Dodge/Burn

13.1.1 Choosing a Brush to Use   [Shift+Ctrl+B]

Menu Location   <Image>/Dialogs/Brushes...

Choosing the right brush for the job is an important skill to learn quickly. There are several ways to access the Brush Selection menu:

- Clicking on <Image>/Dialogs/Brushes...
- Clicking on <Toolbox>/File/Dialogs/Brushes...
- Clicking on the displayed brush in the Toolbox
- Using the hotkey [Shift+Ctrl+B]

In the Brush Selection menu, there is a dialog box showing all the brushes available in the GIMP. See Table 13.1 for descriptions and possible uses of these brushes. If the brush is too big to show, click and hold with the left mouse button, and a larger picture will be shown. You can select brushes by clicking on them with the mouse. The size of the brush is shown in the top-right corner of the Brush menu (see Figure 13.1).

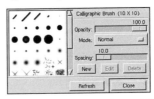

Figure 13.1   *The Brush Selection Window.*

Table 13.1 Brushes and Their Common Uses

Brush Name	Description and Effect	Common Uses
Calligraphic	Pen nib, hard edge	Use with Ink tool to simulate calligraphic pen.
Regular Circle	Hard edge, rough lines	Use for detailed touch-ups.
Fuzzy Circle	Soft edge, smooth lines	Use for drawing lines. Works well with the Eraser, Pencil, or Clone tool.

There are also novelty brushes provided with the GIMP, shown in Figure 13.2:

- Confetti (1)
- Diagonal Star (2)
- GIMP logo (3)
- Galaxy (4)
- Property of XCF (5)
- Sand Dunes (6)
- Square (7)

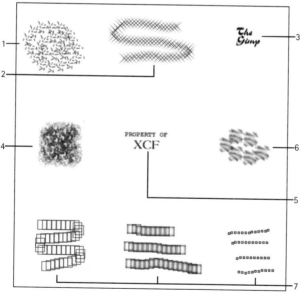

Figure 13.2 *Examples of the various novelty brushes.*

13.1.2   Brush Options

There are three options available for brushes in the GIMP (refer to Figure 13.1):

- **Opacity.** This can range from 0 (fully transparent) to 100 (fully opaque). Opacity is used to change the amount of paint on the brush.

- **Mode** (page 44). This allows you to select how the paint affects the image.

- **Spacing.** This is the distance, in percentage of the brush size, that the mouse is moved before the brush is drawn again. When using tools like the Pencil to draw lines, a small spacing is best. When painting with the novelty brushes, a large spacing is best—otherwise you will just have a big mess of paint.

13.1.3   Creating and Editing Brushes

The GIMP allows you to create your own brushes or edit the existing ones. Creating your own brush can be useful if you need a "stamp" similar to the "Property of XCF" brush that you are going to use many times. It is also useful for making custom textures to paint or blur with.

It is fairly simple to create a brush. Just follow these steps:

1. Create a new grayscale image with a white background ([Ctrl+N]). The size of the brush depends on the application, but generally brushes are small (about 20×20 pixels).

2. Set the foreground color to black.

3. Choose a drawing tool. Using the pencil will give you a brush with hard edges, whereas using the paintbrush or airbrush will give you soft edges.

4. Choose a brush ([Shift+Ctrl+B]). When working with small images like this, use a smaller brush.

5. Create your custom brush. Draw some example strokes on the image[1].

6. Invert the image. (<Image>/Image/Colors/Invert)

7. Save ([Ctrl+S]) the image with the .gbr extension in your ~/.gimp/brushes directory.

   Enter the spacing and the brush name in the dialog box. The spacing here is the default spacing that will be used when painting with the brush. The second option is the name of the brush that shows up in the Brush Selection menu when your brush is chosen. The brush size is shown automatically—it is the dimensions of your image.

8. Click the Refresh button in the Brush Selection menu to make your brush appear.

---

[1] There is also a script called Selection to Brush that will allow you to skip the following steps.

There are a few things to remember when creating brushes:

- Brushes must be grayscale images.

- Brushes must be flattened before saving (see "Flattening Images," page 43).

- Brushes installed on your system will be found in the <Gimp Directory>/ share/gimp/brushes. Copy these to your own ~/.gimp/brushes directory if you are going to edit them so that you have a backup copy.

- GIMP brushes are saved in the .gbr (GIMP BRush) format.

- Always save the brushes you have created in your .gimp/brushes directory so that the GIMP knows where to find them.

- Brushes should be inverted before saving so that they look correct when using them. White areas of brushes are the parts that paint, and black areas are invisible.

13.2 Patterns   [Shift+Ctrl+P]

Menu Location   <Image>/Dialogs/Patterns

Patterns are used to cover large areas with a texture. The tools that use patterns are the Bucket Fill and Clone tools. Some scripts in the Script-Fu menu use patterns as well. There are several ways to access the Pattern Selection menu:

- Clicking on <Image>/Dialogs/Patterns...

- Clicking on <Toolbox>/File/Dialogs/Patterns...

- Clicking on the displayed pattern in the Toolbox

- Using the hotkey [Shift+Ctrl+P]

You can choose patterns by clicking on them in the Pattern Selection menu (see Figure 13.3). If a pattern is too big to display in the window, click and hold the mouse button and the full image will be shown. The name and size of the pattern will be shown in the top-right corner.

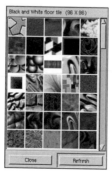

Figure 13.3 *The Pattern Selection window.*

13.2.1 Creating and Editing Patterns

Patterns are just RGB or grayscale images saved in the GIMP's pattern format. Creating your own pattern can be very useful, especially when creating logos and other images for Web pages. Remember to make these images *tileable* so that there aren't any obvious seams in the pattern.

To create your own image, follow these steps:

1. Create a new RGB or Grayscale image ([Ctrl+N]).

2. Draw your new pattern.

3. Use the Make Seamless filter to remove any obvious seams in the image.

4. Save the image with the `.pat` format in `~/.gimp/patterns`.

   The dialog box that pops up here has only one option. This is the name of the pattern that appears in the Pattern Selection menu.

5. Click the Refresh button in the Pattern Selection menu to make your new pattern appear.

13.3 Palettes   [Ctrl+P]

Menu Location   <Image>/Dialogs/Palettes

Palettes are used when you want to paint in a certain color scheme, such as pastel. It is also useful when creating an image that is restricted in the colors it can use (see page 80). There are several ways to access the Palette menu:

- Clicking on <Image>/Dialogs/Palettes...

- Clicking on <Toolbox>/File/Dialogs/Palettes...

- Using the hotkey [Ctrl+P]

A palette in the GIMP is simply a menu with many different colors to choose from. Palettes can be found in `~/.gimp/palettes`.

The Palette Selection menu has several options, accessed via the Edit button (shown in Figure 13.4):

- **Edit.** Click this button to see a menu for performing operations on the palettes available.

  a. **New** creates a new palette to use.

  b. **Delete** removes the current palette from the `~/.gimp/palettes` directory[2].

  c. **Merge** combines two palettes.

  d. **Right-clicking** on a specific color allows you to edit, delete, or add a new color.

---

[2] *Note that if you delete a palette in your* `~/.gimp/palettes` *directory, you must copy it from* <Gimp Directory>/Palettes *to get it back.*

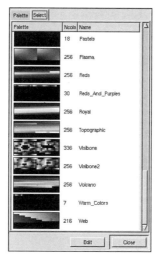

Figure 13.4   *The Palette Selection window.*

To use a color in the palette, simply click on it in the Palette menu, and it will be set to the currently selected color (foreground or background).

The following palettes are available on a stock GIMP install:

- Bears
- Bgold
- Blues
- Borders
- Browns_And_Yellows
- Caramel
- Cascade
- China
- Coldfire
- Cool_Colors
- Cranes
- Dark_Pastels
- Default

- Ega
- Firecode
- Gold
- GrayViolet
- Grayblue
- Grays
- Greens
- Hilite
- Kahki
- Lights
- Muted
- Named_Colors
- News3

- Op2
- Paintjet
- Pastels
- Plasma
- Reds
- Reds_And_Purples
- Royal
- Topographic
- Visibone
- Visibone2
- Volcano
- Warm_Colors
- Web

13.3.1 Creating and Editing Palettes

Palettes can be created two ways: manually, and from an indexed image (see "Saving Palettes," page 65).

To create a palette manually, follow these steps:

1. Open the Palette Selection menu.
2. Click on Edit.
3. Click on New Palette.

   You will be asked for a name for the new palette and this new palette will be created.

4. To add colors to this palette, right-click on an empty position and choose New. This will add the currently selected color (either foreground or background) to the palette.

   To delete this new color, right-click and choose Delete.

Colors can also be edited in existing palettes:

1. The color must be selected in the Edit menu by clicking on it.
2. Right-click the color and choose Edit to bring up the Color Selection menu.
3. Choose a new color and click OK. The old color will become the new color.

   These colors can be named in this menu as well. By default, they are called Untitled, but you can highlight and change them. If you have the Named_Colors palette installed, have a look at it for name suggestions.

13.4 **Gradients**   [Ctrl+G]

> **Menu Location**   <image>/Dialogs/Gradient...

Gradients are most often used with the Blend tool (see "Blend Tool," page 145), but they are occasionally used with Script-Fu. They can also be used with the Paintbrush tool. They give much more control over the colors in blends because you can control specific points for color and transparency changes.

There are several ways to access the Gradient menu:

- Clicking on <Image>/Dialogs/Gradient...
- Clicking on <Toolbox>/File/Dialogs/Gradient...
- Clicking on the displayed gradient in the Toolbox
- Using the hotkey [Shift+Ctrl+B]

To use a gradient that you have created, set the Blend to Custom (from Editor) in the Blend tool options.

13.4.1 The Gradient Editor

The Gradient Editor (see Figure 13.5) is very powerful and has many options:

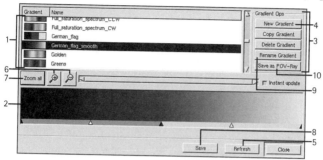

Figure 13.5 *The Gradient Editor menu.*

- Available gradients are listed on the left side (1) and displayed below (2).
- Buttons for editing them are to the right (3).
- Clicking on New Gradient (4) will make a new one. When you create a new gradient or copy an existing one, you will be prompted for a name.
- The Refresh button (5) will re-read the gradients available on your system.
- Zoom buttons (6) are located in the middle to zoom in or out.
- Zoom All (7) will return the display to a 1:1 ratio.
- Save Gradient (8) will save the gradient to disk.
- Rename Gradient (9) will rename the gradient.
- Save as POV-Ray (10) will save the gradient in POV-Ray format.
- The Gradient menu is brought up by right-clicking in the gradient.

Gradients are found in the `<Gimp Directory>/share/gimp/gradients` or in your personal gimp directory, `~/.gimp/gradients`. The Gradient Editor can also be used as a simple palette, since clicking on a color in a gradient will set it as the current color.

13.4.2 Endpoints and Midpoints

Gradients are changed by moving endpoints and midpoints. At the bottom of every gradient are black and white triangles. Black triangles represent endpoints and white triangles represent midpoints. When creating gradients it is important to note what part of it you are editing. This is shown by the dark gray band along the bottom.

To add new endpoints, there are two options in the Gradient menu:

- **Split Segment at Midpoint.** This will create two segments, with their endpoint where the old midpoint was, and two new midpoints.

- **Split Segment Uniformly.** This will bring up a dialog box asking for the number of segments to split it into. You can create as many new segments as you choose.

Adding new segments allows you to add more color changes in that area.

You can move endpoints and midpoints by clicking and dragging with the mouse. The only points that cannot be moved are the endpoints on the extreme left and right. Holding down the Shift key while dragging causes any midpoints or endpoints inside the selection to compress or expand to keep the color blend constant. As the midpoints are moved, note how the color blending shifts. Midpoints can also be centered through the menu by choosing Re-center Midpoints in Selection. Note that this does not adjust endpoints; this must be done with the Re-center Handles in Selection command.

The current segment is shown with the dark gray band along the bottom. You can extend the segment by holding down the Shift key and clicking on the area you wish to extend it to. Segments can be deleted by clicking on Delete Segment inside the menu. Segments can be flipped or duplicated in the Selection Operations portion of the menu.

13.4.3   Colors in Gradients

In this section, the various options for controlling colors are discussed. All of these options are accessed by right-clicking on the current gradient.

13.4.3.1   Selecting Colors

Several options are available for picking colors:

- Choose a color from the selector by clicking on Left's or Right's Endpoint Color.
- Load it from the endpoint's nearest neighbor (In the case of the extreme left endpoint, this is the extreme right endpoint, and vice versa).
- Load it from its own opposite endpoint. This is rather boring; it will make a constant color.
- Load it from the current foreground color.
- Load it from a set of "bookmarks." There are 10 bookmarks available. By default they are somewhat boring colors, but you can replace them through the Save To option in the Gradient menu.

13.4.3.2   Blending Type

You can also change the blending type of the colors (by default, the type is Linear):

- **Curved.** Emphasizes whichever endpoint color has greater length.

- **Sinusoidal.** The opposite of Curved; it emphasizes the endpoint color which has the least length.

- **Spherical (Increasing) and Spherical (Decreasing).** The former emphasizes the color on the right, whereas the latter emphasizes the color on the left. These simulate the color being mapped to a 3D sphere.

In the Selection Operations portion of the menu, there is an option to blend the endpoints' color and opacity. This operation is performed over an extended selection with another endpoint inside it. You will lose the color of any endpoint inside the selection. Flip Segment will reverse the colors inside the selection. Replicate allows you to clone the segment a specified number of times.

13.4.3.3 Coloring Type

The coloring type allows you to choose which color model the gradient uses to fade:

- **Plain RGB.** Works in RGB space, and creates a gradient that you would expect.

- **HSV.** Works in the HSV color scheme, and creates a rainbow effect. You can choose either a clockwise or counter-clockwise direction.

13.4.4 POV-Ray

POV-Ray is an Open Source 3D ray-tracing program available on the Internet. The Gradient Editor allows you to save the gradient you created in a form that POV-Ray can understand. This is very useful because creating the gradients by hand is time consuming. Trying POV-Ray is highly recommended—it creates excellent images.

To save a POV-Ray gradient, simply click on the Save As POV-Ray button in the Gradient Editor menu. This will save the gradient in ASCII format, which is compatible with POV-Ray.

14
Filters

Filters are the basis for all of the impressive effects in the GIMP. They can be run as stand-alone operations, or in combination with others to create interesting effects. This chapter is aimed at providing objective coverage of all filters so that you can see the potential for each one in turn. It is important to remember that these filters can be applied to a whole layer, or to a specific selection. Some filters require specific criteria to use them, which is why sometimes a certain filter is grayed out—meaning that it cannot be used with the current image. See Table 14.1 or the section in this chapter discussing the specific filter for its requirements.

Some of the common effects that can be created with the GIMP are described here, and there are also many tutorials on the Internet that use these filters. In this chapter, only those filters that come with the GIMP are described. Other filters can be downloaded from the GIMP Plug-In Registry, but they are not discussed in this chapter. For information on installing plug-ins, see page 112.

If you have any knowledge of programming in C or related languages, look at the source code for the plug-ins. There is a lot to learn in the source code, and it will give you better understanding of what exactly the filters do.

Remember the hotkeys for the shortcuts found at the top of the Filters menu: Repeat Last [Alt+F] and Re-show Last [Shift+Alt+F]. Repeat Last runs the filter again with the same settings; Re-show Last brings back up the dialog box for the filter, where applicable.

In most filters, scrollbars will be used for previewing images. Some of these filters' preview windows do not use scrollbars—you'll need to click and drag the preview images to see the whole image.

Table 14.1   Filter Requirements (y = Allowed, x = Not Allowed,
            r = Required)

Filter	Page	RGB	Grayscale	Indexed	Layers	Alpha
Adjust FG/BG	197	y	x	x	y	y
Alien Map	197	r	x	x	y	y
Animation Optimize	186	y	y	y	y	y
Animation Playback	187	y	y	y	y	y
Animation Unoptimize	186	y	y	y	y	y
Apply Canvas	188	y	y	x	y	y
Apply Lens	225	y	y	y	y	y
Blinds	207	y	y	x	y	y
Blur	194	y	y	x	y	y
Border Average	199	y	x	x	y	y
Bumpmap	228	y	y	x	y	y
Checkerboard	239	y	y	x	y	y
CML Explorer	238	y	y	x	y	y
Color Exchange	199	r	x	x	y	y
Color Map	200	y	x	x	y	y
Colorify	200	r	x	x	x	x
Cubism	189	y	y	x	y	y
Deinterlace	221	y	y	x	y	y
Depth Merge	204	y	y	x	y	y
Despeckle	221	y	y	x	y	y
Destripe	222	y	y	x	y	y
Diffraction Patterns	239	r	x	x	y	y
Displace	229	y	y	x	y	y
Edge	219	y	y	x	y	y
Emboss	208	r	x	x	x	x
Engrave[1]	209	y	y	x	r	r
Film	206	y	y	y	y	y
Filter All Layers	187	y	y	y	y	y
Flame	241	r	x	x	y	y
FlareFX	226	r	x	x	y	y
Fractal Trace	231	y	y	x	y	y
Gaussian Blur (IIR and RLE)	194	y	y	x	y	y
Gfig	243	y	y	x	y	y

---

[1] *Engrave requires alpha and/or layers*

Filter	Page	RGB	Grayscale	Indexed	Layers	Alpha
Glass Tile	226	y	y	x	y	y
Gradient Map	201	y	y	x	y	y
Grid	249	y	y	x	y	y
Hot	201	r	x	x	x	x
Hurl	238	y	y	y	y	y
IFSCompose	249	y	y	x	y	y
Illusion	231	y	y	x	y	y
IWarp	210	y	y	x	y	y
Laplace	220	y	y	x	y	y
Make Seamless	232	y	y	x	y	y
Map Object	232	r	x	x	y	y
Max RGB	201	r	x	x	y	y
Maze	252	y	y	y	y	y
Mosaic	190	y	y	x	y	y
Motion Blur	195	y	y	x	y	y
NL	222	y	y	x	x	x
Noisify	237	y	y	x	y	y
Oilify	192	y	y	x	y	y
PageCurl	212	y	y	x	r	y
Paper Tile	234	y	y	x	y	y
Pick	238	y	y	y	y	y
Pixelize	196	y	y	x	y	y
Plasma	252	y	y	x	y	y
Polar Coords	213	y	y	x	y	y
Qbist	253	r	x	x	y	y
Ripple	215	y	y	x	y	y
Scatter HSV	202	r	x	x	y	y
Semiflatten	202	r	x	x	r	y
Sharpen	224	y	y	x	y	y
Shift	216	y	y	x	y	y
Sinus	253	y	y	x	y	y
Slur	238	y	y	y	y	y
Small Tiles	234	y	y	x	y	y
Smooth Palette	203	r	x	x	y	y
Solid Noise	255	y	y	x	y	y
Sparkle	226	y	y	x	y	y
Spread	237	y	y	x	y	y
Sobel	220	y	y	x	y	y
Supernova	227	y	y	x	y	y

continues

Table 14.1   Continued.

Filter	Page	RGB	Grayscale	Indexed	Layers	Alpha
Tile	235	y	y	y	y	y
Tileable Blur	197	r	x	x	y	y
Value Invert	204	y	x	y	y	y
Value Propagate	216	y	y	x	y	y
Van Gogh	192	y	x	x	x	x
Video	236	r	x	x	y	y
Waves	218	y	y	x	y	y ·
Whirl and Pinch	218	y	y	x	y	y

14.1   Animation Filters

The first of the filters in the GIMP are the animation-related filters. Different scripts can create animations, or you can create them by hand, but the usefulness of these filters will cause you to revisit this section often.

14.1.1   Animation Optimize and Unoptimize

Animation Optimize and Animation Unoptimize are actually the same plug-in—they are just run in a different order. Animation Optimize applies various optimizations to your layered file that is going to become an animation:

- Compares the layers of the image, and changes any repeated pixels to transparency. This saves a lot of space when saving the animation as a GIF file. The optimization that is going to improve your animation is the addition of transparency.

- Resizes layers to remove any unnecessary transparency. The amount of optimization that occurs depends on the type of image, the number of colors, and the complexity of the animation.

Animation Optimize is best run as the second to last operation on an image that is going to become an animation. The last operation is to convert the image to Indexed, so that it can be saved as a GIF file. Note that Animation Optimize applies a Threshold Alpha operation to the layers, so when you convert the image to Indexed, there should be little change regarding transparency. It does not adjust colors at all; this is left up to you when you convert the image to Indexed.

Animation Unoptimize undoes the optimization of an animation. Editing images that have been optimized is difficult because it is hard to visualize how the changes are going to affect the image. This filter aids in this task by adding the pixels that were removed by Animation Optimize. The layer sizes are all resized to the image size as well. It does not improve the "look" of the transparency of an image, but it does make the editing of the animation much easier.

14.1.2 Animation Playback

The Animation Playback filter is very simple. It does not make any changes to your image—it is just for previewing animations that you have created. The interface (see Figure 14.1) is straightforward. Along the top is a status bar that shows which frame is being displayed. Below the status bar are the control buttons:

- **Play/Stop (1).** Toggles the animation on or off.
- **Rewind (2).** Brings you back to the beginning of the animation.
- **Step (3).** Advances the animation frame by frame.

When you are done previewing your animation, click the Close button (4) at the bottom of the window.

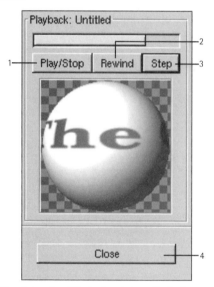

Figure 14.1 *The Animation Playback window displaying a simple animation.*

14.1.3 Filter All Layers

Filter All Layers is useful for creating many different animations using plug-ins that are installed. It applies to every layer and any plug-in available to the GIMP. Filter All Layers can apply the plug-in with constant values, which would make a boring animation, or with varying values. There is no limit to what this filter can do. The only drawback to this filter is that it does not allow you to choose which layers are filtered: The beginning frame will always be affected.

- The first step to this filter is to choose the plug-in that is going to be used. Simply click on the plug-in name (1), as shown in Figure 14.2.

■ Choose the type of application: Apply Constant (2) or Apply Varying (3).

a. **Apply Constant.** Click to bring up the dialog box for the plug-in. Enter any values needed for the plug-in, and click OK. The plug-in is then applied to the first layer. The Filter All Layers dialog box appears, allowing you to save the image as a backup file. In this dialog box, you also can skip the current layer by clicking the Skip <frame number> button. If you want to continue, click the Continue button.

b. **Apply Varying.** Click to view the dialog box for the plug-in. The values entered here are for the first frame. Click OK, and the plug-in is applied. The Filter All Layers dialog box pops up again. Simply click Continue here. The plug-in dialog box again appears. The values entered here are the final values for the plug-in. Filter All Layers automatically calculates the intermediate values. Click OK when the end values are entered. Filter All Layers brings up yet another dialog box, allowing you to back up the image, skip the next frame, or continue applying the plug-in to the layers.

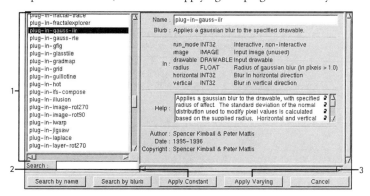

Figure 14.2   *The main interface to Filter All Layers.*

14.2 Artistic Filters

Artistic filters take an image and turn it into a work of art. These filters are all based on common artistic techniques—for instance, turning an image into a mosaic, or making it look like it has been painted on canvas.

14.2.1 Apply Canvas

Apply Canvas adds a subtle texture map to an image (compare Figures 14.3 and 14.4). It makes the image appear as if it has been painted on a canvas. This filter works best on scanned photographs, especially after other filters or scripts have been applied. For example, the Cubism filter (see page 189) works very well with Apply Canvas.

There are two different options for Apply Canvas:

- **Direction of the Light.** This determines where the shadow of the "canvas" appears. The choices are limited to coming from one of the four corners of the image.

- **Depth of the Canvas.** A small depth value will make the image look as if it has been painted on a paper texture. A high depth value will make the image appear to have been painted on a very rough canvas. The depth can range from 1 to 49.

When working with large images, note that patterns of horizontal and vertical lines will appear according to the size of the texture map used.

▶**See Also** Bumpmap (page 228) and Cubism (page 189)

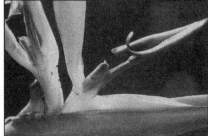

Figure 14.3 *A picture of an orchid before any filters have been applied.*

Figure 14.4 *A picture of an orchid, after Apply Canvas with a depth of 10 has been applied. The direction was Top-right.*

14.2.2 Cubism

The Cubism filter turns an image into something that resembles a Cubist painting (see Figures 14.5 and 14.6). In other words, it gives the image a very "abstract" feel. The original image will usually be barely recognizable in the filtered image. This is a CPU-intensive filter, and may take a few minutes to complete depending on the size of the image. There are three different options for this filter:

- **Toggle the Use of the Background Color On and Off.** When this option is turned on, the background color will appear throughout the image in areas where there are no tiles. By default, the color will be black.

- **Tile Size.** This option determines the size of the tiles used to create the image. Tile size can range from 1.0 to 100.0.

- **Tile Saturation.** High tile saturation will pack the squares very closely together, with a great deal of overlap. This will make the tile sizes seem random. A small saturation value will separate the tiles more, causing them to overlap less. Tile saturation can range from 0.0 to 10.0

Figure 14.5 *Photograph of a waterfall before any filters have been applied.*

Figure 14.6 *A photograph of a waterfall after the Cubism filter has been applied.*

14.2.3 Mosaic

The Mosaic filter transforms your image into a mosaic—a picture made of different colored tiles. It has many options (see Figures 14.7) to give you control in creating pleasing effects (see Figures 14.8 and 14.9). Like Cubism, this filter is also very abstract, and the best results are achieved with images that have areas of solid color. You can create interesting effects when using Mosaic in conjunction with the other artistic filters, especially Cubism.

- **Antialiasing (1).** This option is common throughout the GIMP. It uses Alpha values to smooth out jagged edges. In this case, it smoothes out the tile edges.

- **Color Averaging (2).** This option determines whether you are creating a true mosaic. When Color Averaging is turned on, it averages the colors in each tile area. Each tile is a single color, much like a real mosaic. If this is turned off, the colors in the image are retained. This has the effect of making the image look as if it were painted on a tile floor.

- **Pitted Surfaces (3).** This makes the tiles look "weathered," more like an ancient mosaic.

- **FG/BG Lighting (4).** This determines what colors appear in the "grout" of the tiles. When this option is turned on it uses the foreground and background colors. Turned off, it uses black and white for the grout.

- **Tiling Primitives (5).** These options are the basic shapes of tiles to be used. Squares uses square tiles, Hexagons uses hexagonal tiles, and Octagons and Squares uses both of these shapes.

- **Tile Size (6).** Tile Size determines the average diameter for the tiles in pixels. Size can range from 5.0 to 100.0.

- **Tile Height (7).** This option determines the apparent height of the tiles in pixels. Height can range from 1.0 to 50.0.

- **Tile Spacing (8).** Tile Spacing determines the average space between tiles. Spacing can range from 1.0 to 50.0.

- **Tile Neatness (9).** This option determines the amount of deviation from a perfect tile. A neatness value of 1.0 creates perfectly shaped tiles. Neatness ranges from 0.00 to 1.00.

- **Light Direction (10).** Measured in degrees, this option determines the angle of the light source. This ranges from 0.0 to 360.0. A value of 0.0 means the light is coming from the right; 90.0 means the light is coming from the top of the image.

- **Color Variation (11).** This option allows you to have random coloring. A higher color variation value increases the randomness of the coloring. Variation can range from 0.00 to 1.00.

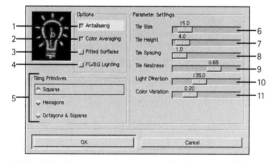

Figure 14.7 *The Mosaic options menu with its many different options.*

Figure 14.8 *A picture of a Porsche before the filter has been applied.*　　**Figure 14.9** *The Porsche after the Mosaic filter has been applied.*

14.2.4 Oilify

The Oilify filter converts an image into something that resembles an oil painting. This is less abstract than the previous filters, but it can still render an image unrecognizable. The options for this filter are simple:

- **Toggle the Intensity Algorithm On and Off.** If this option is turned on, the image created is based on the average intensity of the colors in the mask size. When this option is turned off, it uses the average RGB values in the mask size for each pixel. It is best to use the intensity algorithm, especially when working with images that have distinct color changes.

- **Mask Size.** This option determines the area used to calculate averages for the intensity or RGB algorithm. A larger mask size gives you less detail in an image.

14.2.5 Van Gogh (LIC)

The Van Gogh filter takes an image and turns in into a Van Gogh-esque painting. It also creates some very unique textures. This effect is created by using a map image (usually grayscale) and a blurring effect. An example of the use of this filter is shown in Figures 14.11 to 14.13.

- **Effect Image (1).** This option determines the blurring effect that occurs (see Figure 14.10). The direction is determined by the change of the pixels. Areas of solid color do not affect the image. The Blend tool (see page 145) works well for creating these maps.

- **Filter Length (2).** This option controls the amount of distortion that occurs. The larger the filter length, the more distorted it becomes. Length can range from 0.0 to 64.0.

- **Noise Magnitude (3).** This option controls the amount of random noise that is introduced into the picture. Larger values create a grainier image. Noise Magnitude can range from 1.0 to 5.0.

- **Integration Steps (4).** This option controls how much the effect image affects the source image. A larger number of Integration steps means a greater influence on the image.

- **Maximum Value and Minimum Value (5).** These sliders control the amount of contrast in the new image. When the values are closer together, there is more contrast in the image. Minimum value ranges from −100.0 to 0.0. Maximum value ranges from 0.0 to 100.0

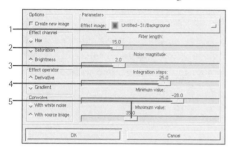

Figure 14.10   *The options menu for the Van Gogh filter.*

Figure 14.11   *The source image used for the Van Gogh filter.*

Figure 14.12   *The effect image used for the Van Gogh filter. This was created with the Blend tool.*

Figure 14.13   *The final image after the filter was run. Note that the blurring that occurs is due to the change in brightness of the effect image.*

14.3   Blur Filters

The Blur filters are very simple. They all distort images by applying some sort of blur. There are many different methods of achieving this, and there are several different filters to create these effects.

14.3.1 Blur

The first filter is the basic Blur (see Figure 14.14). It blurs a layer or selection and makes it appear out of focus. This is done by random number generation. For each pixel, a random number is generated, and if it falls within a percentage range, it is blurred by taking the average value of the surrounding pixels. Blur has a very small effect on the image. This filter does not work well on images that have transparency because it will distort colors. The Blur filter has several options, and the reasons for having them are not entirely obvious:

- **Randomization Seed (1).** The seed helps determine whether a pixel will be blurred or not. Using the current time is a good seed to use. If you need to repeat a blur exactly, enter a number in the Other Value section.

- **Randomization % (2).** This option determines how many pixels actually get blurred. This can range from 0 to 100%.

- **Repeat (3).** Repeat allows you to run the filter several times. This is very useful, because the Blur filter usually has only a small effect on the image. Repeat ranges from 1 to 100.

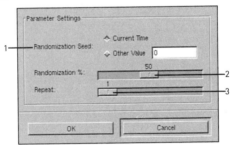

Figure 14.14   *The options menu for the Blur filter.*

14.3.2 Gaussian Blur (IIR and RLE)

There are two types of Gaussian blur, but they are very similar to each other. They both apply a blur operation with a specific radius. The larger the radius, the greater the blurring effect. IIR blurring works best with a large radius for blurring, and for images that are not computer generated, such as scanned photographs. RLE blurring works best on computer-generated images, or images with large areas of constant value.

Gaussian blur can be applied as follows:

- Horizontally
- Vertically
- In both directions

The blur radius needs to be specified to blur the image. Radii less than 1 are invalid because that would mean that a fraction of a pixel would be blurred.

14.3.3   Motion Blur

Motion blur (see Figure 14.15) applies different types of blurring operations to produce the illusion of motion, similar to a photograph taken of a moving object (with a relatively slow shutter speed), like the waterfall in Figure 14.16. The motion can be linear, radial, or zooming. Linear motion (see Figure 14.17) blurring makes the image look as if it is blowing away. When radial blurring (see Figure 14.18) is applied, it appears as though the image is spinning. Zooming (see Figure 14.19) makes the image look as if it is zooming back into the screen. For the three different types of blurring, the options have different effects:

- Linear

    a. The length (1) defines the "distance" the image travels. A greater length creates a more pronounced blurring effect.

    b. The angle (2) determines the direction the image travels.

- Radial

    a. Only the angle (2) is used, length is not. The angle determines the amount that the image is rotated. For complicated images, 45 degrees will blur the image quite well. Values higher than this will take a long time. For simple images, rotating 360 degrees is necessary. The image is "spun" about its center, and currently there is no way of changing this.

- Zoom

    a. This creates the illusion of the image moving away from a camera, like the *USS Enterprise* accelerating to warp speed. Angle does not affect zooming—only length (1). This blurring effect also uses the center of the image to zoom to, and as of this writing there is no way of changing this.

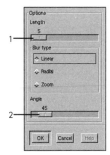

Figure 14.15   *The options menu for the Motion Blur filter.*

Figure 14.16   *A photograph of a waterfall.*

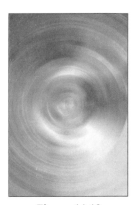

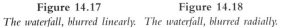

Figure 14.17
The waterfall, blurred linearly.

Figure 14.18
The waterfall, blurred radially.

Figure 14.19
The waterfall, zoom blurred.

14.3.4 Pixelize

The Pixelize filter does the opposite of the other blur filters. Rather than smoothing a rough image out, it takes a smooth image and makes it look chunky and pixelated. This makes images look very computer-generated and creates a "low resolution" feel.

The Pixelize filter only needs one option: the pixel width. This is the new size of pixels to be used. A value of 1 is useless, since the pixels are already 1 pixel wide. Larger values equate to more pixelization, and less detail.

Figure 14.20 *The Linux logo, courtesy of Larry Ewing.*

Figure 14.21 *The Linux logo, after the Pixelize filter with a width of 5 has been applied.*

14.3.5 Tileable Blur

The Tileable blur filter applies a Gaussian blur (IIR or RLE) that works on tileable images so that they retain their symmetry. Tileable blur is actually a script, but it is located in the Filters menu, so it is called a filter. This will take more time than the Gaussian blur filter because it uses a composite of nine images to create the blur.

The options for Tileable blur are the same as the Gaussian blur (see page 194), because it uses the Gaussian blur filters. The only different option is the choice between IIR or RLE blurring.

14.4 Color Filters

The next set of filters is the Color filters. These are filters that perform operations on the colors in an image. Because these filters work with colors, they do not work with grayscale images (except for Gradient Map). These filters tend to be mathematical and somewhat complicated, and it helps to know about the color models used in the GIMP. See the section on Color Models on page 5 for more information.

14.4.1 Adjust Foreground and Background

The Adjust Foreground and Background filter is fairly straightforward. It is the same filter as Color Mapping (see page 200), but slightly simpler. This filter takes any pixel that is the same color as the current foreground color and maps it to black. Any pixel that is the same color as the background color is mapped to white. Other colors are mapped by interpolation.

This filter is not very accurate, especially when you are working with scanned photographs, because it is difficult to tell which pixels will be changed. It is best used with computer-generated images with areas of solid color.

14.4.2 Alien Map

Alien Map is the first filter found in the Color filters menu, and is one of the most complicated filters. It shifts the color intensity (see page 5) of the Red, Green, and Blue channels based on the trigonometric functions sine and cosine. It is easiest to see the effects of this filter when working in individual channels (see page 48) because Alien Map adjusts the intensity for each specific channel.

When mapping to the sine curve, the following occurs:

- Low intensity (0 in the channel) is mapped to medium.
- High intensity (255 in the channel) is mapped to medium as well.

- Medium intensity (127 in the channel) is mapped to full intensity (255 in the channel).

- Intensities of 64 and 191 are mapped to 0 intensity. Intermediate intensities are mapped similarly.

With the cosine curve, the following occurs:

- High intensity is mapped to low intensity.

- Low intensity is unchanged.

- Medium intensity is mapped to high intensity.

See Table 14.2 for a listing of the mapping that occurs.

Table 14.2   Mathematical Result of Alien Map Filter

Original Intensity	Mapped to Sine Curve	Mapped to Cosine Curve
0	127	0
64	0	64
127	255	255
191	0	64
255	127	0

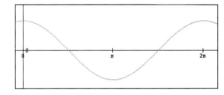

Figure 14.22   *An inverted cosine curve. Note the low negative values at the beginning and end of the curve, and the high value in the middle.*

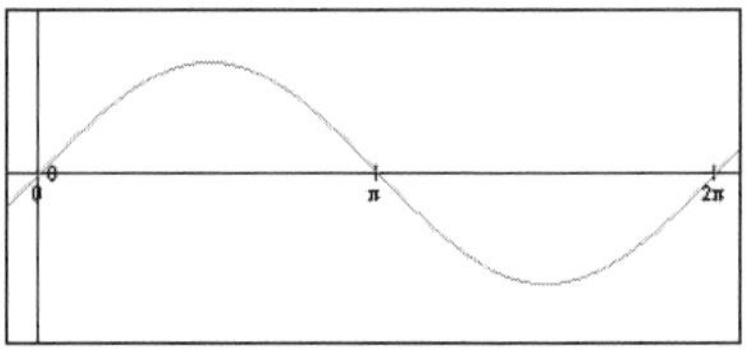

Figure 14.23   *An inverted sine curve. The Alien Map filter does not follow the sine curve exactly because negative intensities are not allowed.*

Figures 14.24 and 14.25 show a Red channel that has been mapped to the cosine curve. With the Alien Map filter, the intensity change can be controlled. The figures shown here are for the maximum change, but they can be lowered. Values of 0 still remain at 0. Table 14.2 summarizes the intensity shifts. The explanation of what happens is very mathematical, and may not be entirely necessary. It is more important to know what will happen to your image when the Alien Map plug-in is used, and experimentation is the best way to learn this.

Figure 14.24 *An example Red channel before the Alien Map filter is applied.*

Figure 14.25 *The Red channel after the Alien Map filter has been applied.*

The options for this complicated plug-in are very simple. For each channel (Red, Green, or Blue), there are two choices:

- Which function to apply to the specific channel. You can choose between Sine, Cosine, or None.

- The amount of intensity change. A high value will give the channel a higher overall intensity; a low value will give it a lower overall intensity.

14.4.3 Border Average

This filter calculates the most common color in a specific range and sets it as the border color. It is useful for finding a good color to use as a border of an image. Using this filter is straightforward. Its options include the following:

- **Thickness.** Thickness determines the size of the border (in pixels) used to calculate the average.

- **Bucket Size.** This option determines the bits used for the bucket size. It defaults to 4 (16-bit color), but if you are running a higher bits per pixel, the bucket size can be set higher. Numbers smaller than 4 do not produce very accurate colors.

14.4.4 Color Exchange

The Color Exchange filter (see Figure 14.26) allows you to take an input color and change it to an arbitrary output color. With it, you can make precise adjustments of the colors in an image. This filter is useful only on images with large areas of solid color. It does not work well with scanned photographs or dithered computer-generated images (it can leave them looking flat). This filter is still under development, and with later versions of the GIMP we should see some additional options that make this plug-in much more useful. The Color Exchange filter's only options are the from and to colors:

- **From Color.** Input Color is always set to the current foreground color, so the Color Picker (see page 176) is very useful with this filter. It can be adjusted manually if needed. You can also set a threshold (see page 3) to allow for subtle changes in color.

- **To Color.** This option must be set manually each time you choose it.

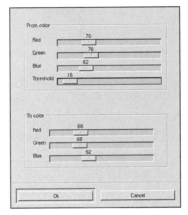

Figure 14.26   *The options menu for the Color Exchange filter.*

14.4.5   Color Mapping

This filter is the more advanced version of the Adjust Foreground and Background filter (see page 197). It takes two source colors and replaces them with two output colors. Intermediate colors are calculated automatically by the filter.

The interface to this filter is only slightly more complicated than the Adjust Foreground and Background filter. There are two From colors, corresponding to the To colors. The From colors are the foreground and background colors by default. Simply click on the colors to change them.

14.4.6   Colorify

The Colorify filter makes your image appear as if it is being viewed through colored glass. This is achieved by replacing each pixel with a specified color with the same intensity. To fully understand what happens with the Colorify filter, use it on an image with red as the selected color. If you look at the channels for the image (see page 48), Red is the only channel with any detail. The Green and Blue

channels do not contain any information at all. This effect differs from placing
a transparent red layer over the image because it completely destroys the
information in the other channels. The image is still a 24-bit image, but one
channel contains information.

Colorify is very easy to use. You are required to choose a color, either from
the standard choices or your own custom color. The filter will then colorify the
image.

14.4.7   Gradient Map

The Gradient Map filter does exactly what its name implies. It maps the active
gradient (see page 179) to the image on the basis of luminosity:

- Pixels with the highest value (usually the white pixels) become the rightmost
  pixel of the gradient.

- Pixels with the least value (usually black pixels) become the leftmost pixel of
  the gradient.

- The intermediate pixels are mapped accordingly.

Gradient Map has no options. It uses the active gradient selected in the Gradient
editor to map.

14.4.8   Hot

Hot is a utility used to ensure that images will display correctly on an NTSC or
PAL system. Computer-generated images have the tendency to generate unsafe
colors for display on these systems. If you are going to be displaying your images
only on your own computer monitor or on paper, this filter is not needed. The
Hot filter has several options:

- **Create a New Layer.** This is recommended so that you do not destroy
  your original image.

- **Display Type.** This is either NTSC or PAL.

- **Action.** Here you must choose the method to deal with the offending
  pixels. You can choose any one of the following:

  a. Reduce luminosity (value).

  b. Reduce saturation.

  c. Make them black to flag them for editing.

14.4.8   Max RGB

The Max RGB filter compares your image's RGB values for each channel. It
then replaces each pixel with the maximum RGB value for the highest channel.

For example, if you have a pixel with the values R 191 G 89 B 234, those values would become R 0 G 0 B 255. Black or white pixels are left unchanged, since they have equal amounts of all colors. Max RGB cannot decide to choose one color over another, so if two values are equal, they are left unchanged.

The only option for Max RGB is whether to use the maximum or minimum values in calculating which channel to use. If minimum is chosen, the channel with the lowest value for each pixel is used instead.

14.4.9   Scatter HSV

The Scatter HSV filter (see Figure 14.27) works with the Hue, Saturation, and Value color model. It is a very versatile tool for creating random noise in an image. This filter introduces random color variations in the image. Scatter HSV is easy to control, and the following options are available:

- **Holdness.** This determines how close the pixels remain to their true color. A low holdness value allows them more freedom to change.

- **Hue.** This slider bar has the greatest effect on the image. The higher the Hue value, the more scattering occurs.

- **Saturation.** Increasing the Saturation gives the scattered pixels higher saturation values, making them look pure.

- **Value.** With a higher Value setting, pixels will have a higher difference between values, making the image spottier.

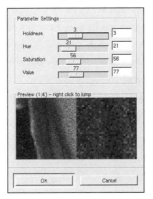

Figure 14.27   *The options menu for the Scatter HSV filter.*

14.4.10   Semiflatten

Semiflatten is the Holy Grail for creating GIFs with transparency. As most Web designers know, GIFs have support for transparency, but only a 1-bit channel (see page 77). This makes images with gradually fading drop shadows or transparent text look horrible. Semiflatten allows you to retain your perfect transparencies. The advantage of doing this over simply flattening the image is that Semiflatten saves some space when the image is saved as a GIF file. The only limitation is that you must display the image on a solid background color. There still is no way to use patterned backgrounds properly with GIF transparency.

When the Semiflatten filter is run, it takes the current background color and uses this for the image's background color. It still uses transparency in the image, but it flattens the parts of the image with Alpha values from 1 to 254. Any part of the image with an Alpha value of 0 is left alone. The effects of this are best shown in Figures 14.28, 14.29, and 14.30.

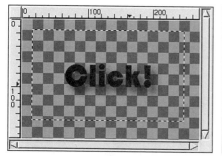

Figure 14.28 *An RGB image with transparency created in the GIMP.*

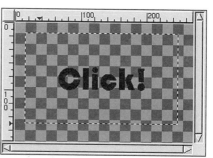

Figure 14.29 *The image, now converted to Indexed, does not look good at all. This is how it would look on a Web page.*

Figure 14.30 *The same image after Semiflatten has been run and then converted to Indexed.*

14.4.11 Smooth Palette

The Smooth Palette filter derives a palette from the colors in your image. This is not the most useful utility by itself, but it can be useful when used in conjunction with other filters and scripts.

When creating a palette with this filter, several options must be specified. The width and height of this new palette need to be chosen. Having a width of 256 means that it creates an image the size of an indexed palette. The height you choose for the image is not as important as the width, although it makes the palette easier to work with. Increasing the search time should give you a wider range of colors, although it may take too long to be effective.

14.4.12 Value Invert

The Value Invert filter inverts the values of pixels in an RGB image (see page 5), meaning that black pixels turn white and vice versa. This filter provides an interesting effect because the color of a pixel does not change. If it is a dark red pixel, it will become bright red. As always, to fully understand the effect of this filter, look at what happens to individual channels (see page 48 for more information on channels). See Figures 14.31 and 14.32 for an example of this filter at work.

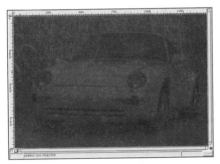   

Figure 14.31 *The Red channel of a Porsche.*   **Figure 14.32** *The Red channel of the Porsche after running Value Invert.*

14.5 Combine Filters

These filters create new images by combining two or more existing images to achieve interesting effects. The two Combine filters found in the stable GIMP distribution are Depth Merge and Film.

14.5.1 Depth Merge

The Depth Merge filter (see Figure 14.33) combines two images using depth maps. This filter takes two layers (1) in an image, or even two different images of the same size, and combines them. It decides between the two images' pixels to use based on values found in depth maps (2). To make things much easier to understand, we will use grayscale depth maps. Black is the "deepest" and white is the "shallowest" in a map. The deepest part between the two depth maps determines the pixel to be shown. The following four figures illustrate this concept:

- Figure 14.34 shows the first image to be merged.
- Figure 14.35 shows the second image to be merged.
- Figure 14.36 shows the depth map used for this image. It is a simple grayscale gradient.
- Figure 14.37 is its depth map.

The results of merging the two can be seen in Figure 14.33. Note that the left side of the first image is fully opaque, where its depth map is completely black. The right side of the second image also is fully opaque, where its depth map is darkest.

The Depth Merge filter comes with several options for greater control over the merging:

- **Overlap (3).** This slider bar allows you to gradually fade the two images together, or create a sharp transition between them. Higher values of overlap result in a smoother transition.
- **Offset (4).** This slider bar changes the darkness values of the depth maps being used. Sliding it to the left, into negative values, makes the first depth map darker. Sliding it to the right makes the second depth map become darker.
- **The Scale (5).** These slider bars at the bottom also control the darkness of the depth maps, but with more precise control. Scale 1 controls the first depth map; Scale 2 controls the second.

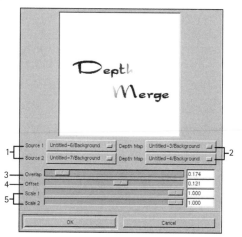

Figure 14.33 *The Depth Merge options menu showing a preview of the merged image.*

Figure 14.34 *The first image to be merged.*

Figure 14.35 *The second image to be merged.*

Figure 14.36 *The first gradient used for merging. Note the black on the left side, which makes the first image show up.*

Figure 14.37 *The second gradient used for merging. Note the black on the right side, which makes the second image appear.*

14.5.2 Film

The Film filter (see Figure 14.38) combines several images onto what looks like a piece of film. This is a quick filter, but the results can look good. The following options are available with this filter:

- **Size of the film (1).** The size can be made to fit the image sizes, or the images can be resized to fit a specific height.
- **Color of the film (2).** Dark brown is a good choice. If you want this to look like a negative, use a light blue and invert the image later.
- **Number the slides (3).** Start from a specific number.
- **Color of numbers (4).**

- **Font of the numbers (5).** If you do not want numbering of the images, simply set the number color to be the same as the film color.

- **Numbers can be placed at the top of the film, at the bottom, or both (6).**

- **Images to be used (7).** Choose the images by using the Add and Remove buttons (8) found under the list of images. Note that the images to be used must currently be open to be used.

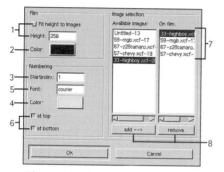

Figure 14.38 *The options menu for the Film filter.*

Figure 14.39 *An example image turned into film.*

14.6 Distortion Filters

The filters found in the Distort menu bend, warp, ripple, pinch, or otherwise distort images. They are most useful when creating logos, or other computer-generated images.

14.6.1 Blinds

The first filter in the Distort menu is Blinds (see Figure 14.40). The Blinds filter make an image look as if it has been pasted on Venetian blinds. This can be accomplished horizontally or vertically, with various sizes, and simulates the opening and closing of blinds. The options behind the Blinds filter are fairly simple:

- **Orientation (1).** Blinds can be placed horizontally or vertically over an image.

- **Background (2).** If you have layers or an Alpha channel in your image, you can choose to have a transparent background for the blinds—otherwise the current background color is used. Note that the preview will show a checkered background rather than the actual layers below the background layer.

- **Displacement (3).** This is the angle at which the blinds are turned. A displacement of 1 means that the blinds are nearly perpendicular to the viewer. A displacement of 90 means that they are parallel to the viewer—almost impossible to see.

- **Num Segments (4).** The number of blinds can be changed from 1 to 10 via the slider bar.

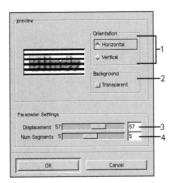

Figure 14.40 *The options menu for the Blinds filter.*

14.6.2   Emboss

The Emboss filter (see Figure 14.41) actually allows you to do two things: emboss or bumpmap an image. This creates a three-dimensional-looking image, as though it has been embossed in metal or another material. When you emboss an image, it loses the color information, but remains an RGB image. If you use bumpmap, it stays as a color image that looks textured. The options for Emboss are similar to those of the Bumpmap filter found in the Map menu (see page 228):

- **Emboss (1).** This effect gives you a grayscale image.

- **Bumpmap (2).** This effect gives you an RGB image.

- **Azimuth (3).** This determines the angle of the "light source," which will give the image its 3D effect.

- **Elevation (4).** The elevation of the light source, given in degrees. This is analogous to the light source's height above the horizon.

- **Depth (5).** This option controls the amount of texture created. A higher depth creates greater contrast between the light and dark areas.

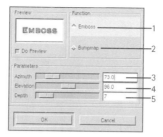

Figure 14.41 *The options menu for the Emboss filter.*

14.6.3 Engrave

The Engrave filter creates images that simulate the look of old grayscale illustrations (see Figures 14.42 and 14.43). The Engrave filter has only two options: Height and Limit Line Width. The Height slider determines the height of the lines created by this filter. You will get better results with low height values. The Limit Line Width toggle button allows you to control the line width, but engravings will generally look more realistic if you leave this unselected.

Figure 14.42 *An example image of a Porsche.*

Figure 14.43   *The Porsche after being engraved.*

14.6.4 IWarp

The IWarp filter (see Figures 14.44 through 14.47) is a program unto itself. It is very similar to Kai's Power Goo. This filter allows you to stretch, shrink, grow, and swirl images. It even allows you to animate these changes. This filter is similar to the Smudge tool (see page 169) and can produce some very pleasing results on scanned images, especially faces. Be careful, however: It can cause you to lose many hours playing around with it.

The IWarp filter is very complex. The first menu, Settings (1), controls the actual image warping:

- The image preview is shown on the left side of the IWarp filter; this is where you click and drag with the mouse to distort the image.
- **Deform Radius (2).** This slider bar determines the size of the warping effect.
- **Deform Amount (3).** This slider bar controls the magnitude of the warping. A larger deform amount results in greater warping.
- The type of warping (4) is selected from a group of option buttons:
    a. **Move.** This allows you to drag parts of the image around.
    b. **Remove.** This option undoes the effects of warping. While this may not seem useful, it does help after warping large areas because you can set it to just reverse small areas.
    c. **Grow.** This enlarges areas of the image when you click on the image.
    d. **Shrink.** This option shrinks an area of the image.

e. **Swirl CCW.** This option swirls the image in a counter-clockwise direction.

f. **Swirl CW.** This swirls the image in a clockwise direction.

■ **Reset (5).** Click this button if you warp too much and want to start over again.

■ **Bilinear (6).** This greatly increases the quality of the warping, but is CPU intensive. If you have a slower computer, consider turning off this option.

■ **Adaptive Supersample (7).** This option makes the warping look much better, but, as with Bilinear, is much slower. If you have a cutting-edge computer with a lot of memory, definitely use this. If time is an issue, and you have a slower computer, leave this turned off.

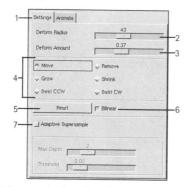

Figure 14.44   *The IWarp Setting menu.*

The second part of the IWarp filter is the Animation section (1). In this menu (see Figure 14.45), you can create animations from your warped images:

■ **Animate (2).** Animation is toggled on and off here (2).

■ **Number of frames (3).** This slider bar controls the number of frames created. A greater number of frames results in better quality, but takes longer.

■ Normally, the animation starts at the original image, and gradually changes to the distorted one. You can also choose from the following options (4):

a. **Reverse.** This option starts the animation at the distorted image and gradually changes to the original image.

b. **Ping-Pong.** This option causes the animation to bounce back and forth between the original and distorted images. The Ping-Pong option should be used for animations that repeat, such as GIFs.

If you use Ping-Pong or Reverse for your animation, remove the original layer, or the animation will have a frame that is out of place.

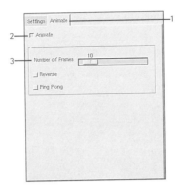

Figure 14.45 *The IWarp Animation menu.*

Figure 14.46 *The original image.*   **Figure 14.47** *The IWarped image.*

14.6.5 PageCurl

The PageCurl filter (see Figure 14.48) simulates the corner of a layer lifting to show the layer or transparency underneath, like a piece of paper curling up. This filter has several different options to suit your image. Unfortunately, the size of the curl cannot be changed, so if you need a small curl, you will need to use selections. The PageCurl filter has the following options:

- **Curl Location (1).** The curl can be placed in any of the four corners of the layer or selection.

- **Curl Orientation (2).** The orientation of the curl can be horizontal or vertical.

- **Shade Under Curl (3).** Toggle the shading underneath the curl as well.

- **Use Current Gradient (4).** The Coloring for the curl normally is the current foreground and background colors, but you can also toggle the use of the current gradient instead.

- **Curl Opacity (5).** This option lets you simulate a transparent material like cellophane that is being peeled off.

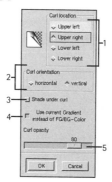

Figure 14.48 *The options menu for the PageCurl filter.*

14.6.6 Polar Coords

The Polar Coords filter remaps an image using polar coordinates and rectangular coordinates. You can remap from either polar to rectangular, or rectangular to polar. Polar Coords essentially maps a rectangle to a circle, or vice versa. This filter can make some very interesting effects, especially when remapping from rectangular to polar. This filter also can be used for making primitive text curves (see Figure 14.49) and circles.

Figure 14.49 *A simple text circle created with the Polar Coords filter.*

There are several options used in the Polar Coords filter (see Figure 14.50):

- **Circle depth in percent.**

  a. When mapping from polar to rectangular, this option adjusts the shape of the circle. At 100%, it is a perfect circle. As the depth gets smaller, the circle becomes less round, and at 0% it becomes a square.

  b. For rectangular to polar mapping, the effect is less obvious. At 100%, this option correctly maps a circle. At 0%, it correctly maps a square. Figures 14.51 through 14.53 demonstrate this quite well.

- **Offset angle.**

  a. For polar to rectangular mapping, this has the effect of moving the beginning (and end) counter clockwise in a circle.

  b. For rectangular to polar mapping, this moves the starting point along horizontally.

- **Map Backwards.** If this option is selected, the image is mapped beginning from the right side instead of the left. For both types of mapping, this has the effect of flipping the image along the vertical axis.

- **Map from Top.**

  a. For polar to rectangular mapping, this reverses the part of the image in the middle, and that which is around the outside.

  b. For rectangular to polar mapping, this determines which part ends up on top and which ends up on the bottom. It essentially flips the image along its horizontal axis.

- **Polar to Rectangular.** This last option switches back and forth between polar to rectangular and rectangular to polar.

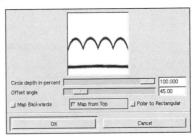

Figure 14.50 *The options menu for the Polar Coords filter.*

Some example images with the Polar Coords filter are shown here (14.51 through 14.53)

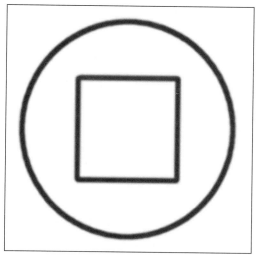

Figure 14.51 *The original image before the Polar Coords filter is used.*

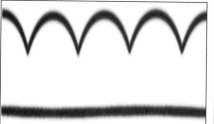

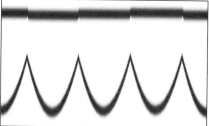

Figure 14.52 *The image after Polar Coords has been applied with 100% circle depth. Note that the circle turns out as a straight line, while the rectangle has become distorted.*

Figure 14.53 *The same image after Polar Coords has been applied with a circle depth of 0%. This time, the rectangle is a straight line, whereas the circle is distorted.*

14.6.7 Ripple

Ripple (see Figure 14.54) is a straightforward filter that distorts an image to look like a reflection in rippling water. Rippling can be done horizontally or vertically, and has many other options, as follows:

- **Antialiasing (1).** This option greatly improves the quality of an image, but takes more time to use.

- **Retain Tileability (2).** This option is useful if you are working with an image that is going to be a background for a Web page, desktop, and so on.

- **Edges (3).** The edges can be treated with the following effects:
  a. **Wrap.** This uses the peaks of the ripples to fill in the valleys.
  b. **Smear.** This just fills in the empty areas by using the colors from the surrounding areas.
  c. **Black.** This simply uses black to fill in the valleys.
- **Orientation (4).** The waves can be horizontal or vertical.
- **Wave Type (5).**
  a. **Sawtooth.** This wave has sharp peaks and valleys.
  b. **Sine.** The sine curve wave is smooth.
- **Period (6).** This determines the distance between two peaks of a wave.
- **Amplitude (7).** This changes the height of the waves.

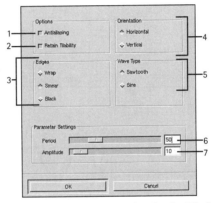

Figure 14.54   *The options window for the Ripple filter.*

14.6.8   Shift

The Shift filter randomly displaces rows or columns of pixels in an image. This can create an interesting noise effect, especially if you apply it both horizontally and vertically.

The options for the Shift filter are fairly simple. The displacement can be done either horizontally or vertically. The shift amount provides the filter with an average density to move. The exact shift is never known, but it will be close to the average density.

14.6.9   Value Propagate

Value Propagate is a versatile filter that adjusts the values for an image. This could include increasing the levels of white or black, changing the amount of midtones, or adjusting the amount of transparency. The number of pixels modified can be changed as well. For the best results, run this filter several times with the same settings. This will give you some engaging artistic effects. Value Propagate has many different options, as follows:

- **Distortion Type**[2]

    a. **More White.** Increases the whiteness of an image by increasing the value for pixels with higher values. This makes brighter pixels whiter.

    b. **More Black.** Does the opposite of More White by darkening the already darker pixels. These first two options work well with photographs, but not with computer-generated images.

    c. **Middle value to Peaks.** Causes contrasting areas to become fuzzy by averaging the color.

    d. **Foreground to Peaks.** Locates the peaks and replaces them with the foreground color. This has the effect of drawing borders around images.

    e. **Only Foreground.** Alters the values for pixels that match the current foreground color.

    f. **Only Background.** Does the same thing as Only Foreground, but uses the background color.

    g. **More Opaque.** Works similarly to More White, but deals with Alpha. The Alpha values of pixels with already high Alpha are increased.

    h. **More Transparent.** Does the opposite of More Opaque. Pixels with already low Alpha values are lowered further.

- **Available pixels to be altered.** The available pixels can be constrained by entering new values into the Low and High thresholds. If a pixel is outside this threshold, it will not be affected. The amount of propagation can be adjusted with the Propagating Rate slider bar.

- **Direction of propagation.** When this filter is used, the pixels are shifted slightly. Normally, this does not have much effect because by default they are shifted in all four directions. When fewer than four directions are selected, the filter has a lesser effect, and it shifts the image slightly in a certain direction. Any combination of these directions can be selected to achieve the desired effect.

    The following directions are available:

    a. Left

    b. Right

    c. Top

    d. Bottom

---

[2]*Options **c** through **h** work better with computer-generated images because they all work by finding areas of larger contrast, similar to the Edge Detection filters.*

14.6.10 Waves

The Waves filter (see Figure 14.55) makes an image look as if it is being reflected in a pool of water after a pebble has been dropped in it. The waves radiate from the center of the image. The size of the waves can be controlled precisely. Moderate values are recommended for this filter; extremely large values will distort the image beyond recognition. The Waves filter's parameters are similar to those of the Ripple plug-in:

- **Amplitude (1).** This determines the height of the waves.

- **Phase (2).** This angle is measured in degrees, and determines where the wave is starting. For example, a phase angle of 0 means that the center wave is at full height. Increasing this angle varies this sinusoidally.

- **Wavelength (3).** This slider bar adjusts the distance between the tops of the waves. A higher wavelength means that the waves are further apart. Higher wavelengths are recommended to keep your image recognizable.

- **Wave Mode (4).** The Wave modes are as follows:

    a. **Smear.** Smears between blank spots.

    b. **Fill.** Fills the areas in with black.

- **Reflective (5).** This option makes the waves interfere with each other.

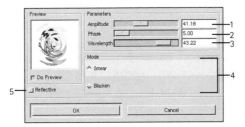

Figure 14.55   *The options menu for the Waves filter.*

14.6.11 Whirl and Pinch

The Whirl and Pinch filter acts similarly to the IWarp Swirl filter, but with more precise control of the swirling. It can make an image look like it is getting sucked into a whirlpool, or provide other interesting effects. The Whirl and Pinch effect is controlled by three slider bars (see Figures 14.56 and 14.57):

- **Whirl Angle (1).** This can range from −360 degrees to 360 degrees. The whirl angle determines how much the image is "swirled."

- **Pinch Amount (2).** This option determines how much the image is "pinched" or sucked into the center. This can range from −1 (exploding out of the screen) to 1 (sucked into the screen).

- **Radius (3).** This option controls the amount of the image affected. This ranges from 0 (none of the image) to 2 (all of the image).

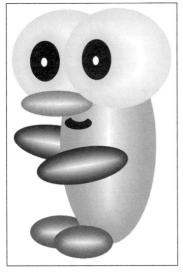

Figure 14.56 *The original image.*

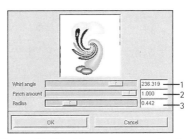

Figure 14.57 *The options menu for the Whirl and Pinch filter.*

14.7 Edge Detect Filters

The Edge Detect filters find color changes in images and highlight them. This creates images with sharp contour lines. Each of these filters uses a different method of detecting edges, and will give you a different result.

14.7.1 Edge

The first of the Edge Detect filters is simply called Edge. It does a simple edge detection on an image. Images that have this filter applied to them will become dark, with light-colored lines showing the edges. The Edge filter has two edge detection options (see Figure 14.58):

- **Amount (1).** The slider bar ranges from 1.0 to 10.0, but larger values can be entered in the box beside it. Low values will result in many bright contour lines, and high values will result in fewer, but darker, contour lines. It is important to use a high enough value to get rid of noise in an image without losing real edges.

- **Empty Spaces (2).**
  a. **Wrap.** Used for tileable images, although with this filter it works well for most images.
  b. **Smear.** Blurs the colors near the empty spaces to fill them in.
  c. **Black.** Puts black in empty spaces. For most filters, black does not produce desirable results, although it tends to work well with this filter.

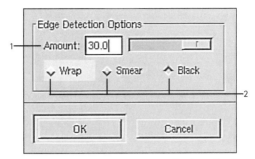

Figure 14.58 *The options menu for the Edge filter.*

14.7.2 Laplace

The Laplace filter is another edge detect filter. It tends to create darker images with more contrast and less color shifting. For best results, use the Gauss IIR filter (see page 194) with a radius between 1.5 to 5.0 before running this filter. As with the Edge filter, the image becomes dark and the contours become light. In this filter, the contours are always one pixel wide. In layers that contain Alpha, the contours become black, and the flat areas become transparent. There are no options for this filter.

14.7.3 Sobel

The Sobel filter works similarly to the Laplace filter. The contour lines can be more than one pixel wide, so it makes thicker lines. The contour lines will have more color to them than Laplace. The lines are usually similar to the inverse of the original colors. There are two options available for the Sobel filter:

- **Edge Detect.** This can be applied in any of three ways:
  a. **Horizontally.** Applying this filter only horizontally detects horizontal edges and ignores vertical ones.
  b. **Vertically.** Applying the filter only vertically does the opposite.
  c. **Both.** Applying the filter both horizontally and vertically detects all edges.
- **Keep Sign of Result.** If you apply this filter in one direction only, there is an option to keep the sign of the result. This gives the new image an embossed look, but it will retain the colored contour lines.

14.8 Enhance Filters

The Enhance filters all improve the look of images, especially scanned photographs and images made from a TV capture card. These filters are very useful as a starting point for improving the quality of an image.

14.8.1 Deinterlace

This first filter, Deinterlace, is used to interpolate fields lost when using a video capture card. Sometimes, only the odd or even fields get captured by these cards, and this filter fills in the lost information. You will have to experiment to see how much the image can be improved.

The only option here is the choice to fill odd or even fields. This must be done using trial and error.

14.8.2 Despeckle

This filter is perfect for removing noise, dust, or scratches from an image. If your image is generally noisy, you will probably want to work on the entire image, using a small radius. If there are particles of dust or scratches on the image, use selections to isolate them, and apply the filter. This filter works by splitting the image up into specific boxes and smoothing the color range in each of them (see example in Figures 14.59 and 14.60).

This is a "quick and dirty" style of filter. Although it can be very useful, there is no replacement for human intuition and the Clone tool. If you are serious about repairing a photograph, there are better techniques that can be used. Also, be careful with this filter, as it can cause unwanted blurring. This filter is somewhat complicated—the following options (see Figure 14.61) are available:

- **Adaptive (1).** This algorithm can be very useful. It attempts to automatically calculate the best size of box to use, and it usually helps stop blurring. Changing the radius can still affect the image, although not as drastically.

- **Recursive (2).** This algorithm also attempts to automatically improve the image, but it will add to the blurring effect.

- **Radius (3).** This is probably the most important setting. Set the radius as small as possible, since larger radii will cause unnecessary blurring and take a long time.

- **Affected pixels.** This allows you to control the pixels that are affected by this filter.

  a. If you have lighter colored scratches, lower the white threshold (4), and set the black threshold (5) to 0.

  b. If the noise on the image is dark, raise the black threshold, and set the white threshold to 255.

Figure 14.59 *An example blemished image.*

Figure 14.60 *The image after the blemish is fixed. The operation took less than 30 seconds.*

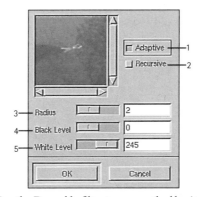

Figure 14.61 *Using the Despeckle filter to remove the blemish in a scanned picture.*

14.8.3 Destripe

The Destripe filter is used to remove stripe patterns from a scanned photograph. This filter is only useful in very specific situations. With the cost of high quality scanners steadily dropping, hopefully the need for this filter will decline.

Using this filter is very easy. The slider bar along the bottom controls the width of the stripes to be removed. Since all pictures are so different, you will have to experiment to find the optimal value. The Histogram button along the side will create a grayscale "histogram" of the image.

14.8.4 NL

The NL filter can be thought of as the non-linear "Swiss army knife" filter. It can apply various operations to scanned images to improve them, and comes with algorithms to reduce noise, smooth images, and also do edge enhancements. This filter is different from the other enhance filters because it uses a seven-pixel hexagon to calculate mean values rather than a 3×3 square of pixels. The NL filter has several different modes in which to work (see Figure 14.62):

- **Alpha Trimmed Mean.** This mode will give similar results to the other enhance filters. Low or 0 Alpha values are best for this mode. For better noise reduction, try an Alpha value of 0.4 and a radius of 0.6.

- **Optimal Estimation.** This mode works on small noise variations. This filter assumes that large variations are meant to be in the image, and it removes only the smaller variations in color. This is well suited for removing dithering in GIFs.

- **Edge Enhancement.** This mode does the opposite of the preceding two modes. It emphasizes the differences in images to improve their quality. Use an Alpha value of 0.3 and a radius of 0.8 for the best results.

For all of these modes, the seven-pixel hexagonal shape is used. Because of this shape, the radius ranges from 0.33 (only one pixel large) to 1.0 (the size of a 3×3 pixel square). Use intermediate values for this, or use a different filter if needed.

This filter can be used several times in succession in different modes. This can be useful in recovering GIF images that have become dithered:

- Use the Optimal Estimation mode with an Alpha of 1.0 and radius 1.0.

- Use the Alpha Trimmed Mean mode with an Alpha of 0.5 and radius 0.55.

- If needed, use the Edge Enhancement mode with an Alpha value of 0.3 and a radius of 0.8. This should give you a better image with which to work.

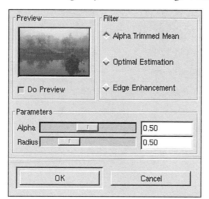

Figure 14.62   *The options menu for the NL filter.*

14.8.5 Sharpen

The Sharpen filter is probably the most useful filter for quickly improving images (see Figures 14.63 through 14.66). Sharpen improves the quality of images by emphasizing color changes in an image. When it detects a color change, it will lighten the pixels on the lighter edge, and darken the pixels on the darker edge. To the human eye, this makes the image much more clear.

Sharpening does have the effect of creating or enhancing noise. Try using a small amount of sharpening on the entire image, and then select certain areas that require additional sharpening. Remember to feather the selection to give it a more natural look. Make sure that you do not create "halos" around objects when using this filter because over-sharpening can make the image look unnatural.

The Sharpen filter is easy to use. The amount of sharpening that occurs is controlled by the slider bar along the bottom of the menu. The preview image is very useful in determining how much sharpening is needed.

Figure 14.63 *This is a close up of the original image.*

Figure 14.64 *This is a close up of the sharpened image. Note the greater contrast between the dark and light areas of the "A".*

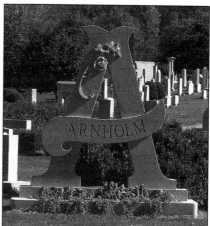

Figure 14.65 *The original, unsharpened image.*

Figure 14.66 *The resulting image after it has been sharpened. This has been over-sharpened to exaggerate the effects of the filter.*

14.9   Glass Effect Filters

These two filters create effects related to "glass," or other semi-opaque images. They create some very fascinating distortions.

14.9.1   Apply Lens

This filter makes an image look as if it is being viewed from behind a lens made of different materials. This filter always occurs at the center of the image or current selection.

The options for this filter are simple. You can either keep the surroundings, or replace them with the background color. The amount of refraction is entered manually and can range from 1.0 to as large as you want to go. Some sample indices of refraction are shown in Table 14.3.

Table 14.3   Sample Indices of Refraction

Substance	Index
Ice	1.31
Water	1.33
Turpentine	1.47
Glass	1.52
Salt	1.54
Quartz	1.54
Dense glass	1.66
Zircon	1.92
Diamond	2.42

14.9.2   Glass Tile

This filter makes an image look like it is being viewed from behind glass tile. It divides the image up into rectangular "glass blocks". The height and width (in pixels) of these blocks are controlled by slider bars.

14.10   Light Effect Filters

The filters found in the Light Effects menu create effects that in real life are caused by light. There are many uses for these filters, especially for creating realistic-looking, computer-generated images.

14.10.1   FlareFX

The first light effect filter is FlareFX. It creates a lens flare at a certain point in an image. Currently, the only option to work with here is where the flare occurs. The coordinates can be entered manually, or you can point and click with the mouse. Hopefully, we will see more options added to this filter in the future.

14.10.2   Sparkle

The Sparkle filter (see Figure 14.67) adds a sparkling effect to an image. Sparkles will occur at the points with the highest value of an image. This filter is very unpredictable, so you may want to use selections or layers to give you greater control. The Sparkle filter is controlled by several slider bars:

- **Luminosity Threshold (1).** Controls the number of pixels affected. Higher luminosity values result in a greater range of affected pixels.
- **Flare Intensity (2).** Controls how "bright" these flares are.
- **Spike Length (3).** Determines how long the average spike is.

- **Spike Points (4).** Controls how many spikes are found in each flare.
- **Spike Angle (5).** Determines where the first spike occurs. This option does not affect the results much if there are several spike points.

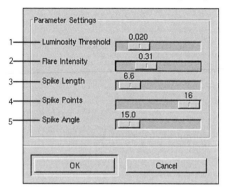

Figure 14.67 *The Sparkle filter's Options menu.*

14.10.3 Supernova

The Supernova filter creates a supernova burst in your image. This filter offers greater control over the result than the FlareFX filter. The only disadvantage to this filter is that there is no preview for the color of the flare. It is best to use the Color Selection menu (see page 12) to pick a color, and manually enter the numbers in the filter's dialog box. This filter has an interface similar to that of the FlareFX plug-in:

- The position of the supernova is entered manually, or using the mouse.
- The color of the supernova is controlled by the slider bars.
- The radius of the burst is also controlled by a slider bar. This radius value only controls the center ball of the supernova—the spokes will spread over the entire image.
- The last slider bar, Spokes, controls the number of spokes radiating from the burst. Low values for the spokes will create very irregular burst shapes.

14.11 Map Filters

These filters deal with "mapping" one image to another, or to an object. This has the effect of creating images that look textured, or have a 3D feel to them. These filters can create some very impressive effects if you know how to use them properly.

14.11.1 Bumpmap

The Bumpmap filter is probably the most frequently used filter in the Map menu. It creates 3D or textured images by combining two images, one as the source image and the other as the map (see Figures 14.68 through 14.70). Map images are usually grayscale images to make them easier to work with. This filter allows you to be very creative. Use this filter for adding textures to logos and other text. The Ripple and Whirl and Pinch filters can create some very interesting images to be used as maps. The controls for this filter are somewhat complicated, however (see figure 14.71):

- **Compensate for Darkening (1).** This should usually be turned on, otherwise the resulting image will become too dark.

- **Invert Bumpmap (2).** This will cause the map's effects to be reversed.

- There are three map types (3):

  a. **Linear Map.** Works directly on the image.

  b. **Spherical Map.** Makes the bumps rounder.

  c. **Sinusoidal Map.** Makes some parts of the map steeper in areas.

- **Bumpmap (4).** The map image to use as the bumpmap is controlled by a drop-down menu. You can use any image for this, but it is best to use a grayscale image.

- **Azimuth (5).** This slider bar simulates the direction of the light (in degrees). This can be thought of as the position of the sun.

- **Elevation (6).** This slider bar controls the height of the light source above the horizon (in degrees). An elevation of 0 means that the light is shining directly horizontally, and large shadows will be created. An elevation of 90 means that the light is directly above the image, and only very small shadows are created. Note that when the elevation is 90 degrees, changing the azimuth does not affect the bumpmap.

- **Depth (7).** This slider bar controls the amount of bumpmapping that occurs. Higher depth values create a greater contrast between light and dark, making the bumpmap seem "deeper."

- **X Offset and Y Offset (8).** The X and Y offsets allow you to precisely place the map over the image. This is useful if you need to align a map with the original image. You can also use the right mouse button to drag around in the preview window to control the offset.

- **Waterlevel (9).** This slider bar determines how pixels with Alpha values in the map image are used. Usually, pixels with Alpha value in them will not affect the image. If, however, you increase the waterlevel, the actual Alpha parts of the map image will affect the original image.

- **Ambient (10).** This slider bar controls how much ambient light there is in the new image. Low amounts of ambient light create more contrast between dark and light areas, and the image is darker overall. High amounts of ambient light result in less contrast, and a brighter image overall.

Figure 14.68   *The base image used for the Bumpmap filter.*

Figure 14.69   *The map image used for Bumpmap filter.*

Figure 14.70   *The resulting image.*

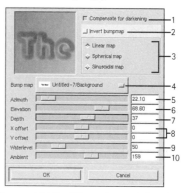

Figure 14.71   *The options window for the Bumpmap filter.*

14.11.2 Displace

The Displace filter is an all-purpose filter used to distort images (see Figures 14.72 through 14.74 for an example).It is especially good for bending text and lines around images, or creating very precise warping and smearing effects. It is in the Map menu because it uses an image (usually grayscale) to get the information for the distortion.

The Displace filter, like most of the Map filters, can be complicated at times. The first concept to learn is how the image used for the map affects the image. For this filter, always use a grayscale image for the map that is the same size as the image you want to distort.The effect the map has on the original image is based on the value of the pixels in the map:

- Any pixel that is black (value 0) will displace it the full amount, either downwards or to the right, or both.

- Any pixel that is white (value 100) will displace the image upwards, to the left, or both.

- Any pixels that are perfectly gray (value 50) will have no effect on the image.
- Pixels that lie between these values will displace the image proportionally to their value, so if a pixel is halfway between black and gray (value 25), it will displace it half the amount.

Also, note that transparent pixels will not affect the image. Using transparency is often more useful than using gray to avoid affecting all areas. Partially transparent pixels will affect the image in proportion to their transparency and color.

Now that you know how the maps work, here are the options for this filter (refer to Figure 14.75):

- The displacement can be done independently for each axis (1). If you want to displace along one axis only, they can be toggled on and off.
- The amount of displacement (2) for each axis is entered here.
- Each map is selected (3).
- The mode for dealing with empty edges is chosen (4):
  a. **Wrap.** This will wrap the edge from the other side.
  b. **Smear.** This is usually the best option for this filter. It fills in empty areas by smudging the edges.
  c. **Black.** Sets empty areas to black.

Figure 14.72 *The original image before the map was applied.*

Figure 14.73 *A sample image used as a map.*

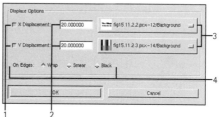

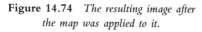

Figure 14.75 *The options menu for the Displace filter.*

Figure 14.74 *The resulting image after the map was applied to it.*

14.11.3 Fractal Trace

The Fractal Trace filter maps your image to a Mandelbrot fractal. This creates very interesting effects on scanned photographs. Be cautious with this filter: It is very CPU intensive and has a tendency to crash.

The Fractal Trace filter has several options for controlling the look of the image:

- **X1.** Determines the scaling factor for the left side of the image.
- **X2.** Controls the right side of the image.
- **Y1.** Controls the scaling for the top of the image.
- **Y2.** Ccontrols the bottom of the image.
- **Depth.** Controls the amount of iterations used to calculate this fractal. The higher the number of iterations, the more detail, although this is not always practical.
- **Edges.** Determines how the edges are dealt with. Experiment with its options to get the best results:
  a. **Smear.** Fills in empty spaces by smudging them together.
  b. **Black.** Fills in empty spaces with black.
  c. **Wrap.** Creates the most attention-getting images.

14.11.4 Illusion

The Illusion filter acts somewhat like a kaleidoscope. It divides an image up into several pieces and displays them over the original image. Using this filter is very simple: You simply enter the number of pieces into which to split the image.

14.11.5 Make Seamless

The Make Seamless filter acts similarly to the Illusion filter. It divides the image up and puts the new tileable layer on top. This makes it perfect for use as a background in a Web page, or anywhere it needs to be tiled. There are no options for this filter.

14.11.6 Map Object

The Map Object filter maps an image to an object—either a sphere or a plane. This filter is great for creating annoying animations for Web pages. It can also be used for creating useful images as well.

This filter is very CPU intensive. When working with this filter, be patient. Updates can take a long time, especially when using anti-aliasing. The following options are available with this filter:

- The Options Menu (see Figure 14.76):
  a. **Map To.** The only available shapes for the map object are a box, cylinder, plane, and sphere, although newer objects are being added as the plug-in develops. Note that when using the box or cylinder, additional options are available for the images to be used.
  b. **Transparent Background.** You can choose to have a transparent background or use the current background color.
  c. **Tile Source Image.** This option toggles the tiling of the source image on and off. This only works when dealing with planes, and makes the transparent background option unnecessary, since there is no background with this option.
  d. **Create New Image.** Either create a new image, or just replace the current one.
  e. **Enable Tooltips.** They appear when you leave your cursor over an option for a short time. They do take up a few of your CPU cycles, so if you really need the performance, disable these.
  f. **Enable Antialiasing.** This should always be used when dealing with this filter because without it, the quality of the new image is poor.
- The Light Menu (see Figure 14.77)
  a. **Lightsource Type.**
    - Point light
    - Directional light
    - None

b. **Lightsource Color.** By default, this is white.

c. **Position.** If you chose point light as the lightsource, the position of the source needs to be entered. This must be done by manually entering coordinates. If you zoom out slightly, there is a blue dot that allows you to place the lightsource.

d. If you selected directional light, you must enter a direction vector for the light to travel in.

- The Material Menu (see Figure 14.78)

    a. **IntensityLevels.** There are two options in this section:

    - **Ambient.** Controls how much of the original color to show when no light hits it. This should be less than 1 to be realistic.

    - **Diffuse.** Determines the intensity of the original color when light does hit it.

    b. **Reflectivity.** There are three options here:

    - **Diffuse.** Controls how much light is reflected from this object.

    - **Specular.** Controls how intense the highlights will be.

    - **Highlight.** Controls how focused these highlights will be.

- The Orientation Menu (see Figure 14.79). This controls the shape and size of the object.

    a. **Show Preview Wireframe.** It is much easier to view the preview wireframe while working with the position. Turn the Show preview wireframe option on.

    b. **Position and Orientation.** This set of options controls the position of the object. A value of 0.5 is in the center.

    - **X Pos.** This controls the X position of the image in three-dimensional space.

    - **Y Pos.** This controls the Y position of the image in three-dimensional space.

    - **Z Pos.** This controls the Z position of the image in three-dimensional space.

    - **XRot.** This slider bar controls the XY rotation around the Z axis.

    - **YRot.** This slider bar controls the YZ rotation around the X axis.

    - **ZRot.** This slider bar controls the XZ rotation around the Y axis.

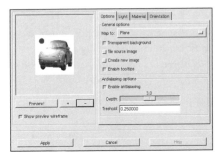

Figure 14.76 *The Options menu for the Map to Object filter.*

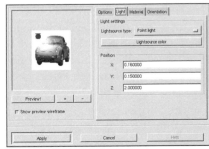

Figure 14.77 *The Light menu for the Map to Object filter.*

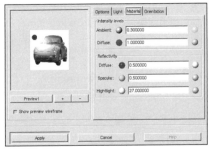

Figure 14.78 *The Material menu for the Map to Object filter.*

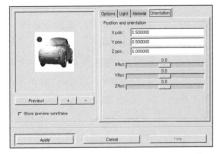

Figure 14.79 *The Orientation menu for the Map to Object filter.*

After you have set the image to your satisfaction, click Apply, and the new image will be created.

14.11.7 Paper Tile

The Paper Tile filter makes an image look as if it has been cut up into squares and placed on a black or white background. These tiles have all moved slightly before they were glued back onto the background.

This filter is easy to use. The width and height of the tiles are entered, as well as the average distance to slide the tiles. The background color is selected here. The only choices are black or white.

14.11.8 Small Tiles

The Small Tiles filter is a very versatile tool for creating complicated tiled images. It allows you to flip certain tiles horizontally, vertically, or around both axes. This gives you precise control to create some very interesting effects. This filter has the following options (see Figure 14.80):

- **Segment Setting (1).** This controls the number of tiles to create. The number displayed here shows the number of tiles in one side of the square (for example, 2 gives you a 2×2 square, or 4 tiles, 3 gives you a 3×3 square, or 9 tiles). This setting ranges from 2 to 6.
- **Flipping.**

  a. Tiles can be flipped horizontally and/or vertically (2).

  b. You can select the tiles to flip (3).

  - **All tiles.**

  - **Alternate tiles.** Starts with the tile in the top-left corner.

  - **Explicit tiles.** These can be specified by entering their coordinates or clicking with the mouse.

  c. **Opacity (4).** If the image has an Alpha channel, its opacity can be controlled via a slider bar.

  d. **Reset (5).** If you have made changes too complicated to fix, simply click on the Reset button to go back to the original settings.

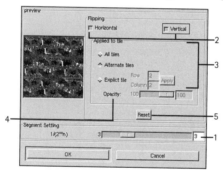

Figure 14.80   *The Options menu for the Small Tiles filter.*

14.11.9 Tile

This filter tiles an image into a new image or layer of arbitrary size. This effect only works if the new image is larger than the previous one. This filter does not provide very precise control, and the Small Tiles filter is better for creating tiled images. This filter is useful, however, for creating tiled images via Script-Fu.

The controls for this filter are simple. The size of the new image is entered in the width and height boxes. The Constrain Ratio toggle button allows you to keep the image's width:height ratio. The New Image toggle button creates a new image; otherwise the current image is simply replaced.

14.12   Miscellaneous Filters

For now, the only filter in this section is the Video filter. This may change with future versions of the GIMP.

14.12.1 Video

This filter makes an image look as if it is being displayed on a low-dot-pitch RGB video monitor (see Figure 14.81). It displays many of the different effects that occur with these low quality monitors. All of these effects are caused by the separation of the R, G, and B channels on a monitor. The interface for this filter is easy to use—the following options are available:

- **Additive.** This option toggles the use of the Additive layer on and off. If this is turned off, the image will usually look too dark.
- **Rotated.** This toggle button rotates the pattern placed on the image by 90 degrees.
- **RGB Pattern Type.**
  a. **Staggered.** Creates a set of staggered rectangles across the image.
  b. **Large Staggered.** Creates the same effect as Staggered, but uses larger rectangles.
  c. **Striped.** Places horizontal rows alternating between red, green, and blue tones across the image.
  d. **Wide-Striped.** Similar to Striped, but the rows are wider.
  e. **Long-Staggered.** Creates the same effect as Staggered, but uses taller rectangles.
  f. **3×3.** Adds red, green, and blue squares on the image.
  g. **Large 3×3.** Uses larger squares than 3×3.
  h. **Hex.** Adds hexagonal shaped objects on the image.
  i. **Dots.** Places small dots of red, green, and blue on the image.

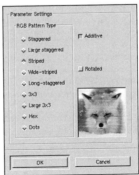

Figure 14.81   *The Options window for the Video filter.*

14.13   Noise Filters

These three filters are used to add noise to an image. Usually, noise is unwanted, and a lot of effort goes into removing it. In some situations where noise is desired, however, these filters can be used.

14.13.1   Noisify

The Noisify filter is used to introduce random noise into an image. The amount of noise for individual channels can be specified. If you are trying to soften a sharp image, add slightly more noise to the Red and Green channels than to the Blue; the Blue channel is often noisy enough already.

This filter is fairly straightforward. The amount of noise in each channel is controlled by a slider bar. The Independent button allows the channels to be adjusted independently. Whether to adjust them independently or not depends on the picture being noisified.

14.13.2   Spread

This filter creates noise in images by moving pixels a random amount in the horizontal and vertical directions. This filter is similar to the Randomize filter in Slur mode, but differs in that it allows you to specify the amount to move in both directions. The amount of spread in an image is constrained by the horizontal and vertical slider bars. These slider bars determine the maximum amount of spread that occurs.

14.14   Random Filters

The Random filters (see Figure 14.82) were previously one filter, but they have been split up. They add random noise to an image. The results of these filters depend on the mode of randomization. The Blur filter (see page 194) was previously part of these filters, so if you are familiar with Blur, these will be easy to learn. The following options are available with these filters:

- **Randomization Seed (1).** Current Time is a good number to use to ensure randomness. If you need to repeat the effects of this filter later, enter your own value in the Other Value text box.

- **Randomization % (2).** This slider bar controls the number of pixels that will be affected by the filter.

- **Repeat (3).** This slider bar controls how many times this filter is run; only applying it once doesn't usually have much effect on an image.

The following randomization types are available:

- **Hurl.** Goes through each pixel in the image and randomizes its color if it is in the randomization range. Hurl usually affects images a lot, so do not repeat it many times.

- **Pick.** Similar to Hurl, but instead of randomizing a color, it chooses a random, nearby pixel's color. This affects the image much less than Hurl.

- **Slur.** Takes an image and randomizes it downward. If a pixel is within its randomization percentage, Slur will shift it. There is an 80% chance that Slur will take the pixel from the line above to move downward; otherwise it uses a pixel to the left or the right of the original (10% chance for each). It has the effect of "melting" an image slightly.

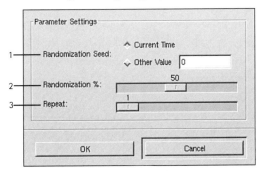

Figure 14.82   *An example Options menu for the Random filters. Note the similarities to the Blur filter.*

14.14   Render Filters

The filters found in this menu are applied to existing images, but rather than affecting the existing images, they create completely new images. These filters are very powerful, and it is well worth your time to become familiar with them.

14.14.1   CML Explorer

CML stands for Coupled Map Lattice, which is a model of complex systems. All you need to know as a GIMP user is that it creates interesting textures based on mathematical formulas. This filter is too complex to explain in detail, so here are some hints about the use of this filter:

- Make small changes to the Power factor and k parameter slider bars.

- Options in the Composition section create the most distinct patterns.

- Use the "Plot Graph" button often to see the result of your changes.

- The Advanced menu creates some interesting patterns. Try adjusting the mutation rates.

14.14.2 Checkerboard

This filter is a lot easier to use than CML Explorer. It simply creates checkerboard patterns on an image. The colors used are taken from the foreground and background colors set in the Toolbox. The Checkerboard filter is controlled by the Check Size slider bar. This bar determines the dimensions of the checks. If you choose the Psychobilly option, it creates a checkerboard that looks like it is bulging outwards (see Figures 14.83 and 14.84). For the Psychobilly option, the only check that is the size specified by the slider bar is the center one. All other tiles scale smaller proportionally to their distance from the center check. Checks to the left or right shrink in width; checks above or below the center shrink in height.

Figure 14.83 *A regular checkerboard with a check size of 20.*

Figure 14.84 *A psychobilly checkerboard with a check size of 20.*

14.14.3 Diffraction Patterns

The Diffraction Patterns filter renders unique patterns from a variety of settings. It is useful for creating strange symmetric patterns for backgrounds or layers.

This filter takes a long time to render images, so the preview is not updated automatically. You must click on the Preview button each time you make a change. The following options are available with this filter:

- Frequencies menu (see Figure 14.85)
  a. This menu controls the frequency for each channel.
  b. Low frequencies create large "waves" with gradual color changes.
  c. Higher frequencies create very small "waves" with sharp color changes.
  d. The frequency affects the amount of color created by each channel. When the frequencies are all similar, the image is made up of equal parts of all colors. When one channel is different from the other two, it emphasizes or subdues that color in the image.

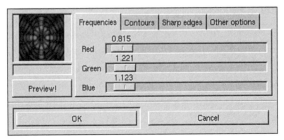

Figure 14.85   *The Frequencies notebook page for the Diffraction Patterns filter.*

- Contours menu (see Figure 14.86)
  a. For each channel, it controls the roundness and brightness.
  b. Large values make images look very random and noisy, so values of approximately 1.0 are optimal.
- Sharp Edges menu (see Figure 14.87)
  a. This menu provides greater control of the brightness of each channel, but has very little effect on the shape of the pattern.
- Other Options menu (see Figure 14.88)
  a. **Brightness.** This option controls the levels for the entire image. This means that black areas become lighter, and the image looks washed out.
  b. **Scattering.** For more vivid colors, lower the brightness and increase the amount of scattering with the Scattering slider bar.
  c. **Polarization.** This option controls the amount of interference created between waves. This slider bar depends on the settings in the other menus, so it is hard to describe its effects in every situation. Experiment with this value, as it will usually create the most engaging patterns.

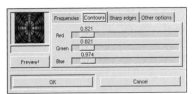

Figure 14.86   *The Contours menu for the Diffraction Patterns filter.*

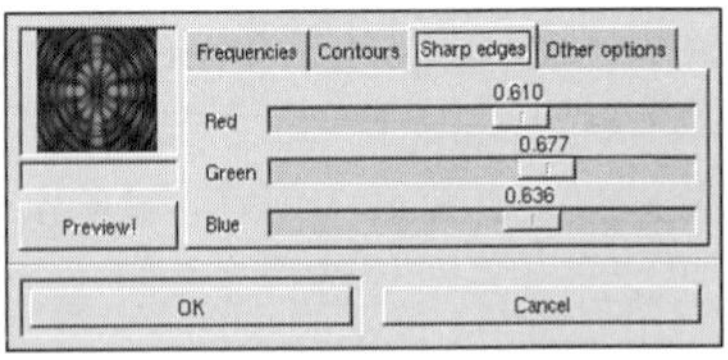

Figure 14.87   *The Sharp Edges menu for the Diffraction Patterns filter.*

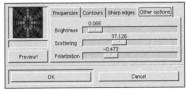

Figure 14.88   *The Other Options menu for the Diffraction Patterns filter.*

14.14.4 Flame

The Flame filter creates random shapes based on a colormap and different mathematical functions. This colormap can be a gradient from the Gradient Editor, one of several included colormaps, or based on the colors in an image. The Smooth palette works well for creating colormaps. The options for this filter can be somewhat complicated—the following options are available (see Figure 14.89):

- **Rendering.** This section controls the look of the image, regardless of the shape.

    a. **Brightness.** This controls the brightness of the shape.

    b. **Contrast.** This adjusts the contrast in the image. This may not be apparent in the preview, but it is noticeable in the final output.

    c. **Gamma.** This slider bar controls the gamma correction for the image. It determines how the gradient is actually mapped to the flame. It is best to keep the default value of 2.00.

    d. **Sample Density.** This is the most important option in the Rendering menu. It controls the level of detail in the final image. The preview windows always display the low-quality versions of the image; changing the quality will not affect the previews.

    e. **Spatial Oversample.** This changes the detail level.

    f. **Spatial Filter Radius.** This option also controls the detail level. The default values are recommended for this filter. Raising these values will increase detail level and quality, but they increase the rendering time as well.

    g. **Colormap.** This changes the colormap that is to be used in the image. There are several choices for colormaps:

        - **Custom gradient.** This is selected in the Gradient Editor (see page 179).

        - **Included colormaps.**

        - **Existing image.** The Smooth Palette filter (see page 203) is perfectly suited for this.

- **Camera.** This section defines the look of the shape to be rendered.

    a. **Zoom.**

    b. **X and Y offsets.**

- **Shape Edit.** (See Figure 14.90.) This option allows you to control the look of the flame. It is accessed by clicking on the Shape Edit button. There are nine preview windows showing images. The center image is the currently selected one. They can be randomized by clicking on the center image, or by clicking on the Randomize button. You can replace the center image with any one of the eight surrounding images by clicking. The Speed slider bar along the bottom varies the speed of rendering the images. Higher values give more detail in the shapes. The variation of the shapes can be controlled as well:

a. **Same.** Uses the default shapes.

b. **Randomize.** Uses random shapes.

c. **Linear.** Gives you shapes with bunches of straight lines.

d. **Sinusoidal.** Uses the trigonometric function to generate shapes.

e. **Spherical.** Gives very round shapes.

f. **Swirl.** Generates swirling shapes.

g. **Horseshoe.** Creates swirling shapes as well, but they often bend back on themselves.

h. **Polar.** Uses polar coordinates to generate shapes. They are very irregular shapes.

i. **Bent.** Similar to Linear, but the lines will often have "kinks" in them, or seem to slowly curve.

■ **Load.** This button loads previously created shapes.

■ **Store.** This option allows you to store these shapes for later use.

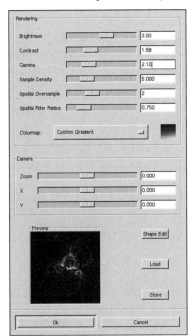

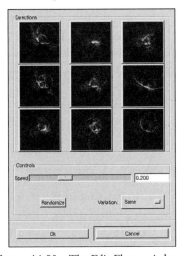

Figure 14.90   *The Edit Flame window for the Flame filter.*

Figure 14.89   *The Options window for the Flame filter.*

14.14.5   Gfig

The Gfig filter is used to draw various shapes with different brushes, tools, and colors. It is a very versatile program, and could easily stand alone as a simple drawing program. This is the filter to use when you need to draw objects with shapes like lines, circles, Bezier curves, and so on. Note that this filter does not work with selections—this is because Gfig uses selections to draw on the image. The following options are available with this filter:

- **Operations menu.** This menu has a toolbar with all of the tools used for drawing (See Figure 14.91).

    a. **Line.** This tool draws simple straight lines. Click and drag with the mouse to draw them. To draw connected lines, hold down the Shift key while clicking.

    b. **Circle.** This tool draws simple circles. Click where the center of the circle is to be placed, and drag to set the radius.

    c. **Ellipse.** This tool works similarly to Circle.

    d. **Curve.** This tool draws partial circles, not Bezier curves. The first mouse click sets the first point. The next mouse click determines the highest point of the curve. The last mouse click sets the last point, and the curve is drawn.

    e. **Poly.** This tool creates regular polygons. The number of sides is chosen by double-clicking on the tool's icon. The slider bar allows you to roughly choose a value, but it is best to enter values manually here. Polygons are created like circles: Click for the center, and drag to define the radius.

    f. **Star.** This tool creates stars. The number of points is controlled by double-clicking on the Star tool's icon. The size of the spikes are controlled by dragging the square between the center and the points.

    g. **Spiral.** This tool creates round spirals. The number of turns and the direction of the spiral is determined in the Spiral tool's options.

    h. **Bezier.** This tool creates primitive Bezier curves. Curves are created by clicking on control points. When you are finished, hold down the Shift key and click for the last control point. There are two options for this tool. The first is whether to create a closed or open curve. The second is to show the square frame when creating Bezier curves. This option is not always useful because it can clutter up the screen with useless lines.

    i. With all tools, right-click and use the **Snap to Grid** option to constrain the control points to points on the grid.

    j. **Move.** Use this tool to move objects around by clicking on their control points. If you hold down this Shift key while dragging, any objects connected to the one being moved will be moved as well.

k. **Move Point.** This tool lets you move specific control points in images. This gives you very precise control of the shapes of objects, especially the more complex ones, such as stars. It also allows you to break a complex object up into individual lines: Hold down the Shift key while clicking the object.

l. **Copy.** This tool enables you to copy an object by clicking and dragging. There is no Paste tool in this filter.

m. **Delete.** You can delete an object by clicking on any control point.

n. **< and >.** If your object is cluttered, specific objects can be viewed by using these buttons.

o. **==.** You can view any object again by clicking on the **==** button.

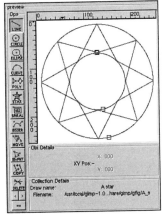

Figure 14.91   *The Operations toolbox, also showing the preview window.*

- **Grid menu.** (See Figure 14.92.)

  a. **Display Grid (1).** For creating precise drawings, a grid can be superimposed on the image.

  b. **Snap to Grid (2).** You can also choose to snap to the grid points.

  c. **Grid Spacing (3).** The size of the grid is controlled by a slider bar. The grid size can range from 10 pixel squares to 50 pixels.

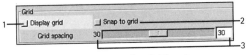

Figure 14.92   *The Grid options.*

- **Object menu.** (See Figure 14.93.) This section allows you to save and load drawings. Several example drawings are included here. You can view a small preview of the drawing (1) and a listing of available Gfig files (2). You can choose to merge one of these drawings into your current one by clicking on it to select it, then clicking the Merge button (3). If you just want to edit the drawing, click on the Edit button (4). There are some other file management tools here:

a. **Rescan (5).** This button allows you to refresh the directories in which the Gfig files are kept. It also allows you to add new directories in which to search for Gfig files.

b. **Load (6).** This button loads specific Gfig object files from an arbitrary directory.

c. **New (7).** This button creates a new Gfig object file.

d. **Delete (8).** This button removes the selected file from the Gfig directories.

Figure 14.93 *The Object Manager.*

■ **Paint menu.** (See Figure 14.94.) This menu determines what to use when painting on the image.

a. **Using (1).**

■ **Brush.** This may not be the best term, because this choice allows you to use the Brush, Airbrush, Pencil, or Pattern tool.

■ **Selection.** This creates an active selection on your image.

■ **Selection + Fill.** This means that an active selection is created, and filled.

b. **Draw On (2).**

■ **Original.** This is the original image.

■ **New.** This makes a layer (for the entire object).

■ **Multiple.** This creates a new layer for each object.

c. **With BG Of (3).** The background appearance.

■ **Transparent.**

■ **Current background color.**

■ **White.**

■ **Copy.** Copy takes the previous layer, copies it, and draws the new object on top.

■ **Selection.** The option to create new/multiple layers is not available using Selection.

■ **Background Types.** This option is not available unless you are creating new/multiple layers.

d. **Reverse Line (4).** If this option is selected, the lines are drawn in reverse.

e. **Scale to Image (5).** Normally, the scale is a 1:1 ratio, but it can be adjusted via this slider bar.

f. **Approx. Circles/Ellipses (6).** This option allows the Fadeout option to work with circles and ellipses.

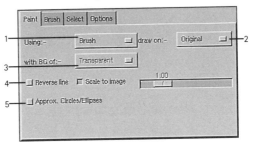

Figure 14.94 *The Paint menu.*

■ **Brush menu.** (See Figure 14.95.)

a. The currently selected brush shape is displayed in this menu.

b. The tool type can be selected here (1):

■ **Brush.** With the brush, you can choose to use the Fadeout option.

■ **Airbrush.** When using the Airbrush tool, you can choose the pressure to use via a slider bar.

■ **Pencil.**

■ **Pattern.**

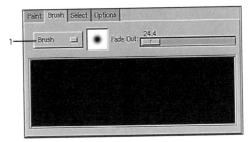

Figure 14.95 *The Brush menu.*

■ **Select menu**[3]. (See Figure 14.96.)

a. **Selection Type (1).** (See page 24 for more information on selections.)

■ **Add**

■ **Subtract**

- Replace
- Intersect

b. **Antialiasing (2).** This should always be turned on.

c. **Feather (3).** This option turns on feathering for the selection. The Feather Radius slider bar controls the amount of feathering in the selection (see page xxx).

d. **Fill Type (4).** This determines what kind of paint is used to fill the selection.

- Pattern
- Foreground color
- Background color

e. **Fill Opacity (5).** This is controlled by a slider bar.

f. **Fill After (6).** This option determines when the fill takes place. This option only makes sense if you are using opacity and/or patterns that will overlap.

- Each Selection
- All Selections

g. **Arc As (7).** This option determines how arcs are created.

- **Segment.** This creates a straight line between the beginning and ending control points.

- **Sector.** This creates the selection by drawing a line from the beginning control point to the center of the "circle" and then to the end control point. This creates a selection that is shaped like a slice of pie.

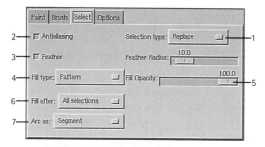

Figure 14.96 *The Select menu.*

---

³ *When working with selections, ensure that you do not use any lines; otherwise, the entire image will end up selected, and the filter will not work. Also, Bezier curves will automatically be closed when working with selections.*

- **Options menu.** (See Figure 14.97.)

    a. **Show Image (1).** This allows you to view the image behind the object.

    b. **Reload Image (2).** This button reloads the image after changes have been made.

    c. **Hide Cntr Pnts (3).** This toggle hides controls points on objects. It can be useful when you have a complicated image that is cluttering up the window.

    d. **Grid Type (4).** Changes the type of grid used. The following grid types are available:

        - **Rectangular**

        - **Polar**

        - **Isometric**

    e. **Grid Color (5).** This changes the color of lines used to draw the grid.

    f. **Max Undo (6).** This slider bar changes the levels of undo available to this filter. This ranges from 1 to 10.

    g. **Show Tool Tips (7).** This option turns tool tips on and off. They are helpful, so it recommended that this option remain on.

    h. **Show Pos (8).** This option displays the coordinates of the cursor below the preview window.

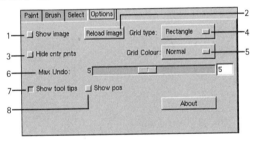

Figure 14.97   *The Options menu.*

After you have created an object, and you are ready to transfer it to your image, click on the Paint button. This will "paint" with the settings (that is, create selections and new layers if needed). If you are done with your "painting" and have saved any changed objects, click on the Done button. If you do not want to save your changes to the object, click the Cancel button. The Save button saves the current changed object. If you want to start over, click the Clear button. Note that this does not clear your image—only the object.

14.14.6 Grid

The Grid filter creates a grid system on an image. It draws lines that are one pixel wide, dividing the image up into rectangles. This filter uses the following options:

- **Size (X/Y).** This determines the width and height of the rectangles.
- **Offset (X/Y).** This determines the offset of the first square downward and to the right. Negative values are allowed.

14.14.7 IFSCompose

This filter creates an Iterated Function System fractal (see Figure 14.98). It can create shapes similar to ones found in nature. It is especially useful for creating leaves and spirals. It is very versatile, and has created some of the more interesting GIMP art found on the Internet. This filter's menu is split up into several areas:

- The design area exhibits a wireframe display of the fractals (1). By default, they are triangular, and numbered 0 to 2.
- Fractals can be added or deleted by using the buttons at the bottom. The center of the fractals is represented by a small cross-hair.
- Fractals are selected by clicking on them. If you wish to select multiple fractals, hold the Shift key while clicking.
- You can modify these fractals by clicking and dragging with the mouse. Use small mouse movements; otherwise, you can ruin your image. The operation is selected by clicking on the buttons, or by right-clicking in the design area.

The following operations can be performed on the fractals:

- **Move (2).** Hotkey [M]
- **Rotate/Scale (3).** Hotkey [R]
- **Stretch (4).** Hotkey [S]
- **Select All.** Accessed by right-clicking.
- **Recompute Center.** Accessed by right-clicking. Hotkey [Ctrl+A]
- **Undo/Redo.** Accessed by right-clicking. Hotkey [Alt+R]

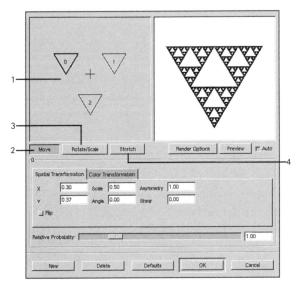

Figure 14.98   *The Wireframe window showing three fractals.*

The Spatial Transformation page displays the information about the currently selected fractal. The values can be edited. The following parameters are available for each fractal (shown in Figure 14.99):

- **X.** The X coordinate.
- **Y.** The Y coordinate.
- **Scale.** Increases or decreases the size of the fractal. The larger the fractal, the greater impact it has on the image.
- **Angle.** Determines the direction in which the fractal is pointing.
- **Asymmetry.** Shrinks or widens the base of the fractal.
- **Shear.** Moves the tip of the fractal from side to side.
- **Flip.** Flips the fractal around its center.
- **Relative Probability.** Controls the amount of impact a specific fractal has on the image.

Figure 14.99   *The Spatial Transformation page.*

In the Color Transformation page (see Figure 14.100), the color of the currently selected fractal can be adjusted. By default, the fractal's color is set to the current foreground color, but it can be changed. There are two ways of achieving this:

- **Simple (1).** This method automatically calculates the color shift for you. The original color is displayed in the first box. The new color is displayed in the second box. Click on the second box to change its color. By changing the Hue and Value, you change the way the color shift is calculated.

- **Full (2).** This method manually adjusts different color ranges. Each box affects a different color range. The colors are shifted here by changing the colors in the boxes. For example, if you have a fractal that is mainly red, and change the red box to yellow, the fractal will become mainly yellow. The following boxes are available:

  a. **Red**

  b. **Green**

  c. **Blue**

  d. **Black**

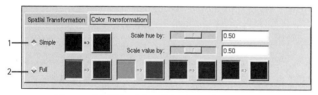

Figure 14.100   *The Color Transformation page.*

The second part of this filter is the preview area. This controls the preview of the image, and also the rendering options. Automatic previewing can be turned on and off here.

The following rendering options are available by clicking on the Render Options button:

- **Max Memory.** Determines the maximum amount of memory used by this filter. Increasing this value will make it render more quickly. Enter values in multiples of 4096.

- **Iterations.** Determines how many times the fractal repeats itself.

- **Subdivide.** Controls the level of detail in the image.

- **Spot Radius.** Determines the thickness of the brush-strokes used to paint the image. A larger spot radius results in a longer rendering time.

If you have changed the settings in this filter beyond recognition, use the Defaults button to reset the filter. Once you have an image to your liking, click OK. If you want to cancel these operations, click on the Cancel button.

14.14.8   Maze

This filter creates a random maze on an image. It uses the foreground color for the walls and the background color for the passages. There are two sections in this filter:

- **Options menu.** The following options are available:

    a. **Tileable.** If this toggle is turned on, it creates a tileable maze.

    b. **Width (Pixels).** This option determines the width of the walls and passages of the maze.

    c. **Pieces.** Pieces determines the number of vertical pieces in the maze.

    d. **Height (Pixels).** This option determines the height of the walls and passages in the maze.

    e. **Pieces.** Here, Pieces determines the number of horizontal pieces in the maze.

- **Advanced Menu.** The following options are available:

    a. **Multiple.** This should be left at 57 in order to create proper mazes.

    b. **Offset.** This option should also be left at its default value. The author of the plug-in borrowed the code to generate the maze, and he doesn't know what it does.

    c. **Seed.** This option determines the randomness of the maze. Using the current time is good for generating a random one. To be able to repeat the creation of a maze, enter a value in this section and turn off the Time option.

    d. **Algorithm.** There are two options in this menu:

        - **Depth's First.** This algorithm creates a maze by computing one branch at a time.

        - **Prim's Algorithm.** This algorithm creates a maze by computing a whole tree with multiple branches at once.

14.14.9   Plasma

The Plasma filter creates a colorful, random pattern that simulates a plasma cloud. The following options are available for this filter:

- **Seed.** This option determines the randomness of the plasma cloud. Using the current time is a good value. To be able to repeat the creation of a plasma cloud, enter a value in this section and turn off the Time option.

- **Turbulence.** This slider determines the turbulence, or randomness, of the cloud.

14.14.10 Qbist

This filter generates very interesting random patterns. The filter generates nine sample images. The center image is the one that is actually created. To select an image that is not in the center, simply click on it. This will move it to the center, and generate new random patterns based on the center image. Clicking on the center image will generate the nine new images. Images can be saved and loaded for later use. When there is a satisfactory image in the center, click on the OK button.

14.14.11 Sinus

The Sinus filter generates random textures based on sinusoidal functions. There are three menus for this filter:

- **Settings menu.** (See Figure 14.101.)

  a. **X scale (1).** This slider scales the function to cycle more often in the X axis.

  b. **Y scale (2).** This slider scales the function to cycle more often in the Y axis.

  c. **Complexity (3).** This option makes the image more complicated by increasing the number of waves in the image.

  d. **Random Seed (4).** This option provides a random number used to generate the texture. By default the number is 42, an obvious choice.

  e. **Force Tiling (5).** This option makes the image tileable, which will distort the image.

  f. **Ideal (6).** When force tiling is turned on, this algorithm creates a perfectly symmetrical image.

  g. **Distorted (7).** This algorithm slightly distorts the image, making it seem much more random.

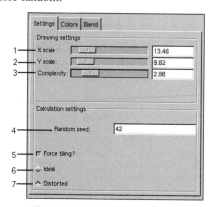

Figure 14.101 *The Settings menu.*

- **Colors Menu.** (See Figure 14.102.)

    a. **Black & White (1).**

    b. **Foreground & Background (2).**

    c. **Choose Here (3).** The two colors can be chosen using the GIMP's color selector.

    d. **Alpha Channels (4).** The Alpha value for each color can be controlled here via slider bars.

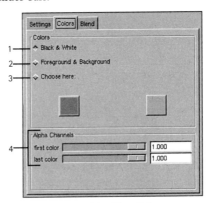

Figure 14.102   *The Colors menu.*

- **Blend menu.** (See Figure 14.103.)

    a. **The Gradient.** This option allows you to select the gradient with which to color the texture. The following options are available:

       - **Linear.** This uses a basic linear gradient, which can create some jagged edges, so it is not always recommended.

       - **Bilinear.** This uses a bilinear gradient for blending the colors. It creates a much smoother transition between colors.

       - **Sinusoidal.** This option uses a sinusoidal texture for blending colors. It creates a sharper transition between colors, but it is still smooth.

    b. **Exponent.** This slider bar controls the emphasis of one color over another.

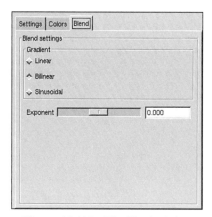

Figure 14.103   *The Blend window.*

14.14.12   Solid Noise

This filter generates solid noise, grayscale textures on an image. These can be tileable, and are excellent for random bumpmaps.

The following options are available with this filter:

- **Seed.** This provides a random number for generating the image. A number can be entered here, or the current time can be used.

- **Detail.** Determines the detail level of the noise. Larger numbers create more detail in the image, but the image then takes longer to render.

- **Turbulent.** This gives the image greater variation between the light and dark areas.

- **Tileable.** This toggle makes the image tileable, perfect for Web page backgrounds or patterns.

- **X Size.** This scales the image in the X direction.

- **Y Size.** This scales the image in the Y direction.

15
Script-Fu

Script-Fu is the GIMP's own scripting language, equivalent to macros in the Windows world. Despite their similarities, Script-Fu is much more powerful than macros because it allows you to change variables and turn different effects on and off. The scripts included here will give you a good idea of what can be done with the GIMP. If you need to perform the same or similar tasks with many photos, read about writing your own Script-Fu on page 83. This chapter assumes you are familiar with all of the filters found in Chapter 14. If you are not familiar with the filters, you will still be able to use these scripts, but you may not understand how they work.

If a script is not running properly, make sure you are using the correct settings. A common error is to try using a script with a font that is not installed on your system.

All of the scripts in Table 15.1 are found in the <Image>/Script-Fu menu unless otherwise noted.

Table 15.1 Scripts by Name (y = Allowed, x = Not Allowed, and r = Required)

Script	Page	RGB	Grayscale	Indexed	Layers	Alpha
Add Bevel	259	y	y	x	y	y
Add Border	264	r	x	x	y	y
ASCII 2 Image Layer	265	y	y	y	y	y
Blend	266	y	y	x	y	y
Carve-It	268	x	r	x	x	x
Chrome-It	268	x	r	x	x	x
Circuit	259	y	y	x	y	y
Clothify	269	y	y	x	y	y
Coffee Stain	259	r	x	x	y	y

continues

Table 15.1   Continued

Script	Page	RGB	Grayscale	Indexed	Layers	Alpha
Color Cycling	266	r	x	x	y	y
Distress Selection	271	r	x	x	y	y
Draw HSV Graph	265	r	x	x	y	y
Drop Shadow	272	y	y	x	y	y
Erase Every Other Row	269	y	y	y	y	y
Fade Outline	271	y	y	x	y	y
Fuzzy Border	260	y	y	x	y	y
Lava	261	y	y	x	y	y
Line Nova	274	y	y	y	y	y
Make Grid System	273	y	y	y	y	y
Old Photo	262	y	y	x	y	y
Perspective	273	y	y	x	y	y
Predator	262	r	x	x	y	y
Rippling	267	y	y	x	y	y
Round	272	y	y	y	y	y
Round Corners	263	y	y	x	x	x
Show Image Structure	265	y	y	x	y	y
Slide	263	y	y	x	x	x
Spinning Globe	267	y	y	x	y	y
To Brush	271	y	y	x	y	y
To Image	272	y	y	x	y	y
Unsharp Mask	270	y	y	x	y	y
Waves	268	y	y	x	y	y
Weave	270	y	y	x	y	y
Xach Effect	263	y	y	x	y	y

15.1   Decor

This section contains scripts that add decoration to your image. They can be useful for improving computer-generated images.

15.1.1 Add Bevel

This script uses a bumpmap to create a beveling effect on a layer. It is best used on images that contain alpha. If it is used on a layer with no alpha, it will bevel the edges of the layer, which is probably not the desired effect. The following options are available with this script:

- **Thickness.** This option determines the size of the bevel in pixels, ranging from 0 to 30.

- **Work On Copy.** When you turn on this option, you create a new image rather than working on the original image.

- **Keep Bump Layer.** This keeps the layer used for the bumpmap instead of deleting it. This option is useful for seeing the effect of the Add Bevel script.

▸**See Also** "Bumpmap" (page 228)

15.1.2 Circuit

This script creates a layer that looks like a circuit board. It is useful for creating a random texture. Currently, the circuit will always be black and white. The Circuit script uses the following options:

- **Oilify Mask Size.** Determines the amount of oil painting that occurs. Any reasonable value can be entered here.

- **Circuit Seed.** A seed number used to generate the circuit board. Note that this is random: Using the same seed number will not give you the same image. Any value can be entered here.

- **No Background.** Only available if you are using a separate layer. Does not fill in black background; it remains transparent.

- **Keep Selection.** When this is turned on, the selection is not deleted after the script is finished running.

- **Separate Layer.** Creates a separate layer rather than drawing on the active layer.

▸**See Also** "Oilify" (page 192) and "Maze" (page 252)

15.1.3 Coffee Stain

This is one of the more interesting scripts. It simulates coffee stains on an image (see Figure 15.1). It works particularly well on scanned images. The script uses the following options:

- **Stains.** The number of stains that appear on the image.

- **Darken Only.** This makes the stains look more realistic, but it works better on lighter images.

Figure 15.1 *A coffee-stained image.*

▶**See Also** "Distress Selection" (page 271)

15.1.4 Fuzzy Border

This script takes a layer or selection and makes its border "fuzzy." The edges of the border are slightly random, and the degree of their fuzziness can be controlled. This script has the following options:

- **Color.** Determines the color outside the border.

- **Border Size.** Determines the average width of the border in pixels. This is an arbitrary value, but it should not exceed half the total size of the selection or layer.

- **Blur Border.** When turned on, this option blurs the border to make it more fuzzy.

- **Granularity.** Determines the roughness of the border. Lower numbers result in rougher borders.

- **Add Shadow.** This option adds a drop shadow to the border.

- **Shadow-Weight.** This is only available when Shadow-Weight is turned on. It determines the opacity of the shadow in percentage.

- **Work On Copy.** When turned on, the script will create a new image, instead of working on the original.

- **Flatten Layers.** This toggle will flatten the image after it has finished creating the border.

Figure 15.2   *An example fuzzy border.*

▶**See Also** "Drop Shadow" (page 272) and "Spread" (page 237)

15.1.5   Lava

This script creates a layer of "lava." It creates a random image, and maps a gradient to it. With the German_flag_smooth gradient, this simulates lava. The Lava script uses the following options:

- **Seed.** This is used for a random seed number for the Solid Noise filter.
- **Size.** Determines the tile size used in the Cubism filter.
- **Roughness.** Determines the roughness used for the Oilify filter.
- **Gradient.** Allows you to type in the name of the gradient to use. It is often easier to use the current gradient, described later in this list.
- **Keep Selection.** When this is turned on, the selection is not deleted after the script is finished running.
- **Separate Layer.** Creates a separate layer rather than drawing on the active layer.
- **Use Current Gradient.** This option uses the current gradient, and overrides the name of the gradient entered in this menu.

Figure 15.3   *A logo with a Lava background.*

▶**See Also** "Solid Noise" (page 255), "Cubism" (page 189), "Oilify" (page 192), "Edge Detect" (page 219), and "Gradient Map" (page 201)

15.1.6   Old Photo

This script turns an image into an old photo, complete with stains and defects. For best results, use on scanned photos. The Old Photo script uses the following options:

- **Defocus.** Blurs the image slightly to simulate being out of focus.
- **Sepia.** Adds a sepia tone to the image.
- **Border.** Adds a fuzzy border to the image, making the image look as if it is fading at the edges.
- **Mottle.** Introduces random defects into the image.
- **Work on Copy.** When turned on, the script will create a new image, instead of working on the original.

▶**See Also** "Fuzzy Border" (page 260) and "Gaussian Blur" (page 194)

15.1.7   Predator

This script changes a layer's colors so that they form what looks like a thermal image, similar to what the Predator sees in the movie of the same name. The following options are available for the Predator script:

- **Edge Detect.** Determines the amount of edge detection. This ranges from 0 to 24.
- **Pixelize.** This toggle turns pixelization on. This ranges from 1 to 16.
- **Pixel Amount.** Determines the pixel width. This option is not used unless Pixelize is turned on.
- **Keep Selection.** When this is turned on, the selection is not deleted after the script has finished running.
- **Separate Layer.** Creates a separate layer rather than drawing on the active layer.

Figure 15.4   *A Porsche seen from the Predator's eyes.*

▶**See Also** "Pixelize" (page 196), "Max RGB" (page 201), and "Edge" (page 219)

15.1.8 Round Corners

This script rounds the corners of an image by removing circular selections. It can also add a drop shadow effect to the image. The following options are available with this script:

- **Radius of Edges.** Determines the radius (in pixels) of the rounded corners. This can be any number, although it should be less than half the size of the layer.

- **Add Drop Shadow.** Turns on the Drop Shadow script.

- **Shadow X.** Offset of the shadow in the x direction. This can be any reasonable value.

- **Shadow Y.** Offset of the shadow in the y direction. This also can be any reasonable value.

- **Blur Radius.** The amount of blurring that occurs on the shadow. This can be a value greater than 1.

- **Add Background.** Adds a background layer to the image.

- **Work on Copy.** When turned on, the script creates a new image, instead of working on the original.

▸**See Also** "Drop Shadow" (page 272)

15.1.9 Slide

This script turns your image into a slide. It uses the Film filter to achieve this effect. The image is first cropped into an aspect ratio of 1:1.5. It is then turned into a slide. The Slide script uses the following options:

- **Text.** Determines the title of the slide.

- **Number.** Determines the number of the slide.

- **Font.** Determines the font used to write on the slide.

- **Font Color.**

- **Work on Copy.** When turned on, the script creates a new image rather than working on the original.

▸**See Also** "Film" (page 206)

15.1.10 Xach Effect

This script creates a very slight 3D effect on a selection. It creates a slight drop shadow on the image, and often is better than the Drop Shadow script itself when only a subtle shadow is needed. This script works best with an active selection, but it will run without one. To achieve a smoother change, try using the Add Bevel script after this script is run. The following options are available for this script:

- **Highlight X Offset.** Determines the x direction shift in the highlight layer. This ranges from 100 to −100.

- **Highlight Y Offset.** Determines the y direction shift in the highlight layer. This ranges from 100 to −100.

- **Highlight Color.** Determines what color to use as the highlight layer background.

- **Opacity.** Determines the color to use for the opacity in the highlight layer. This ranges from 1 to 255.

- **Drop Shadow Color.** Determines the color to use for the shadow.

- **Drop Shadow Opacity.** Determines the opacity of the drop shadow.

- **Drop Shadow Blur Radius.** Determines the amount of blurring of the shadow.

- **Drop Shadow X Offset.** Determines the x direction shift of the shadow.

- **Drop Shadow Y Offset.** Determines the y direction shift of the shadow.

- **Keep Selection.** When this is turned on, the selection is not deleted after the script is finished running.

▶**See Also** "Offset" (page 60) and "Drop Shadow" (page 272)

15.2 Modify

Currently, there is only one script found in the Modify section: Add Border.

15.2.1 Add Border

The Add Border script creates a 3D-looking border around a layer. This script supports the following options:

- **Border X Size.** Determines the border size on the sides.

- **Border Y Size.** Determines the thickness of the border on the top and bottom.

- **Border Color.** Determines the color of the border.

- **Delta Value on Color.** Determines the amount of color change on the border. A value of 0 means no color change. A value of 255 makes the border white at the top, black at the bottom, lighter on the left, and darker on the right. Lower values are best for this script.

15.3 Utils

The scripts in this section of scripts do not actually create effects to be used on an image. They are more useful in describing your image.

15.3.1 ASCII 2 Image Layer

This script does not fit very well into this section. It creates a text layer from the input of an ASCII 2 file. It does allow you to do some simple batch text processing in the GIMP. The input file is read, and each line is created as a layer. This script is not smart enough to realize when it is drawing outside of the image, so some experimentation may be necessary. The following options are available with this script:

- **File Name.** The name of the input file.
- **Font.** The name of the font to be used.
- **Font Size.** The size of the text (in pixels).
- **Text Color.** The color of the text created.
- **Flatten Image.** If this option is selected, it flattens the image rather than leaving each line as a separate layer.

15.3.2 Draw HSV Graph

This script draws a graph of the image in HSV space. The red line represents Hue, the green line represents Saturation, and the blue line represents Value. This script uses the following options:

- **Graph Scale.** Determines the amount of scaling to be done.
- **BG Opacity.** Determines the opacity (in percent) of the background for the new image.
- **Use Selection Bounds Instead of Belows.** This toggle uses only the active selection instead of the dimensions described below. If there is no active selection, this toggle selects the entire image.
- **From Top-Left to Bottom-Right.** Analyzes the graph diagonally rather than straight across.
- **Start X.** Determines the starting x coordinate.
- **Start Y.** Determines the starting y coordinate.
- **End X.** Determines the ending x coordinate.
- **End Y.** Determines the ending y coordinate.

15.3.3 Show Image Structure

This script is quite interesting. It breaks a layered image up into all of its parts and displays them. It simulates viewing them at an angle, whereas normally they are viewed directly from above. This script uses the Shear tool, so it may take a while for your computer to complete the effect. The following options are available:

- **Make New Image.** Either create a new image or use the existing one.
- **Space Between Layers.** Determines the space between layers (in pixels).

- **Shear Length.** Changes the angle which the layers are viewed. This value must be greater than 0.

- **Outer Border.** Determines the space around the sheared layers.

- **Apply Layer Mask.** Determines how layer masks are treated (either applied or discarded).

- **Layer Name.** Toggles whether to insert layer names.

- **Padding for Transparent Regions.** Toggles whether to pad areas with transparency.

- **Pad Color.** The color to use as padding.

- **Pad Opacity.** The opacity (in percent) of the padding.

- **Background Color.** The color of the background in the new image.

15.4 Animators

These scripts create excellent animations. They work very well for creating animated GIFs on Web pages. Remember to use the Animation Optimize filter on the new images. Note that using the default values will not create an animation.

15.4.1 Blend

This script takes a minimum of two layers (plus a background layer) and blends them together using transparency and blurring. It uses the following options:

- **Intermediate Frames.** Determines the number of frames creating between the originals.

- **Max Blur Radius.** Determines the maximum amount of blurring that occurs.

- **Looped.** Loops the animation.

15.4.2 Color Cycling

This script cycles the colors in an image. Color Cycling is based on the AlienMap filter (see page 197). It is best to use the AlienMap filter first to find optimal values for the starting and ending points, and then run the script. The Color Cycling script uses the following options:

- **Number of Frames.** Determines the number of frames in the animation. The greater number of frames, the smoother the color transition.

- **Start Intensity Factor.** (Red, Green, and Blue channels.) The starting intensity value for each channel. This can range from 0 to 128.

- **End Intensity Factor.** (Red, Green, and Blue channels.) The ending intensity value for each channel. This can range from 0 to 128.

- **Color Mode.** (Red, Green, and Blue channels.) The type of function to use for mapping:

  a. Sine

  b. Cosine

  c. None

- **Inversion Before Transformation.** (Red, Green, and Blue channels.) A toggle that inverts the channel before transformation occurs.

- **Start: Phase Displacement.** (Red, Green, and Blue channels.) Determines the displacement of the channels in the starting frame. Measured in radians.

- **End: Phase Displacement.** (Red, Green, and Blue channels.) Determines the displacement of the channels in the ending frame. Measured in radians.

- **Start: Frequency.** (Red, Green and Blue channels.) Determines the frequency of the channels in the starting frame.

- **End: Frequency.** (Red, Green and Blue channels.) Determines the frequency of the channels in the ending frame.

- **Inversion Before Transformation.** (Red, Green, and Blue channels.) A toggle that inverts the channel before transformation occurs.

15.4.3 Rippling

This script creates a rippling effect on an image, similar to that of a flag waving in the wind. It works very well, especially when a larger number of frames are used. It is based on the Ripple filter (see page 215). The following options are available with this script:

- **Rippling Strength.** Determines the amount of rippling.
- **Number of Frames.**

15.4.4 Spinning Globe

This script maps an image to a spinning globe, like those found on Web pages. This script works best with a square image. The following options are available:

- **Frames.** The number of frames used to create the animation.
- **Turn from Left to Right.** Determines the direction of spinning.
- **Transparent Background.** Either uses the current background color or creates a transparent background.
- **Index of n Colors.** Converts the image to Indexed with n number of colors. Enter **0** to maintain an RGB image.
- **Work on Copy.** When turned on, the script will create a new image rather than working on the original.

15.4.5 Waves

This script creates an animation with the Waves filter (see page 218).
The following options are available with this script:

- **Amplitude.** Determines the height of the waves.
- **Wavelength.** Determines the distance between peaks of waves.
- **Number of Frames.**
- **Invert Direction.** Causes the waves to travel inward to a point instead of spreading outward.

15.5   Stencil Ops

These scripts use single-layer grayscale images for stencils to draw with.

15.5.1   Carve-It

The Carve-It script is an extension to the Emboss filter (see page 208). It carves a grayscale image into an RGB or Grayscale image. It uses the grayscale image as a layer mask. Note that a single-layer grayscale image is required for carving. If the script still isn't available, make sure you have flattened the image first. This script supports the following options:

- **Image to Carve.** Select the image to be carved here. This image can be either RGB or grayscale. It can have layers and alpha as well.
- **Carve White Areas.** This toggle determines what part carves the image. Either black or white areas carve more deeply. This option simply inverts the grayscale image.

15.5.2   Chrome-It

This script "chromes" an image using an environment map and specific colors for highlights. It operates only on grayscale images. This script is the basis for the SOTA Chrome script. This script creates four layers:

- **Chrome.** This layer has the basic picture of the environment map with grayscale image used as a layer mask.
- **Highlight.** Highlight has the environment map on it with a slightly distorted grayscale image used as a layer mask.
- **Drop Shadow.** The Drop Shadow layer is a black-to-transparent blend.
- **Background.** This layer has the Marble #1 pattern on it.

This script has the following options:

- **Chrome Saturation.** Determines the saturation amount for the Chrome layer. This value ranges between 100 and −100.

- **Chrome Lightness.** The average lightness of the Chrome layer. This value ranges between 100 and −100.
- **Chrome Factor.** Determines how "chromed" the image becomes. The higher the number, the greater detail in the environment map.
- **Environment Map.** The image that is mapped to the grayscale image. By default, this is a JPEG of a cat.
- **Highlight Balance.** The color used for the Highlight layer in the image. This is the color that "reflects" off of the bright parts of the chrome.
- **Chrome Balance.** The base color used for the Chrome layer.
- **Chrome White Areas.** Determines which part of the image is used for the chrome effects. If this is selected, it uses white areas for the chrome effect, and black areas become transparent. When it is not selected, it has the opposite effect.

15.6 Alchemy

These scripts all perform a transformation on the image. The most useful script found here is Unsharp Mask, which is used for improving the quality of scanned photographs. It is similar to PhotoShop's Unsharp Mask filter.

15.6.1 Clothify

This script gives a layer a cloth-like texture by adding noise to the image and bumpmapping it. It is mostly based on the Bumpmap filter. This script has the following options:

- **X Blur.** The amount of blurring in the x direction.
- **Y Blur.** The amount of blurring in the y direction.
- **Azimuth.** The direction of the light source (see the Bumpmap filter, page 228).
- **Elevation.** The height of the light source (see the Bumpmap filter, page 228).
- **Depth.** The amount of bumpmapping (see the Bumpmap filter, page 228).

15.6.2 Erase Every Other Row

This script simply erases every other row or column. It is erased to the background color, or if the image contains an alpha channel, it is erased to transparency. This script supports the following options:

- **Rows/Cols.** Specify which to erase. Must be written in the form `'rows` or `'cols`.
- **Even/Odd.** Specify which to erase. Must be written in the form `'even` or `'odd`.

15.6.3 Unsharp Mask

This script is for sharpening scanned photographs. It creates two layer masks that sharpen the image. It works very well. To get the best results, adjust the transparency of the two layer masks after the script has finished running. This script only has one option: Mask Size. The larger the mask size, the more the script tries to sharpen. The only disadvantage to sharpening too much is that it can emphasize scanner noise or photographic defects. This script often works better than the Sharpen filter (see page 224) when a quick fix is needed.

15.6.4 Weave

The Weave script makes an image look as though it has been created by weaving threads together, as shown in Figure 15.5. The Weave script uses the following options:

- **Ribbon Width.** The average width (in pixels) of the ribbons.
- **Ribbon Spacing.** The average space between ribbons.
- **Shadow Darkness.** The darkness value of the shadow between the ribbons. A larger value make the ribbons seem to move further.
- **Shadow Depth.** The depth of the shadows. A larger value means the ribbons bend more around each other.
- **Thread Length.** The average length of the threads in the ribbons. Different values make the ribbons seem to be made of different material.
- **Thread Density.** Determines how closely packed the ribbons are.
- **Thread Intensity.** Determines the brightness of the ribbons. A lower value makes the ribbons brighter.

Figure 15.5 *An image of a flower after the weave script has been applied.*

15.7 Selection

The scripts in this section deal with selections. They modify or perform operations on selections.

15.7.1 Distress Selection

Distress Selection randomly distorts a selection and is the basis for the Coffee script. This script has the following options:

- **Threshold.** Controls the size change of the selection. 1 will enlarge the selection; 255 will shrink the selection.

- **Spread.** Determines how much the selection spreads out. A higher value will give more random spreading.

- **Granularity.** Determines the roughness of the selection. 1 will make the selection the roughest.

- **Smooth.** Determines the amount of smoothing that occurs. This is done by the Gaussian Blur filter (see page 194).

- **Smooth Horizontally.**

- **Smooth Vertically.**

15.7.2 Fade Outline

This script fades anything outside a selection to transparency. This is useful for creating quick logos and icons. The following options are available with this script:

- **Border Size.** Determines the amount of fading that occurs. The higher the number, the longer it takes to fade.

- **Apply Generated Layermask.** Toggles whether to apply the layer mask or leave it unapplied.

- **Clear Unselected Mask Area.** Clears anything outside the selected area.

15.7.3 To Brush

This script converts a selection into a GIMP brush. It uses the following options:

- **Description.** The name that will appear in the Brush selection dialog.

- **Filename.** The actual filename that will appear in your `~/.gimp` directory.

- **Spacing.** The default spacing of the brush.

15.7.4 To Image

This script creates a new image from a selection. The new image will be a single-layer image of the same type (for example, an RGB image with layers will become a single-layer RGB image). All other layers in the image are ignored. Any alpha will be replaced with the current background color. If the selection is not perfectly rectangular, anything outside the selection will be set to the background color in order to make the image rectangular. If you have multiple selections, To Image will fit all of them into a rectangular image, and set any outside areas to the background color.

15.7.5 Round

This script rounds the corners of a selection. The relative radius of the circle is entered here. The relative radius describes the radius of the corner circles relative to the height and width of the selection.

15.8 Shadow

The scripts found here create shadows of layers. These are extremely useful for logos and icons for Web pages.

15.8.1 Drop Shadow

This script simulates the layer floating above the background with its shadow appearing below. The following options are available with this script:

- **X Offset.** Determines the distance the shadow is shifted in the x direction.
- **Y Offset.** Determines the distance the shadow is shifted in the y direction.
- **Blur Radius.** Determines the amount of blurring that occurs. Having a blur of 0 means that the shadow is not blurred at all. This makes the object appear to have thickness.
- **Color.** Determines the color of the shadow.
- **Opacity.** Determines the opacity of the shadow layer.
- **Allow resizing.** Allows resizing of the image. This option is rarely desirable.

Figure 15.6 *A logo using a white drop shadow behind the text, and black drop shadow behind the base.*

15.8.2 Perspective

This script creates a shadow that simulates light shining from a distance, giving it a 3D look. The following options are available with this script:

- **Angle.** Determines the angle at which the shadow is placed.
- **Relative Horizon Distance.** Determines how far the object is away from the horizon. A larger value here will make the shadow slightly wider because it is closer to the light source.
- **Relative Shadow Length.** Determines how large the shadow is compared to the actual object.
- **Blur Radius.** Determines the amount of blurring that occurs. Lower blur radii are better for this script compared to the Drop Shadow script.
- **Color.** Determines the color of the shadow.
- **Opacity.** Determines the opacity of the shadow layer.
- **Interpolate.** Reduces jagged lines in the shadow.
- **Allow Resizing.** Toggles resizing of the image on and off. This is generally not used.

15.9 Render

These scripts draw onto an image. They can create some interesting effects when used creatively.

15.9.1 Make Grid System

This script renders grid lines onto an image. The outcome of the script is determined in the menu. For both the x and y directions, the grid is described. They must be entered in the form ' (<data>). For example, an entry of ' (1 2) for the x directionof and ' (1 3) for the Y directionof creates the grid shown in Figure 15.7. The rows in the image are 1 unit wide, then 2 units wide. The columns in the image are 1 unit wide, then 3 units wide. Another option to use is g, the Golden Ratio. It is approximately equal to 1.618. You can also use the fraction 1/g, which is approximately equal to 0.618. The color and size of the grid lines depend on the current foreground color, and the currently selected brush.

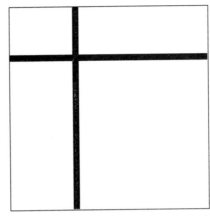

Figure 15.7 *A grid created with the parameters X: '(1 2) and Y: '(1 2).*

15.9.2 Line Nova

This script creates supernova effects by drawing lines on an image. The following options are available with this script:

- **Number of Lines.**
- **Sharpness.** Determines how wide the lines are in degrees.
- **Offset Radius.**
- **Randomness.** Determines the randomness of the length of the lines.

15.10 Xtns

The following scripts are found in the <Toolbox>/Xtns/Script-Fu menu. They are standalone scripts, which means that they do not work on existing images—rather, they create their own. The scripts found here can create excellent logos and icons for Web pages.

15.10.1 Logos

There are many logos included with the GIMP. These are perfect for quickly creating logos for Web pages. Experiment with using different fonts and options here to get in idea of what they can do. These scripts are also good to look at for help in creating your own script. The following logos are available with the GIMP:

- **3D Outline.** Creates a 3D outline of a text string.
- **Alien Glow.** Creates a logo with a strange glow behind it.
- **Basic I.** A basic blend logo with a drop shadow.

- **Basic II.** Another basic blend logo.
- **Blended.** Creates a texture logo with a blend background.
- **Bovination.** A text logo that looks as if it has been made from cowhide.
- **Carved.** Creates a text logo that looks as if it has been carved in marble.
- **Chalk.** Creates a logo that looks as if it has been drawn in chalk.
- **Chip Away.** Creates a logo of raised text where the background has been chipped away.
- **Chrome.** A basic chrome logo.
- **Comic Book.** Creates text that looks like writing from a comic book.
- **Cool Metal.** An excellent logo that looks as if it is being reflected off of shiny metal.
- **Crystal.** A logo that looks as if it has been made from crystal.
- **Frosty.** Creates a sparkling logo.
- **Glossy.** A complicated script that creates excellent glossy text.
- **Glowing Hot.** Creates a text logo that looks as if it is glowing hot.
- **Gradient Bevel.** An interesting blended, beveled logo.
- **Imigre-26.** Creates a text logo that looks as if it has been done roughly by hand.
- **Neon.** Creates a glowing neon text logo.
- **SOTA Chrome.** Another interesting text logo.
- **Starburst.** A logo with a starburst inside it.
- **Starscape.** Creates a logo with a starburst behind it, making it glow.
- **Particle Trace.** Creates a logo that looks like a cutout of a particle tracing.
- **Text Circle.** Creates a circle of text. This is one of the most useful logos here.
- **Textured.** An interesting text logo with a textured background.
- **Web Title Header.** A basic text logo for a Web page.

15.10.2   Patterns

The scripts in this section create tileable patterns for use as Web page backgrounds, or patterns for the GIMP. The following patterns are available:

- **3D Truchet.** Creates an interesting pattern made of curved tubes.
- **Camouflage.** Renders a camouflage pattern.
- **Flatland.** Creates a random pattern, more similar to lava than flatland.
- **Land.** Creates a random pattern that looks like landmasses.
- **Render Map.** Renders an image that looks like a map, with oceans and islands.

- **Swirl-Tile.** Creates a tileable image that looks like swirling sand.
- **Swirly (Tileable).** Creates a simple tileable image of several swirls.
- **Trochoid.** Draws a colorful trochoid pattern, like something drawn by a spirograph.
- **Truchet.** Creates a simpler truchet pattern than that of the 3D version.

15.10.3 Web Page Themes

These scripts create images with a common theme for a Web page.

15.10.3.1 Alien Glow

This theme is the same as the Alien Glow logo. It creates images that are backlit with a glowing color. There are four objects that can be created here:

- **Arrow.** Creates an arrow for a navigation bar. It can go in four directions: 'right, 'left, 'up, and 'down.
- **Hrule.** Creates a glowing horizontal bar, like the hrule in HTML.
- **Bullet.** Creates a glowing bullet.
- **Button.** Creates a button with text.

15.10.3.2 Beveled Pattern

This theme creates beveled objects. Various patterns can be used for the base—by default it is wood. Marble is another good pattern to use. Five different objects can be created with this theme:

- **Arrow.** Creates an arrow for a navigation bar. It can go in four directions: 'right, 'left, 'up, and 'down.
- **Bullet.** Creates a beveled bullet.
- **Button.** Creates a simple beveled button with text.
- **Heading.** Creates a larger text logo for a heading.
- **Hrule.** Creates a beveled horizontal bar, like the hrule in HTML.

15.10.3.3 GIMP.Org

This theme creates the same images used on the GIMP's Web site, http://www.gimp.org. There are a variety of scripts here. If you are serious about creating Web sites with an overall theme, use these scripts as a model to create your own Script-Fu. There are six different objects that can be created here:

- **Big Header.** Creates a large text header.
- **Small Header.** Creates a smaller text header.
- **Tube Button Label.** Creates a button label.

- **Tube Sub-Button Label.** Another smaller button label.
- **Tube Sub-Sub-Button Label.** An even smaller button label.
- **General Tube Header.** A general text logo used as a header.

15.10.4 Utils

These scripts are aimed at creating images that would be useful for creating other images.

There are three scripts in this menu:

- **ASCII 2 Image.** Creates a new image from a text file. See the ASCII 2 Image Layer script (page 265) for more information.
- **Font Map.** Creates an image that demonstrates the fonts available to the GIMP.
- **Custom Gradient.** Creates an image using the current gradient.

15.10.5 Buttons

Currently, there is only one button in this menu: Simple Beveled Button. It creates a beveled button with a blended background.

15.10.6 Make Brush

The scripts in this menu create brushes to use in the GIMP. It is automatically saved in your ~/.gimp directory. There are four different types of brushes that can be created:

- **Rectangular.** A basic rectangular brush.
- **Rectangular, Feathered.** A rectangular brush with feathered edges.
- **Elliptical.** A basic elliptical brush.
- **Elliptical, Feathered.** An elliptical brush with feathered edges.

15.10.7 Misc

There is only one script in this menu: Make Sphere. It creates a 3D-looking sphere with an optional shadow.

Installing the GIMP

A

Installation of the GIMP can be a difficult and frustrating task for someone who is new to Linux or Unix because many libraries are required before you can begin to install the GIMP. Most Linux distributions come with the GIMP pre-installed. If you wish to run a "bleeding-edge" version of the GIMP or its libraries, the information in this appendix is essential. Although binaries, RPMs, or DEBs of the GIMP are available, you will also learn how to install from the source code to fully customize the GIMP.

All of these programs must be installed by the root user to be available to everyone. If you do not have root access to your computer, ask your system administrator to install the programs. If you cannot do this, it is possible to install the GIMP for your own use, but it becomes complicated. Binary installations are not covered here because not all of the required libraries are available for every Linux distribution. Source code can be compiled on almost every Linux system in existence today. The major Linux distributions will be able to install these programs. If you are using a distribution other than one of the "standard" Linux distributions—Slackware, RedHat (its derivatives), Debian, SuSE, or Caldera—you may need to do some additional work.

Warning—due to the many distributions and versions available, this appendix cannot cover every system variation. Read the README and INSTALL files very carefully before installing any software. Be careful when using a package manager to install packages automatically.

A.1   Installing RedHat Packages

The RedHat Package Manager (RPM) is a program that allows you easily install software packages. Most RedHat distributions come with all of the required graphics libraries, so you must install only the GTK, glib, and GIMP packages. The glib and GTK packages are found here:

```
ftp://ftp.gimp.org/pub/gtk/binary/RPMS/
```

Enter the correct directory for your system (for example, "i386" for Intel systems). Download the two latest package files. Next, go to the GIMP package, found here:

```
ftp://ftp.gimp.org/pub/gimp/binary/RPMS/
```

Download the latest version of the GIMP that is in this directory. Installing these packages is fairly simple:

1. Type `rpm -ivh glib.<version info>.rpm` to install glib.

2. Type `rpm -ivh gtk.<version info>.rpm` to install GTK.

3. Type `rpm -ivh gimp.<version info>.rpm` to install the GIMP.

If you already have older versions installed, use `rpm -Uvh` instead of `rpm -ivh`.

A.2 Installing Debian Packages

The Debian package manager program allows you to easily install packages on your Debian system. Debian is very strict about only allowing Open Source software in their distribution, so GIF support may not be included, but most other graphics libraries will be installed. To keep your system current, you must install the latest versions of glib, GTK, and the GIMP. The latest version of glib and GTK can be found here:

`ftp://ftp.gimp.org/pub/gtk/binary/DEBIAN/stable/`

The latest version of the GIMP is found here:

`ftp://ftp.gimp.org/pub/gimp/binary/DEBIAN/1.2/stable/`

Installation is fast and straightforward:

1. Type **dpkg --install glib_<version number>.deb** to install glib.
2. Type **dpkg --install gtk_<version number>.deb** to install GTK.
3. Type **dpkg --install gimp_<version number>.deb** to install the GIMP.

A.3 Installing the Required Image Libraries from Source

Prior to installing the GIMP, several image libraries must be installed. These are necessary in order to read and write various image formats. If you have older versions of these libraries on your machine, it is best to remove them before you begin. This is done through your distribution's package manager. Old libraries present on your computer will just cause problems in the future.

A.3.1 Installation Guidelines

To keep your directories tidy, it is best to unpack all of your files into /usr/ local/src. Most packages will be compressed with tar and gzip, or tar and bzip2. bzip2 provides better compression, but is less common than gzip. If you have bzip2 installed, choose those files to save yourself, and the ftp server, some time. To unpack the packages, you must type the full path to the file unless it is in your current directory.

To unpack the a gzipped archive, type the following:

    gzip -dc <path to file> ¦ tar xvf -

To unpack a bzip2 archive, type the following:

    bzip2 -dc <path to file> ¦ tar xvf -

This will create a new directory with the unpacked files in it. The general process for building libraries will be to change to the directory, and type each of the following in order:

1. `/configure`
2. `make`
3. `make install`
4. `ldconfig`

This is the standard GNU way of installing a program from the source code, but some libraries do not follow this method. It is essential to read the README and/or INSTALL files included in the packages to avoid compilation problems. If you run into problems installing, and want to start fresh, type the following:

`make distclean`

This will clean the directories out, and you can start over.

A.3.2 Jpeglib

The first library to install is jpeglib. It can be found here:

`ftp://ftp.uu.net/graphics/jpeg/`

Unpack the downloaded file into /usr/local/src. Change into the newly created directory and type the following:

`./configure`

By default, this will install into your /usr/local/lib directory. This will configure the program to compile on your computer. When it is finished running, type the following:

`make && make test`

If there are no errors, type the following:

`make install`

At this point, edit the file called /etc/ld.so.conf. If you do not see /usr/local/lib in this file, add it to the last line. Next, type the following:

`/sbin/ldconfig -v ¦ more`

You should see several files starting with libjpeg* in the output.

Zlib

Zlib is a compression library required to use the PNG file format. It can be downloaded from this location:

`ftp://ftp.cdrom.com/pub/infozip/zlib/`

Unpack this package and change into the new directory. Zlib uses a different configure script for installation, but the command line options are similar. Type the following to set it up to be compiled:

`./configure`

Use the `--prefix` option to set a different install location:

`make test`

This should run without any errors. If you do encounter errors using make test, check the README file for additional instructions. Assuming that it runs without any errors, type the following:

`make install && ldconfig`

A.3.3 PNG

The PNG library is required to read and write PNG files. It can be obtained here:

`ftp://ftp.uu.net/graphics/png/src/`

Zlib must be installed and working before PNG can be installed. PNG's installation process is not a standard method, so it is important that you read the INSTALL file carefully. To begin, when you are in the `libpng` directory, type the following:

`cp scripts/makefile.lnx makefile`

Next, edit `pngconf.h` to make any necessary configuration changes. Standard Linux systems should not need any changes.

Note that if you are running a PowerPC processor, uncomment the line that refers to `PNG_READ_BIG_ENDIAN_SUPPORTED`.

Next, type the following:

`make test`

This will run a small test program that reads a sample PNG file and saves it in an alternate file. If these two PNG files are identical, the PNG library is ready to compile. If you have problems at this point, go back and make sure zlib is installed correctly. If you ran `make test` in the zlib directory, and it worked, zlib is installed correctly. Next, type the following:

`make install && ldconfig`

PNG is now installed on your system.

A.3.4 Libtiff

Libtiff is very easy to install. It can be found here:

`ftp://ftp.sgi.com/graphics/tiff`

Unpack this file and change to the tiff-<version number> directory.

Documentation for this is in the `html` directory. If you wish, read the `index.html` file and its instructions. If you have a standard Linux system, type the following:

```
./configure && make
```

If there are no errors, type the following:

```
make install && ldconfig
```

The libraries described previously are all that are necessary to run a functional GIMP. Other libraries can be installed, but they have very specific purposes, and most users will not need them. The next library, GTK+, is necessary to run the GIMP.

A.4 Installing GTK+

GTK+, or the GIMP ToolKit, is an extremely flexible library for creating graphical user interfaces for the X Window System. Many applications for Linux use this library, and you will find it very useful to have installed on your system. Because of its popularity, GTK+ may already be installed on your system. This may cause difficulties if it is out of date, so unless you have the latest version of GTK+, remove the old library and install the newer version.

A.4.1 Building and Installing Glib and GTK+

If you decided to upgrade or install GTK+, it is necessary to download it. The GTK+ homepage is `http://www.gtk.org`, and the files are located here:

```
ftp://ftp.gtk.org/pub/gtk
```

The first step is to install glib. glib was previously included in GTK+, but has grown enough to warrant its own distribution. It will be located in the same directory as GTK+. Unpack the glib archive first, and change into that directory. Type the following to configure the archive for your system:

```
./configure — disable-debug
```

When that has completed, type the following:

```
make
```

The most common error with this library has to do with threads. If an error occurs regarding threads, reconfigure glib with the `—enable-threads=no` option.

If glib finished installing with no errors, type the following:

```
make install && ldconfig
```

glib will be configured for your system. After this has completed, change back into the `/usr/local/src` directory and unpack the GTK+ archive. To configure this package, type the following:

```
./configure — disable-debug
```

Typing `--disable-debug` removes the debugging information from the binaries, giving you smaller and faster programs. If you are interested in troubleshooting and helping the development of GTK+, you can enable debugging. This is only necessary if you are hacking the GTK+ code.

If you have a pen tablet, you will also want to include XInput support. This is done by adding `--with-xinput=xfree` to the configure command.

If the compile finished with no errors, type the following:

```
make && make install && ldconfig
```

If you encounter errors referring to `gettext` when compiling GTK+, add the command `--disable-nls` when running configure.

A.5 The GIMP

After all of the libraries required by the GIMP are working and installed, it is finally time to install the GIMP. After installing all of these other libraries, the installation of the GIMP should be very straightforward. Be prepared to go out and grab a cup of coffee, though. The GIMP will take more than three times as long as the Linux kernel to compile. Dual Pentium IIs come in very handy at this point.

A.5.1 Which Version is Right for Me?

The "right" version to use depends on what you are using the GIMP for. If you need bleeding-edge features, use the development version of the GIMP. If you want a program that will not crash unexpectedly, use the stable version. For an explanation of the numbering system the GIMP uses, see page 2.

The GIMP package can be found here:

```
ftp://ftp.gimp.org/pub/gimp
```

If you are installing the stable version of the GIMP, download the `gimp-data-extras-1.0.0` package as well. This gives you many extra patterns, gradients, brushes, and so on, to use.

A.5.2 Building and Installing the GIMP

After the download is complete, unpack the GIMP archive and change into the new directory. Type the following to configure the GIMP for your system:

```
./configure --disable-debug
```

When this has completed, check in the `config.log` file to see if any errors were generated. A common error is that the "AA library" is not found. The logfile will read as follows:

```
/usr/bin/ld: cannot open -laa: No such file or directory
```

This library can be found at `http://horac.ta.jcu.cz/aa/`. The GIMP will run safely without it, however.

Another common error is that the MPEG library is not found. The logfile will read as follows:

```
/usr/bin/ld: cannot open -lmpeg: No such file or directory
```

This library is also not necessary, but if you find that you need it, you can download the MPEG library from `ftp://yorick.mni.mcgill.ca/pub/mpeg/`.

If any errors occur while you are checking for the JPEG, PNG, or TIFF library, go back and make sure that the libraries are installed correctly. If these libraries are not working, you won't be able use that type of image—that is, the GIMP will compile correctly, but will refuse to open those images. When you are sure that everything is ready, type the following:

make

This will take a long time (go grab that cup of coffee). When it has finished compiling, type the following:

make install && ldconfig

This will install all of the binaries for the GIMP. If you downloaded the extra data files, unpack that archive into `/usr/local/src`, and change into that directory. Type the following:

./configure && make install

This will install the extra data files into your GIMP directory.

You now have a working copy of the GIMP[1]! It's time to begin using it. It is not recommended to work while you are the root user, so log in as a regular user. Start X Windows. Most new window managers will come with a GIMP entry on the Start menu. It is time to load it. If you don't have a GIMP entry, open up an xterm and type the following:

gimp

A dialog box will pop up asking if you want to set up your GIMP directory. Click on the Install button. The GIMP startup screen will pop up, and then the main GIMP toolbar will appear.

---

[1] *A new feature in GIMP 1.2 is the GIMP-Perl scripting extension. This extension is beta currently, and the installation can be difficult. Adventurous users may want to attempt installation of this, but for most people it is not really necessary. If you do want to attempt the installation, you will need to install three more packages:*

*1. **GTK-Perl.** The latest version is 0.5121, available from `ftp://ftp.gimp.org/ pub/gtk/perl`.*

*2. **PDL.** This is available from `ftp://ftp.aao.gov.au/pub/perldl/`.*

*3. **Parse.** This is available from `http://www.cpan.org/modules/by-module/Parse/`.*

Using Multiple Versions of the GIMP

Sometimes you will want to have two versions of the GIMP installed on your system—one version for all the new, cool features, and the other for daily work.

A.5.3 Building and Installing the Development Version of the GIMP

The development version of the GIMP comes with many improvements over the older, stable version. It sacrifices stability to do this, so don't be surprised if it crashes or doesn't even compile. It can be downloaded from here:

```
ftp://ftp.gimp.org/pub/gimp/unstable
```

There will be two directories at this location. The latest version of the GIMP will be in the numbered directory—for example, 1.1.8/. The directory old/ contains all of the previous development versions. Only use packages from this directory if you are having problems with the latest version. Download and unpack the latest package into /usr/local/src. Change into the new directory and type the following:

```
./configure --enable-debug=no --prefix=/usr/local/gimp-1.1.6
```

When the configure script has finished setting up the GIMP for your system, type the following:

```
make && make install
```

If you encounter problems during the compilation, you may need to install the gettext package, or use the one provided by the GIMP. This can be done by appending --with-included-gettext to the configure script that was previously run. Installing the gettext package from the GNU site may be the better choice. The latest version can be found here:

```
ftp://ftp.gnu.org/pub/gnu/gettext/
```

Alternatively, if you do not need native language support, append --disable-nls to the configure script. After the configure script has completed, type the following:

```
make && make install
```

When the GIMP has completed building, you must make the system aware of the new library files. There are two methods you can use:

- **Edit the /etc/ld.so.conf file.** This is the easiest method if you have superuser access. Simply add the /usr/local/gimp-1.1.6/lib directory to the /etc/ld.so.conf file. Save the file and then type the following:
  ```
  ldconfig -v ¦ more
  ```

You should see an entry similar to this:

```
/usr/local/gimp-1.1.6/lib:
libgck-1.1.so.6 => libgck-1.1.so.6.0.0
libgimpui-1.1.so.6 => libgimpui-1.1.so.6.0.0
libgimp-1.1.so.6 => libgimp-1.1.so.6.0.0
```

- **Use an environment variable.** Using the bash shell, add the following to your ~/.profile file:

```
export LD_LIBRARY_PATH="$LD_LIBRARY_PATH:/usr/local/
gimp-1.1.6/lib"
```

And then type the following:

```
source ~/.profile
```

At this point you may want to try running the GIMP. You will have to do this from an xterm, or create an entry in your window manager to execute the file /usr/local/gimp-1.1.6/bin/gimp. When you first run the development version of the GIMP, it will ask you to install several files. Click on the Install button to do this. This will create a new directory called .gimp-1.1 that contains the necessary configuration files. After you have verified that it works, you can close it down.

A.5.4 Building and Installing the Stable Version of the GIMP

Now that the development version is installed, it is time to compile the stable version of the GIMP. It can be downloaded from here:

```
ftp://ftp.gimp.org/pub/gimp/v1.0
```

Unpack the archive and change into the new directory. Type the following to set up the GIMP for your machine:

```
./configure --prefix=/usr/local/gimp-1.0.4
```

Then type the following to build the GIMP:

```
make && make install
```

When the GIMP has completed building, you must make the system aware of the new library files. There are two methods you can use:

- **Edit the /etc/ld.so.conf file.** This is the easiest to do if you have superuser access. Simply add the /usr/local/gimp-1.0.4/lib directory to the /etc/ld.so.conf file. Save the file and then type the following:

```
ldconfig -v ¦ more
```

Look for an entry similar to this:

```
/usr/local/gimp-1.0.4/lib:
        libgck.so.1 => libgck.so.1.0.0
        libgimpui.so.1 => libgimpui.so.1.0.4
        libgimp.so.1 => libgimp.so.1.0.4
```

- **Use an environment variable.** Using the bash shell, add the following to your ~/.profile file:

```
export LD_LIBRARY_PATH="$LD_LIBRARY_PATH:/usr/local/
gimp-1.0.4/lib"
```

Then type the following:
source ~/.profile

At this point, you might also want to install the gimp-data-extras package.

The installation is finally complete, and you should now have two working copies of the GIMP installed. Test the stable version of the GIMP by typing **/usr/local/gimp-1.0.4/bin/gimp**, and a similar installation screen should pop up. Choose to install, and a .gimp directory will be created for the stable version's configuration files. The GIMP is now ready to go.

B
Window Managers and the GIMP

A *window manager* is a strange concept to new users. It is a part of the Graphical User Interface used by Linux. It controls how windows are displayed, moved, resized, closed, and so on. The X server is the other part of the GUI that controls the more basic interface, drawing on the monitor, and so on.

There are many different window managers available to use on a Unix system. All of them will run with the GIMP. However, with the window managers becoming more complicated, there may be some idiosyncrasies.

B.1 Command-Line Options for the GIMP

The GIMP is usually run by issuing the `gimp` command. Sometimes additional parameters need to be passed to a program. The GIMP recognizes the following parameters:

Table B.1 `gimp` Parameters

Parameter	Effect
`-h --help`	Display a text help message.
`-v --version`	Display the GIMP's version.
`-b --batch commands`	Run the GIMP in batch mode.
`-n --no-interface`	Run without a user interface. This is used in conjunction with batch mode.
`--no-data`	Do not load any patterns, gradients, palettes, or brushes.
`--verbose`	Show startup messages.
`--no-splash`	Do not show the startup window.
`--no-splash-image`	Do not add an image to the startup window.
`--no-shm`	Do not use shared memory between GIMP and its plug-ins.
`--no-xshm`	Disable use of the X Shared Memory extension. This option shouldn't be used unless you are using an X server over a network.

continues

Table B.1   Continued

Parameter	Effect
--console-messages	Display all warnings to the console instead of a dialog box from the GIMP. This is useful if you want to log any error messages.
--debug-handlers	Enable debugging signal handlers.
--display display	Use the designated X display.

B.2   Common Window Managers

The descriptions of these window managers are very general. Different distributions install them in different places, so the filenames here may not be correct. Most of the configuration files are located in a share directory. This could be /usr/share, /usr/X11R6/share, /usr/local/share, or something similar.

B.2.1   AfterStep

AfterStep runs the GIMP out of the box. It is located in the Root menu in Applications/Multimedia/The Gimp. The configuration file for the GIMP is in ~/GNUstep/Library/AfterStep/start/Applications/Multimedia/4_gimp. AfterStep's home page is located at http://www.afterstep.org.

B.2.2   Blackbox

Blackbox is a lightweight window manager. The GIMP is located in the Root menu in Graphics/The Gimp. The configuration file for the GIMP is found in the ~/.blackbox/Menu file. Blackbox's home page is located at http://blackbox.alug.org.

B.2.3   Enlightenment

Enlightenment is a highly configurable window manager that uses a great deal of your system's resources. The GIMP is located in the Root menu in Applications/Gimp. The configuration file can be found in share/enlightenment/config/menus.cfg.

B.2.4   GNOME

GNOME is a desktop environment. It works together with a window manager. The GIMP is located inside the Gnome Foot menu in Graphics/The Gimp. The configuration file for the GIMP is found in share/gnome/apps/Graphics/GIMP.desktop. If you want to add your own entry, it would be found in ~/.gnome/apps. After an entry is added using the Gnome Menu Editor tool, it appears here. Trying to add it by hand would be difficult.

B.2.5 IceWM

IceWM is another lightweight window manager. The GIMP is located in the Start menu in `Applications/Graphics/Gimp`. The configuration file for the GIMP is located in `~/.icewm/menu`. The IceWM home page is found at `http://www.kiss.uni-lj.si/~k4fr0235/icewm/`.

B.2.6 KDE

KDE is another desktop environment that uses its own window manager, KWM. The GIMP is found in the KDE Gears menu under `non-KDE Apps/Graphics/Gimp`. The configuration file for the GIMP is found in `~/.kde/share/applnk/apps/Graphic/gimp.kdelnk`. The KDE home page is located at `http://www.kde.org/`.

B.2.7 WindowMaker

WindowMaker is a window manager similar to AfterStep. The GIMP is in the Root menu under `Applications/Graphics/Gimp`. The configuration file for the GIMP is found in `~/GNUStep/Library/WindowMaker/menu`. The Window-Maker home page is located at `http://www.windowmaker.org/`.

C

Internet Resources for the GIMP

Obviously, the GIMP has many Web pages devoted to it. This is just a sampling of what you might find on the Internet. The GIMP's Web site hosts many developers' Web pages, and provides pointers to other home pages. Tigert's home page (`http://tigert.gimp.org/`) is a good example of a developer's site. For other sites, try typing the developer's email address to find the page, such as `username.gimp.org`. Other people can be found at `www.gimp.org/~username`.

Table C.1   GIMP Online Resources

Location	Title	Description
`http://www.gimp.org/links.html`	GIMP.ORG -> links	Important links for the GIMP.
`http://www.gtk.org`	The GIMP ToolKit	The GIMP ToolKit's home page. Provides links to the latest software.
`http://registry.gimp.org`	GIMP Plug-In Registry	A list of plug-ins for the stable and unstable versions of the GIMP.
`comp.graphics.apps.gimp`	The GIMP's Newsgroup	This is a good place to ask your GIMP-related questions.
`http://tigert.gimp.org/`	tigert.gimp.org	An excellent page of GIMP art and resources.
`http://www.xach.com/gimp/news/index.html`	Xach's GIMP News	Up-to-date news on the GIMP. Also many excellent tutorials.
`http://luthien.nuclecu.unam.mx/~federico/gimp/`	Everybody Loves the GIMP	Quartic's GIMP resource page. Many plug-ins can be found here.

continues

Table C.1   Continued

Location	Title	Description
http://www.rru.com/ ~meo/gimp/	GIMP FAQs	Frequently asked questions about the GIMP.
http://www.gimp.org/ mailing_list.html	Archives of the GIMP Mailing Lists	A useful archive of the GIMP mailing list. Check here before posting questions.
http://www.cooltext.com	CoolText.Com	An excellent example of Net-Fu.
http://www.isc.tamu.edu/ ~lewing/gimp/	Larry Ewing's GIMP Page	The home of the Linux logo.

D
Function Reference for Scripts

331   **gimp_display_new**—Create a new display for the specified image.

332   **gimp_layer_set_opacity**—Set the opacity of the specified layer.

332   **gimp_edit_fill**—Fill selected area of drawable.

332   **gimp_image_set_component_visible**—Set the specified component's visibility.

333   **gimp_drawable_set_pixel**—Set the value of the pixel at the specified coordinates.

333   **gimp_layer_is_floating_sel**—Determine whether the specified layer is a floating selection.

333   **gimp_drawable_height**—Return the height of the drawable.

334   **gimp_edit_copy**—Copy from the specified drawable.

334   **gimp_image_remove_layer**—Remove the specified layer from the image.

334   **gimp_image_disable_undo**—Disable the image's undo stack.

335   **gimp_layer_get_opacity**—Get the opacity of the specified layer.

335   **gimp_image_clean_all**—Set the image dirty count to 0.

335   **gimp_image_raise_layer**—Raise the specified layer in the image's layer stack.

D.1 Script Reference

D.1.1 gimp_drawable_get_pixel

Description This procedure gets the pixel value at the specified coordinates. The num_channels argument must always be equal to the bytes-per-pixel value for the specified drawable.

Table D.1 gimp_drawable_get_pixel Variables

Variable Name	Type	Description
drawable	PDB_DRAWABLE	The drawable
num_channels	PDB_INT32	The number of channels for the pixel
pixel	PDB_INT8ARRAY	The pixel value
x coordinate	PDB_INT32	The x coordinate
y coordinate	PDB_INT32	The y coordinate

D.1.2 gimp_layer_add_alpha

Description This procedure adds an additional component to the specified layer if it does not already possess an Alpha channel. An Alpha channel makes it possible to move a layer from the bottom of the layer stack and to clear and erase to transparency rather than the background color. This transforms images of type RGB to RGBA, Gray to GrayA, and Indexed to IndexedA.

Table D.2 gimp_layer_add_alpha Variable

Variable Name	Type	Description
layer	PDB_LAYER	The layer

D.1.3 gimp_layer_set_mode

Description This tool sets the combination mode of the specified layer.

Table D.3 gimp_layer_set_mode Layers

Variable Name	Type	Description
layer	PDB_LAYER	The layer
mode	PDB_INT32	The new layer combination mode

D.1.4 gimp_bucket_fill

Description This tool requires information about the paint application mode, and the fill mode, which can either be in the foreground color, or in the currently active pattern. If there is no selection, a seed fill is executed at the specified coordinates and extends outward in keeping with the threshold parameter. If there is a selection in the target image, the threshold, sample merged, x, and y arguments are unused. If the sample_merged parameter is non-zero, the data of the composite image will be used instead of that for the specified drawable. This is equivalent to sampling for colors after merging all visible layers. In the case of merged sampling, the x, y coordinates are relative to the image's origin; otherwise, they are relative to the drawable's origin.

Table D.4 gimp_bucket_fill Variables

Variable Name	Type	Description
drawable	PDB_DRAWABLE	The affected drawable.
fill_mode	PDB_INT32	The types of fill: FG-BUCKET-FILL (0), BG-BUCKET-FILL (1), PATTERN-BUCKET-FILL (2).
image	PDB_IMAGE	The image.
opacity	PDB_FLOAT	The opacity of the final bucket fill (0 <= opacity <= 100).
paint_mode	PDB_INT32	The paint application modes: NORMAL (0), DISSOLVE (1), BEHIND (2), MULTIPLY (3), SCREEN (4), OVERLAY (5), DIFFERENCE (6), ADDITION (7), SUBTRACT (8), DARKEN-ONLY (9), LIGHTEN-ONLY (10), HUE (11), SATURATION (12), COLOR (13), VALUE (14).
sample_merged	PDB_INT32	Uses the composite image, not the drawable.
threshold	PDB_FLOAT	The threshold determines how extensive the seed fill will be. Its value is specified in terms of intensity levels (0 <= threshold <= 255). This parameter is valid only when there is no selection in the specified image.
x	PDB_FLOAT	The x coordinate of this bucket fill's application. This parameter is valid only when there is no selection in the specified image.
y	PDB_FLOAT	The y coordinate of this bucket fill's application. This parameter is valid only when there is no selection in the specified image.

D.1.5 gimp_invert

Description This procedure inverts the contents of the specified drawable. Each intensity channel is inverted independently. The inverted intensity is given as inten' = (255 × inten). Indexed color drawables are not valid for this operation.

Table D.5 gimp_invert Variables

Variable Name	Type	Description
drawable	PDB_DRAWABLE	The drawable
image	PDB_IMAGE	The image

D.1.6 gimp_floating_sel_remove

Description This procedure removes the floating selection completely, without any side effects. The associated drawable is then set to active.

Table D.6 gimp_floating_sel_remove Variable

Variable Name	Type	Description
floating_sel	PDB_LAYER	The floating selection

D.1.7 gimp_brightness_contrast

Description This procedure allows the brightness and contrast of the specified drawable to be modified. Both brightness and contrast parameters are defined between -127 and 127.

Table D.7 gimp_brightness_contrast Variables

Variable Name	Type	Description
brightness	PDB_INT32	Brightness adjustment: $(-127 <= $ brightness $<= 127)$
contrast	PDB_INT32	Constrast adjustment: $(-127 <= $ contrast $<= 127)$
drawable	PDB_DRAWABLE	The drawable
image	PDB_IMAGE	The image

D.1.8 gimp_text

Description This tool adds text at the specified location as a floating selection or new layer. It requires font information in the form of seven parameters: size, foundry, family, weight, slant, set_width, spacing. The font size can be specified in units of either pixels or points, and the appropriate metric is specified using the size_type argument. The x and y parameters together control the placement of the new text by specifying the upper-left corner of the text bounding box. If the antialias parameter is non-zero, the generated text will blend more smoothly with underlying layers. This option requires more time and memory to compute than non-antialiased text; the resulting floating selection or layer, however, will require the same amount of memory with or without antialiasing. If the specified drawable parameter is valid, the text will be created as a floating selection attached to the drawable.

If the drawable parameter is not valid (-1), the text will appear as a new layer. Finally, a border can be specified around the final rendered text. The border is measured in pixels.

Table D.8 `gimp_text` Variables

Variable Name	Type	Description
antialias	PDB_INT32	Generates antialiased text
border	PDB_INT32	The size of the border: (border >= 0)
drawable	PDB_DRAWABLE	The affected drawable: -1 for a new text layer
family	PDB_STRING	The font family, * for any
foundry	PDB_STRING	The font foundry, * for any
image	PDB_IMAGE	The image
set_width	PDB_STRING	The font set-width parameter, * for any
size	PDB_FLOAT	The size of text in either pixels or points
size_type	PDB_INT32	The units of the specified size: PIXELS (0), POINTS (1)
slant	PDB_STRING	The font slant, * for any
spacing	PDB_STRING	The font spacing, * for any
text	PDB_STRING	The text to generate
text_layer	PDB_LAYER	The new text layer
weight	PDB_STRING	The font weight, * for any
x	PDB_FLOAT	The x coordinate for the left side of text bounding box
y	PDB_FLOAT	The y coordinate for the top of text bounding box

D.1.9 `gimp_image_get_layers`

Description This procedure returns the list of layers contained in the specified image. The order of layers is from topmost to bottommost.

Table D.9 `gimp_image_get_layers` Variables

Variable Name	Type	Description
image	PDB_IMAGE	The image
layer_ids	PDB_INT32ARRAY	The list of layers contained in the image
num_layers	PDB_INT32	The number of layers contained in the image

D.1.10 gimp_image_floating_selection

Description This procedure returns the image's floating_sel, if it exists. If it doesn't exist, -1 is returned as the layer ID.

Table D.10   gimp_image_floating_selection Variables

Variable Name	Type	Description
floating_sel	PDB_LAYER	The image's floating selection
image	PDB_IMAGE	The image

D.1.11 gimp_image_flatten

Description This procedure flattens all visible layers into a single layer; it combines the visible layers in a manner analogous to merging with the ClipToImage merge type. Non-visible layers are discarded, and the resulting image is stripped of its Alpha channel.

Table D.11   gimp_image_flatten Variables

Variable Name	Type	Description
image	PDB_IMAGE	The image
layer	PDB_LAYER	The resulting layer

D.1.12 gimp_selection_all

Description This procedure sets the selection mask to completely encompass the image. Every pixel in the selection channel is set to 255.

Table D.12   gimp_selection_all Variable

Variable Name	Type	Description
image	PDB_IMAGE	The image

D.1.13 gimp_layer_copy

Description This procedure copies the specified layer and returns the copy. The newly copied layer is for use within the original layer's image. It should not be subsequently added to any other image. The copied layer can optionally have an added Alpha channel. This is useful if the background layer in an image is being copied and added to the same image.

Table D.13 gimp_layer_copy Variables

Variable Name	Type	Description
add_alpha	PDB_INT32	Add an Alpha channel to the copied layer
layer	PDB_LAYER	The layer to copy
layer_copy	PDB_LAYER	The newly copied layer

D.1.14 gimp_palette_get_background

Description This procedure retrieves the current GIMP background color. The background color is used in a variety of tools such as blending, erasing (with non-Alpha images), and image filling.

Table D.14 gimp_palette_get_background Variable

Variable Name	Type	Description
background	PDB_COLOR	The background color

D.1.15 gimp_layer_get_preserve_trans

Description This procedure returns the specified layer's preserve transparency setting.

Table D.15 gimp_layer_get_preserve_trans Variables

Variable Name	Type	Description
layer	PDB_LAYER	The layer
preserve_trans	PDB_INT32	The layer's preserve transparency setting

D.1.16 gimp_selection_layer_alpha

Description This procedure requires a layer with an Alpha channel. The Alpha channel information is used to create a selection mask such that for any pixel in the image defined in the specified layer, that layer pixel's Alpha value is transferred to the selection mask. If the layer is undefined at a particular image pixel, the associated selection mask value is set to 0.

Table D.16 gimp_selection_layer_alpha Variables

Variable Name	Type	Description
image	PDB_IMAGE	The image
layer	PDB_LAYER	The layer with Alpha

D.1.17   `gimp_layer_translate`

Description   This procedure translates the layer by the amounts specified in the x and y arguments. These can be negative, and are considered offsets from the current position. This command works only if the layer has been added to an image. All additional layers contained in the image which have the linked flag set to TRUE will also be translated by the specified offsets.

Table D.17   `gimp_layer_translate` Variables

Variable Name	Type	Description
layer	PDB_LAYER	The layer
offx	PDB_INT32	Offset in X direction
offy	PDB_INT32	Offset in Y direction

D.1.18   `gimp_layer_get_name`

Description   This procedure returns the name of the specified layer.

Table D.18   `gimp_layer_get_name` Variables

Variable Name	Type	Description
layer	PDB_LAYER	The layer
name	PDB_STRING	The layer name

D.1.19   `gimp_palette_set_foreground`

Description   This procedure sets the current GIMP foreground color. After this is set, operations that use foreground such as paint tools, blending, and bucket fill will use the new value.

Table D.19   `gimp_palette_set_foreground` Variable

Variable Name	Type	Description
foreground	PDB_COLOR	The foreground color

D.1.20 `gimp_drawable_type`

Description This procedure returns the drawable's type.

Table D.20 `gimp_drawable_type` Variables

Variable Name	Type	Description
drawable	PDB_DRAWABLE	The drawable
type	PDB_INT32	The drawable's types: RGB (0), RGBA (1), GRAY (2), GRAYA (3), INDEXED (4), INDEXEDA (5)

D.1.21 `gimp_image_get_active_layer`

Description If there is an active layer, its ID will be returned; otherwise, -1 is returned. If a channel is currently active, then no layer will be. If a layer mask is active, then this will return the associated layer.

Table D.21 `gimp_image_get_active_layer` Variables

Variable Name	Type	Description
image	PDB_IMAGE	The image
layer_ID	PDB_LAYER	The ID of the active layer

D.1.22 `gimp_channel_ops_offset`

Description This procedure offsets the specified drawable by the amounts specified by `offset_x` and `offset_y`. If `wrap_around` is set to TRUE, then portions of the drawable that are offset out of bounds are wrapped around. Alternatively, the undefined regions of the drawable can be filled with transparency or the background color, as specified by the `fill_type` parameter.

Table D.22 `gimp_channel_ops_offset` Variables

Variable Name	Type	Description
drawable	PDB_DRAWABLE	The drawable to offset
fill_type	PDB_INT32	Fills vacated regions of drawable with background or transparent: OFFSET_BACKGROUND (0), OFFSET_TRANSPARENT (1)
image	PDB_IMAGE	The image

continues

Table D.22   Continued.

Variable Name	Type	Description
offset_x	PDB_INT32	Offset by this amount in X direction
offset_y	PDB_INT32	Offset by this amount in Y direction
wrap_around	PDB_INT32	Wraps image around or fills vacated regions

D.1.23   `gimp_layer_scale`

Description   This procedure scales the layer so that its new width and height are equal to the supplied parameters. The `local_origin` parameter specifies whether to scale from the center of the layer or from the image origin. This operation works only if the layer has been added to an image.

Table D.23   `gimp_layer_scale` Variables

Variable Name	Type	Description
layer	PDB_LAYER	The layer
local_origin	PDB_INT32	Determines whether to use a local origin or the image origin
new_height	PDB_INT32	New layer height: (new_height > 0)
new_width	PDB_INT32	New layer width: (new_width > 0)

D.1.24   `gimp_selection_feather`

Description   This procedure feathers the selection. Feathering is implemented using a Gaussian blur.

Table D.24   `gimp_selection_feather` Variables

Variable Name	Type	Description
image	PDB_IMAGE	The image
radius	PDB_FLOAT	Radius of feather (in pixels)

D.1.25 `gimp_gradients_get_active`

Description This procedure returns the name of the active gradient in the gradient editor.

Table D.25 `gimp_gradients_get_active` **Variable**

Variable Name	Type	Description
name	PDB_STRING	The name of the active gradient

D.1.26 `gimp_layer_delete`

Description This procedure deletes the specified layer. This does not need to be done if a gimage containing this layer was already deleted.

Table D.26 `gimp_layer_delete` **Variable**

Variable Name	Type	Description
layer	PDB_LAYER	The layer to delete

D.1.27 `gimp_image_width`

Description This procedure returns the image's width. This value is independent of any of the layers in this image. This is the \canvas\ width.

Table D.27 `gimp_image_width` **Variables**

Variable Name	Type	Description
image	PDB_IMAGE	The image
width	PDB_INT32	The image's width

D.1.28 `gimp_selection_value`

Description This procedure returns the value of the selection at the specified coordinates. If the coordinates lie out of bounds, 0 is returned.

Table D.28 `gimp_selection_value` **Variables**

Variable Name	Type	Description
image	PDB_IMAGE	The image
value	PDB_INT32	Value of the selection: (0 <= **value** <= 255)
x	PDB_INT32	x coordinate of value
y	PDB_INT32	y coordinate of value

D.1.29 gimp_layer_resize

Description This procedure resizes the layer so that its new width and height are equal to the supplied parameters. Offsets are also provided that describe the position of the previous layer's content. No bounds checking is currently provided, so don't supply parameters that are out of bounds. This operation works only if the layer has been added to an image.

Table D.29 gimp_layer_resize Variables

Variable Name	Type	Description
layer	PDB_LAYER	The layer
new_height	PDB_INT32	New layer height: (new_height > 0)
new_width	PDB_INT32	New layer width: (new_width > 0)
offx	PDB_INT32	x offset between upper-left corner of old and new layers: (new - old)
offy	PDB_INT32	y offset between upper-left corner of old and new layers: (new - old)

D.1.30 gimp_selection_sharpen

Description This procedure sharpens the selection mask. For every pixel in the selection channel, if the value is > 0, the new pixel is assigned a value of 255. This removes any antialiasing that might exist in the selection mask's boundary.

Table D.30 gimp_selection_sharpen Variable

Variable Name	Type	Description
image	PDB_IMAGE	The image

D.1.31 gimp_drawable_type_with_alpha

Description This procedure returns the drawable's type if an Alpha channel was added. If the type is currently Gray, for instance, the returned type would be GrayA. If the drawable already has an Alpha channel, the drawable's type is simply returned.

Table D.31 `gimp_drawable_type_with_alpha` Variables

Variable Name	Type	Description
drawable	PDB_DRAWABLE	The drawable
type_with_alpha	PDB_INT32	The drawable's type with Alpha: RGBA (0), GRAYA (1), INDEXEDA (2)

D.1.32 `gimp_image_delete`

Description   If there are no other references to this image it will be deleted. Other references are possible when more than one view to an image exists.

Table D.32 `gimp_image_delete` Variable

Variable Name	Type	Description
image	PDB_IMAGE	The image ID

D.1.33 `gimp_layer_get_visible`

Description   This procedure returns the specified layer's visibility.

Table D.33 `gimp_layer_get_visible` Variables

Variable Name	Type	Description
layer	PDB_LAYER	The layer
visible	PDB_INT32	The layer visibility

D.1.34 `plug_in_rotate`

Description   This plug-in rotates the active layer or the whole image clockwise by multiples of 90 degrees. When the whole image is chosen, the image is resized if necessary.

Table D.34 `plug_in_rotate` Variables

Variable Name	Type	Description
angle	PDB_INT32	Angle: 90 (1), 180 (2), 270 (3)
drawable	PDB_DRAWABLE	Input drawable
everything	PDB_INT32	Determines whether to rotate the whole image: { TRUE, FALSE }
image	PDB_IMAGE	Input image
run_mode	PDB_INT32	Interactive, non-interactive

D.1.35 `gimp_image_resize`

Description   This procedure resizes the image so that its new width and height are equal to the supplied parameters. Offsets are also provided that describe the position of the previous image's content. No bounds checking is currently provided, so don't supply parameters that are out of bounds. All channels within the image are resized according to the specified parameters; this includes the image selection mask. All layers within the image are repositioned according to the specified offsets.

Table D.35   `gimp_image_resize` Variables

Variable Name	Type	Description
image	PDB_IMAGE	The image
new_height	PDB_INT32	New image height: (new_height > 0)
new_width	PDB_INT32	New image width: (new_width > 0)
offx	PDB_INT32	x offset between upper-left corner of old and new images: (new − old)
offy	PDB_INT32	y offset between upper-left corner of old and new images: (new - old)

D.1.36 `plug_in_semiflatten`

Description   This plug-in flattens pixels in an RGBA image that aren't completely transparent against the current GIMP background color.

Table D.36   `plug_in_semiflatten` Variables

Variable Name	Type	Description
drawable	PDB_DRAWABLE	Input drawable
image	PDB_IMAGE	Input image (unused)
run_mode	PDB_INT32	Interactive, non-interactive

D.1.37 `gimp_selection_is_empty`

Description   This procedure returns non-zero if the selection for the specified image is not empty.

Table D.37   gimp_selection_is_empty Variables

Variable Name	Type	Description
image	PDB_IMAGE	The image
is_empty	PDB_INT32	Determines whether the selection is empty

D.1.38   gimp_selection_float

Description   This procedure determines the region of the specified drawable that lies beneath the current selection. The region is then cut from the drawable and the resulting data is made into a new layer, which is instantiated as a floating selection. The offsets allow initial positioning of the new floating selection.

Table D.38   gimp_selection_float Variables

Variable Name	Type	Description
drawable	PDB_DRAWABLE	The drawable from which to float selection
image	PDB_IMAGE	The image
layer	PDB_LAYER	The floated layer
offset_x	PDB_INT32	x offset for translation
offset_y	PDB_INT32	y offset for translation

D.1.39   gimp_selection_shrink

Description   This procedure shrinks the selection. Shrinking involves trimming the existing selection boundary on all sides by the specified number of pixels.

Table D.39   gimp_selection_shrink Variables

Variable Name	Type	Description
image	PDB_IMAGE	The image
radius	PDB_INT32	Radius of shrink (pixels)

D.1.40   gimp_drawable_update

Description   This procedure updates the specified region of the drawable. The (x, y) coordinate pair is relative to the drawable's origin, not to the image origin. Therefore, the entire drawable can be updated with: {x->0, y->0, w->width, h->height}.

Table D.40   gimp_drawable_update Variables

Variable Name	Type	Description
drawable	PDB_DRAWABLE	The drawable
h	PDB_INT32	Height of update region
w	PDB_INT32	Width of update region
x	PDB_INT32	x coordinate of upper-left corner of update region
y	PDB_INT32	y coordinate of upper-left corner of update region

D.1.41   gimp_layer_set_name

Description   This procedure sets the specified layer's name to the supplied name.

Table D.41   gimp_layer_set_name Variables

Variable Name	Type	Description
layer	PDB_LAYER	The layer
name	PDB_STRING	The new layer name

D.1.42   gimp_floating_sel_to_layer

Description   This procedure transforms the specified floating selection into a layer with the same offsets and extents. The composited image will look precisely the same, but the floating selection layer will no longer be clipped to the extents of the drawable to which it was attached. The floating selection will become the active layer. This procedure will not work if the floating selection has a different base type from the underlying image. This might be the case if the floating selection is above an auxiliary channel or a layer mask.

Table D.42   gimp_floating_sel_to_layer Variable

Variable Name	Type	Description
floating_sel	PDB_LAYER	The floating selection

D.1.43 file_print

Description   Prints images to PostScript, PCL, or ESC/P2 printers.

Table D.43 file_print Variables

Variable Name	Type	Description
brightness	PDB_INT32	Brightness (0–200%)
drawable	PDB_DRAWABLE	Input drawable
driver	PDB_STRING	Printer driver short name
image	PDB_IMAGE	Input image
left	PDB_INT32	Left offset (points, -1 = centered)
media_size	PDB_STRING	Media size (Letter, A4, and so on)
media_source	PDB_STRING	Media source (Tray1, Manual, and so on)
media_type	PDB_STRING	Media type (Plain, Glossy, and so on)
orientation	PDB_INT32	Output orientation (-1 = auto, 0 = portrait, 1 = landscape)
output_to	PDB_STRING	Print command or filename (¦ to pipe to command)
output_type	PDB_INT32	Output type (0 = gray, 1 = color)
ppd_file	PDB_STRING	PPD file
resolution	PDB_STRING	Resolution (300, 720, and so on)
run_mode	PDB_INT32	Interactive, non-interactive
scaling	PDB_FLOAT	Output scaling (0–100%, -PPI)
top	PDB_INT32	Top offset (points, -1 = centered)

D.1.44 plug_in_despeckle

Description   This plug-in selectively performs a median or adaptive box filter on an image. This filter is typically used to "despeckle" a photographic image.

Table D.44 plug_in_despeckle Variables

Variable Name	Type	Description
black	PDB_INT32	Black level (0 to 255)
drawable	PDB_DRAWABLE	Input drawable
image	PDB_IMAGE	Input image
radius	PDB_INT32	Filter box radius (default = 3)

continues

Table D.44   Continued.

Variable Name	Type	Description
run_mode	PDB_INT32	Interactive, non-interactive
type	PDB_INT32	Filter type (0 = median, 1 = adaptive, 2 = recursive-median, 3 = recursive-adaptive)
white	PDB_INT32	White level (0 to 255)

D.1.45   gimp_drawable_image

Description   This procedure returns the drawable's image.

Table D.45   gimp_drawable_image Variables

Variable Name	Type	Description
drawable	PDB_DRAWABLE	The drawable
image	PDB_IMAGE	The drawable's image

D.1.46   plug_in_gauss_iir

Description   Applies a Gaussian blur to the drawable, with specified radius of affect. The standard deviation of the normal distribution used to modify pixel values is calculated based on the supplied radius. Horizontal and vertical blurring can be independently invoked by specifying only one to run. The IIR Gaussian blurring works best for large radius values and for images that are not computer generated. Values for radius less than 1.0 are invalid because they will generate spurious results.

Table D.46   plug_in_gauss_iir Variables

Variable Name	Type	Description
drawable	PDB_DRAWABLE	Input drawable
horizontal	PDB_INT32	Blur in horizontal direction
image	PDB_IMAGE	Input image (unused)
radius	PDB_FLOAT	Radius of Gaussian blur (in pixels > 1.0)
run_mode	PDB_INT32	Interactive, non-interactive
vertical	PDB_INT32	Blur in vertical direction

D.1.47 gimp_image_set_active_layer

Description   If the layer exists, it is set as the active layer in the image. Any previous active layer or channel is set to inactive. An exception is a previously existing floating selection, in which case this procedure will return an execution error.

Table D.47   gimp_image_set_active_layer Variables

Variable Name	Type	Description
image	PDB_IMAGE	The image
layer	PDB_LAYER	The layer to be set active

D.1.48 gimp_selection_none

Description   This procedure deselects the entire image. Every pixel in the selection channel is set to 0.

Table D.48   gimp_selection_none Variable

Variable Name	Type	Description
image	PDB_IMAGE	The image

D.1.49 gimp_palette_set_background

Description   This procedure sets the current GIMP background color. After this is set, operations that use background such as blending, filling images, clearing, and erasing (in non–Alpha images) will use the new value.

Table D.49   gimp_palette_set_background Variable

Variable Name	Type	Description
background	PDB_COLOR	The background color

D.1.50 gimp_edit_cut

Description   If there is a selection in the image, then the area specified by the selection is cut from the specified drawable and placed in an internal GIMP edit buffer. It can subsequently be retrieved using the gimp-edit-paste command. If there is no selection, then the specified drawable will be removed and its contents stored in the internal GIMP edit buffer. The drawable must belong to the specified image, or an error is returned.

Table D.50 `gimp_edit_cut` Variables

Variable Name	Type	Description
drawable	PDB_DRAWABLE	The drawable to cut from
image	PDB_IMAGE	The image

D.1.51 `gimp_image_get_selection`

Description This will always return a valid ID for a selection, which is represented as a channel internally.

Table D.51 `gimp_image_get_selection` Variables

Variable Name	Type	Description
image	PDB_IMAGE	The image
selection mask ID	PDB_SELECTION	The ID of the selection channel

D.1.52 `gimp_image_height`

Description This procedure returns the image's height. This value is independent of any of the layers in this image. This is the canvas height.

Table D.52 `gimp_image_height` Variables

Variable Name	Type	Description
height	PDB_INT32	The image's height
image	PDB_IMAGE	The image

D.1.53 `gimp_selection_clear`

Description This procedure sets the selection mask to empty, assigning the value 0 to every pixel in the selection channel.

Table D.53 `gimp_selection_clear` Variable

Variable Name	Type	Description
image	PDB_IMAGE	The image

D.1.54 gimp_channel_ops_duplicate

Description This procedure duplicates the specified image, copying all layers, channels, and image information.

Table D.54 gimp_channel_ops_duplicate Variables

Variable Name	Type	Description
image	PDB_IMAGE	The image
new_image	PDB_IMAGE	The new, duplicated image

D.1.55 gimp_drawable_layer

Description This procedure returns non-zero if the specified drawable is a layer.

Table D.55 gimp_drawable_layer Variables

Variable Name	Type	Description
drawable	PDB_DRAWABLE	The drawable
layer	PDB_INT32	Non-zero if the drawable is a layer

D.1.56 gimp_crop

Description This procedure crops the image so that its new width and height are equal to the supplied parameters. Offsets are also provided that describe the position of the previous image's content. All channels and layers within the image are cropped to the new image extents; this includes the image selection mask. If any parameters are out of range, an error is returned.

Table D.56 gimp_crop Variables

Variable Name	Type	Description
image	PDB_IMAGE	The image
new_height	PDB_INT32	New image height: (0 < new_height <= height)
new_width	PDB_INT32	New image width: (0 < new_width <= width)
offx	PDB_INT32	x offset: (0 <= offx <= (width − new_width))
offy	PDB_INT32	y offset: (0 <= offy <= (height − new_height))

D.1.57 gimp_message

Description   Displays a dialog box with a message. Useful for status or error reporting.

Table D.57   gimp_message Variable

Variable Name	Type	Description
message	PDB_STRING	Message to display in the dialog box

D.1.58 gimp_image_set_component_active

Description   This procedure sets whether the specified component is active or inactive—that is, whether it can be affected during painting operations. If the specified component is not valid for the image type, an error is returned.

Table D.58   gimp_image_set_component_active Variables

Variable Name	Type	Description
active	PDB_INT32	Determines whether component is active (1 for true, 0 for false)
component	PDB_INT32	The image component: RED-CHANNEL (0), GREEN-CHANNEL (1), BLUE-CHANNEL (2), GRAY-CHANNEL (3), INDEXED-CHANNEL (4)
image	PDB_IMAGE	The image

D.1.59 gimp_scale

Description   This tool scales the specified drawable if no selection exists. If a selection exists, the portion of the drawable that lies under the selection is cut from the drawable and made into a floating selection, which is then scaled by the specified amount. The interpolation parameter can be set to TRUE to indicate that either linear or cubic interpolation should be used to smooth the resulting scaled drawable. The return value is the ID of the scaled drawable. If there was no selection, this will be equal to the drawable ID supplied as input. Otherwise, this will be the newly created and scaled drawable.

Table D.59   gimp_scale Variables

Variable Name	Type	Description
drawable	PDB_DRAWABLE	The affected drawable
drawable	PDB_DRAWABLE	The resulting drawable
image	PDB_IMAGE	The image
interpolation	PDB_INT32	Whether to use interpolation
x1	PDB_FLOAT	The x coordinate of the upper-left corner of newly scaled region
x2	PDB_FLOAT	The x coordinate of the lower-right corner of newly scaled region
y1	PDB_FLOAT	The y coordinate of the upper-left corner of newly scaled region
y2	PDB_FLOAT	The y coordinate of the lower-right corner of newly scaled region

D.1.60   gimp_edit_clear

Description This procedure clears the specified drawable. If the drawable has an Alpha channel, the cleared pixels will become transparent. If the drawable does not have an Alpha channel, cleared pixels will be set to the background color. This procedure affects regions within a selection only if there is a selection active.

Table D.60   gimp_edit_clear Variables

Variable Name	Type	Description
drawable	PDB_DRAWABLE	The drawable to clear from
image	PDB_IMAGE	The image

D.1.61   gimp_floating_sel_anchor

Description This procedure anchors the floating selection to its associated drawable. This is similar to merging with a merge type of ClipToBottomLayer. The floating selection layer is no longer valid after this operation.

Table D.61   gimp_floating_sel_anchor Variable

Variable Name	Type	Description
floating_sel	PDB_LAYER	The floating selection

D.1.62 `gimp_selection_invert`

Description This procedure inverts the selection mask. For every pixel in the selection channel, its new value is calculated as (255–old_value).

Table D.62 `gimp_selection_invert` Variable

Variable Name	Type	Description
image	PDB_IMAGE	The image

D.1.63 `gimp_rect_select`

Description This tool creates a rectangular selection over the specified image. The rectangular region can be either added to or subtracted from, or replace the contents of the previous selection mask. If the feather option is enabled, the resulting selection is blurred before combining. The blur is a Gaussian blur with the specified feather radius.

Table D.63 `gimp_rect_select` Variables

Variable Name	Type	Description
feather	PDB_INT32	Feather option for selections
feather_radius	PDB_FLOAT	Radius for feather operation
height	PDB_FLOAT	The height of the rectangle: (height > 0)
image	PDB_IMAGE	The image
operation	PDB_INT32	The selection operation: ADD (0), SUB (1), REPLACE (2), INTER-SECT (3)
width	PDB_FLOAT	The width of the rectangle: (width > 0)
x	PDB_FLOAT	x coordinate of upper-left corner of rectangle
y	PDB_FLOAT	y coordinate of upper-left corner of rectangle

D.1.64 `gimp_edit_paste`

Description This procedure pastes a copy of the internal GIMP edit buffer to the specified drawable. The GIMP edit buffer will be empty unless a call was previously made to either `gimp-edit-cut` or `gimp-edit-copy`. The `paste_into` option specifies whether to clear the current image selection or to paste the buffer behind the selection. This allows the selection to act as a mask for the pasted buffer. Anywhere that the selection mask is non-zero, the pasted buffer will show through. The pasted buffer will be a new layer in the image that is designated as the image floating selection. If the image has a floating selection at the time of pasting, the old floating selection will be anchored to its drawable before the new floating selection is added. This procedure returns the new floating layer. The resulting floating selection will already be attached to the specified drawable, and a subsequent call to `floating_sel_attach` is not needed.

Table D.64 `gimp_edit_paste` Variables

Variable Name	Type	Description
drawable	PDB_DRAWABLE	The drawable to paste from
floating_sel	PDB_LAYER	The new floating selection
image	PDB_IMAGE	The image
paste_into	PDB_INT32	Determines whether to clear selection or paste behind it

D.1.65 `gimp_image_lower_layer`

Description This procedure lowers the specified layer one step in the existing layer stack. It will not move the layer if there is no layer below it, or the layer has no Alpha channel.

Table D.65 `gimp_image_lower_layer` Variables

Variable Name	Type	Description
image	PDB_IMAGE	The image
layer	PDB_LAYER	The layer to lower

D.1.66 `gimp_selection_load`

Description This procedure loads the specified channel into the selection mask. This essentially involves a copy of the channel's content in to the selection mask. Therefore, the channel must have the same width and height of the image or an error is returned.

Table D.66 `gimp_selection_load` Variables

Variable Name	Type	Description
channel	PDB_CHANNEL	The channel
image	PDB_IMAGE	The image

D.1.67 `gimp_image_enable_undo`

Description This procedure enables the image's undo stack, allowing subsequent operations to store their undo steps. This is generally called in conjunction with `gimp_image_disable` `_undo` to temporarily disable an image undo stack.

Table D.67 `gimp_image_enable_undo` Variables

Variable Name	Type	Description
enabled	PDB_INT32	True if the image undo has been enabled
image	PDB_IMAGE	The image

D.1.68 `gimp_image_merge_visible_layers`

Description This procedure combines the visible layers into a single layer using the specified merge type. A merge type of EXPAND-AS-NECESSARY expands the final layer to encompass the areas of the visible layers. A merge type of CLIP-TO-IMAGE clips the final layer to the extents of the image. A merge type of CLIP-TO-BOTTOM-LAYER clips the final layer to the size of the bottommost layer.

Table D.68 `gimp_image_merge_visible_layers` Variables

Variable Name	Type	Description
image	PDB_IMAGE	The image
layer	PDB_LAYER	The resulting layer
merge_type	PDB_INT32	The type of merge: EXPAND-AS-NECESSARY (0), CLIP-TO-IMAGE (1), CLIP-TO-BOTTOM-LAYER (2)

D.1.69 `gimp_image_scale`

Description This procedure scales the image so that its new width and height are equal to the supplied parameters. Offsets are also provided that describe the position of the previous image's content. No bounds checking is currently provided, so don't supply parameters that are out of bounds. All channels within the image are scaled according to the specified parameters; this includes the image selection mask. All layers within the image are repositioned according to the specified offsets.

Table D.69 gimp_image_scale Variables

Variable Name	Type	Description
image	PDB_IMAGE	The image
new_width	PDB_INT32	New image width: (new_width > 0)
new_height	PDB_INT32	New image height: (new_height > 0)

D.1.70 gimp_selection_border

Description This procedure borders the selection. Bordering creates a new selection that is defined along the boundary of the previous selection at every point within the specified radius.

Table D.70 gimp_selection_border Variables

Variable Name	Type	Description
image	PDB_IMAGE	The image
radius	PDB_INT32	The radius of border (pixels)

D.1.71 gimp_image_active_drawable

Description This procedure returns the ID of the image's active drawable. This can be a layer, channel, or layer mask. The active image channel specifies the active drawable. If that is -1, then it is the active image layer. If the active image layer has a layer mask and the layer mask is in edit mode, then the layer mask is the active drawable.

Table D.71 gimp_image_active_drawable Variables

Variable Name	Type	Description
drawable	PDB_DRAWABLE	The active drawable
image	PDB_IMAGE	The image

D.1.72 gimp_image_new

Description Creates a new image, undisplayed with the specified extents and type. A layer should be created and added before this image is displayed, or subsequent calls to gimp_display_new with this image as an argument will fail. Layers can be created using the gimp_layer_new commands. They can be added to an image using the gimp_image_add_layer command.

Table D.72 `gimp_image_new` **Variables**

Variable Name	Type	Description
height	PDB_INT32	The height of the image
image	PDB_IMAGE	The ID of the newly created image
type	PDB_INT32	The type of image: RGB (0), GRAY (1), INDEXED (2)
width	PDB_INT32	The width of the image

D.1.73 `gimp_layer_get_mode`

Description This procedure returns the specified layer's combination mode.

Table D.73 `gimp_layer_get_mode` **Variables**

Variable Name	Type	Description
layer	PDB_LAYER	The layer
mode	PDB_INT32	The layer combination mode: NORMAL (0), DISSOLVE (1), MULTIPLY (3), SCREEN (4), OVERLAY (5), DIFFERENCE (6), ADDITION (7), SUBTRACT (8), DARKEN-ONLY (9), LIGHTEN-ONLY (10), HUE (11), SATURATION (12), COLOR (13), VALUE (14)

D.1.74 `gimp_image_add_layer`

Description This procedure adds the specified layer to the gimage at the given position. If the position is specified as -1, then the layer is inserted at the top of the layer stack. If the layer to be added has no Alpha channel, it must be added at position 0. The layer type must be compatible with the image base type.

Table D.74 `gimp_image_add_layer` **Variables**

Variable Name	Type	Description
image	PDB_IMAGE	The image
layer	PDB_LAYER	The layer
position	PDB_INT32	The layer position

D.1.75 `gimp_drawable_width`

Description This procedure returns the specified drawable's width in pixels.

Table D.75 `gimp_drawable_width` Variables

Variable Name	Type	Description
drawable	PDB_DRAWABLE	The drawable
width	PDB_INT32	The width of drawable

D.1.76 `plug_in_gauss_rle`

Description Applies a Gaussian blur to the drawable, with specified radius of affect. The standard deviation of the normal distribution used to modify pixel values is calculated based on the supplied radius. Horizontal and vertical blurring can be independently invoked by specifying only one to run. The RLE Gaussian blurring performs most efficiently on computer-generated images or images with large areas of constant intensity. Values for radii less than 1.0 are invalid because they will generate spurious results.

Table D.76 `plug_in_gauss_rle` Variables

Variable Name	Type	Description
drawable	PDB_DRAWABLE	Input drawable
horizontal	PDB_INT32	Blurs in horizontal direction
image	PDB_IMAGE	Input image (unused)
radius	PDB_FLOAT	Radius of Gaussian blur (in pixels > 1.0)
run_mode	PDB_INT32	Interactive, non-interactive
vertical	PDB_INT32	Blurs in vertical direction

D.1.77 `gimp_palette_get_foreground`

Description This procedure retrieves the current GIMP foreground color. The foreground color is used in a variety of tools such as paint tools, blending, and bucket fill.

Table D.77 `gimp_palette_get_foreground` Variable

Variable Name	Type	Description
foreground	PDB_COLOR	The foreground color

D.1.78   `gimp_image_get_component_active`

Description   This procedure returns information about whether the specified image component (such as the Red, Green, or Blue intensity channel in an RGB image) is active or inactive—that is, whether or not it can be modified. If the specified component is not valid for the image type, an error is returned.

Table D.78   `gimp_image_get_component_active` Variables

Variable Name	Type	Description
active	PDB_INT32	1 for active, 0 for inactive
component	PDB_INT32	The image component: RED-CHANNEL (0), GREEN-CHANNEL (1), BLUE-CHANNEL (2), GRAY-CHANNEL (3), INDEXED-CHANNEL (4)
image	PDB_IMAGE	The image

D.1.79   `gimp_drawable_indexed`

Description   This procedure returns non-zero if the specified drawable is of type { Indexed, IndexedA }.

Table D.79   `gimp_drawable_indexed` Variables

Variable Name	Type	Description
drawable	PDB_DRAWABLE	The drawable
indexed	PDB_INT32	Non-zero if the drawable is a indexed type

D.1.80   `gimp_selection_grow`

Description   This procedure grows the selection. *Growing* involves expanding the boundary in all directions by the specified pixel amount.

Table D.80   `gimp_selection_grow` Variables

Variable Name	Type	Description
image	PDB_IMAGE	The image
steps	PDB_INT32	Steps of growth (pixels)

D.1.81 `gimp_layer_new`

Description This procedure creates a new layer with the specified width, height, and type. Name, opacity, and mode are also supplied parameters. The new layer still needs to be added to the image, as this is not automatic. Add the new layer with the `gimp_image_add_layer` command. Other attributes such as layer mask modes and offsets should be set with explicit procedure calls.

Table D.81 `gimp_layer_new` Variables

Variable Name	Type	Description
height	PDB_INT32	The layer height: (height > 0)
image	PDB_IMAGE	The image to which to add the layer
layer	PDB_LAYER	The newly created layer
mode	PDB_INT32	The layer combination modes: NORMAL (0), DISSOLVE (1), MULTIPLY (3), SCREEN (4), OVERLAY (5), DIFFERENCE (6), ADDITION (7), SUBTRACT (8), DARKEN-ONLY (9), LIGHTEN-ONLY (10), HUE (11), SATURATION (12), COLOR (13), VALUE (14)
name	PDB_STRING	The layer name
opacity	PDB_FLOAT	The layer opacity: (0 <= opacity <= 100)
type	PDB_INT32	The layer types: RGB_IMAGE (0), RGBA_IMAGE (1), GRAY_IMAGE (2), GRAYA_IMAGE (3), INDEXED_IMAGE (4), INDEXEDA_IMAGE (5)
width	PDB_INT32	The layer width: (width > 0)

D.1.82 `gimp_display_new`

Description Creates a new display for the specified image. If the image already has a display, another is added. Multiple displays are handled transparently by the GIMP. The newly created display is returned and can be subsequently destroyed with a call to `gimp_display_delete`. This procedure makes sense only for use with the GIMP UI.

Table D.82 `gimp_display_new` Variables

Variable Name	Type	Description
display	PDB_DISPLAY	The new display
image	PDB_IMAGE	The image

D.1.83 `gimp_layer_set_opacity`

Description This procedure sets the specified layer's opacity.

Table D.83 `gimp_layer_set_opacity` Variables

Variable Name	Type	Description
layer	PDB_LAYER	The layer
opacity	PDB_FLOAT	The new layer opacity: (0 <= `opacity` <= 100)

D.1.84 `gimp_edit_fill`

Description This procedure fills the specified drawable with the background color. This procedure affects regions within a selection only if there is a selection active.

Table D.84 `gimp_edit_fill` Variables

Variable Name	Type	Description
drawable	PDB_DRAWABLE	The drawable to fill from
image	PDB_IMAGE	The image

D.1.85 `gimp_image_set_component_visible`

Description This procedure sets whether the specified component is visible or invisible. If the specified component is not valid for the image type, an error is returned.

Table D.85 `gimp_image_set_component_visible` Variables

Variable Name	Type	Description
component	PDB_INT32	The image component: RED-CHANNEL (0), GREEN-CHANNEL (1), BLUE-CHANNEL (2), GRAY-CHANNEL (3), INDEXED-CHANNEL (4)
image	PDB_IMAGE	The image
visible	PDB_INT32	Determines whether the component is visible: 1 for true, 0 for false

D.1.86 gimp_drawable_set_pixel

Description This procedure sets the pixel value at the specified coordinates. The num_channels argument must always be equal to the bytes-per-pixel value for the specified drawable.

Table D.86 gimp_drawable_set_pixel Variables

Variable Name	Type	Description
drawable	PDB_DRAWABLE	The drawable
num_channels	PDB_INT32	The number of channels for the pixel
pixel	PDB_INT8ARRAY	The pixel value
x coordinate	PDB_INT32	The x coordinate
y coordinate	PDB_INT32	The y coordinate

D.1.87 gimp_layer_is_floating_sel

Description This procedure returns whether the layer is a floating selection. *Floating selections* are special cases of layers that are attached to a specific drawable.

Table D.87 gimp_layer_is_floating_sel Variables

Variable Name	Type	Description
layer	PDB_LAYER	The layer
is_floating_sel	PDB_CHANNEL	Non-zero if the layer is a floating selection

D.1.88 gimp_drawable_height

Description This procedure returns the height of the specified drawable in pixels

Table D.88 gimp_drawable_height Variables

Variable Name	Type	Description
drawable	PDB_DRAWABLE	The drawable
height	PDB_INT32	The height of the drawable

D.1.89 gimp_edit_copy

Description   If there is a selection in the image, then the area specified by the selection is copied from the specified drawable and placed in an internal GIMP edit buffer. It can subsequently be retrieved using the gimp-edit-paste command. If there is no selection, then the specified drawable's contents will be stored in the internal GIMP edit buffer. The drawable must belong to the specified image or an error is returned.

Table D.89   gimp_edit_copy Variables

Variable Name	Type	Description
drawable	PDB_DRAWABLE	The drawable to copy from
image	PDB_IMAGE	The image

D.1.90 gimp_image_remove_layer

Description   This procedure removes the specified layer from the image. If the layer doesn't exist, an error is returned. If there are no layers left in the image, this call will fail. If this layer is the last layer remaining, the image will become empty and have no active layer.

Table D.90   gimp_image_remove_layer Variables

Variable Name	Type	Description
image	PDB_IMAGE	The image
layer	PDB_LAYER	The layer

D.1.91 gimp_image_disable_undo

Description   This procedure disables the image's undo stack, allowing subsequent operations to ignore their undo steps. This is generally called in conjunction with gimp_image_enable_undo to temporarily disable an image undo stack. This is advantageous because saving undo steps can be time and memory intensive.

Table D.91   gimp_image_disable_undo Variables

Variable Name	Type	Description
disabled	PDB_INT32	True if the image undo has been disabled
image	PDB_IMAGE	The image

D.1.92 gimp_layer_get_opacity

Description This procedure returns the specified layer's opacity.

Table D.92 gimp_layer_get_opacity Variables

Variable Name	Type	Description
layer	PDB_LAYER	The layer
opacity	PDB_FLOAT	The layer opacity

D.1.93 gimp_image_clean_all

Description This procedure sets the specified image's dirty count to 0, allowing operations to occur without having a "dirtied" image. This is especially useful for creating and loading images that should not initially be considered dirty, even though layers must be created, filled, and installed in the image.

Table D.93 gimp_image_clean_all Variable

Variable Name	Type	Description
image	PDB_IMAGE	the image

D.1.94 gimp_image_raise_layer

Description This procedure raises the specified layer one step in the existing layer stack. It will not move the layer if there is no layer above it, or the layer has no Alpha channel.

Table D.94 gimp_image_raise_layer Variables

Variable Name	Type	Description
image	PDB_IMAGE	The image
layer	PDB_LAYER	The layer to raise

Index

Symbols

A

G

Galaxy brush, 173

gamma correction (XSane menu), 134

GAP (GIMP Animation Plug-In), 111

Gaussian filter
IIR, 194–195
RLE, 194–195

GBR (Brush Format), 72

Gfig filter, 243–248
Brush menu, 246
Grid menu, 244
Object menu, 244–245
Operations menu, 243–244
Options menu, 248
Paint menu, 245–246
Select menu, 246–247

GhostScript, 32

GIF (Graphics Interchange Format), 77–80
animations for Web, 81
interlaced, 74
supported options, 77

GIMP (GNU Image Manipulation Program)
color models, 5
Grayscale model, 6
HSV model, 6
Indexed model, 6
RGB model, 5
customizing, 115
gtkrc files, 115–117
themes, 117
file formats, 69
BMP, 78
GBR, 72
GIF, 77
image compression, 73–75
JPEG, 76
PAT, 72
PNG, 76-77
PostScript, 75-76
PSD, 78
TIFF, 75
XCF, 71-72
XPM, 77
XWD, 78

hotkeys, 117
installation, 280–286
deciding which version to use, 285
image libraries, 281-284
introduction, 2
parameters, 291–292
plug-ins, 111–115
imagemap, 113-115
installation, 112-113
resolution, 6
monitor, 6
printer, 7
script references. *See* script references
system requirements, 3
Toolbox, 4, 10
color selection, 12-15
creating new images, 11-12
drawing techniques, 12
File and Xtns menus, 10
layout, 10
tool options, 16
Undo/Redo, 16
versions, 287
development, 287-288
numbering scheme, 2
stable, 288
Web site, 3
window managers, 291–292
AfterStep, 292
Blackbox, 292
Enlightenment, 292
Gnome, 292
IceWM, 293
KDE, 293
WindowMaker, 293

GIMP Animation Plug-In, 111

GIMP FAQs Web site, 296

GIMP Logo brush, 173

GIMP method (color selection), 13–14

GIMP Newsgroup Web site, 295

GIMP Plug In Registry Web site, 295

GIMP Toolkit Web site, 295

GIMP Toolkit. *See* GTK+

GIMP.org links Web site, 295

GIMP.org Web page theme script, 276–277

New Riders\

We Want to Know What You Think

To better serve you, we would like your opinion on the content and quality of this book. Please complete this card and mail it to us or fax it to 317-581-4663.

Name_____

Address _____

City _____State _____Zip _____

Phone _____

Email Address _____

Occupation _____

Operating System(s) that you use _____

What influenced your purchase of this book?

❑ Recommendation ❑ Cover Design
❑ Table of Contents ❑ Index
❑ Magazine Review ❑ Advertisement
❑ New Riders' Reputation ❑ Author Name

How would you rate the contents of this book?

❑ Excellent ❑ Very Good
❑ Good ❑ Fair
❑ Below Average ❑ Poor

How do you plan to use this book?

❑ Quick reference ❑ Self-training
❑ Classroom ❑ Other

What do you like most about this book?
Check all that apply.

❑ Content ❑ Writing Style
❑ Accuracy ❑ Examples
❑ Listings ❑ Design
❑ Index ❑ Page Count
❑ Price ❑ Illustrations

What do you like least about this book?
Check all that apply.

❑ Content ❑ Writing Style
❑ Accuracy ❑ Examples
❑ Listings ❑ Design
❑ Index ❑ Page Count
❑ Price ❑ Illustrations

What would be a useful follow-up book to this one for you? _____

Where did you purchase this book? _____

Can you name a similar book that you like better than this one, or one that is as good? Why?
_____
_____

How many New Riders books do you own? _____

What are your favorite computer books? _____
_____

What other titles would you like to see us develop? _____
_____

Any comments for us? _____
_____
_____
_____

GIMP Essential Reference, 0-7357-0911-4

Fold here and tape to mail

New Riders Publishing
201 W. 103rd St.
Indianapolis, IN 46290

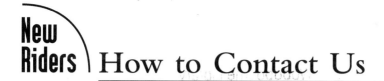

How to Contact Us

Visit Our Web Site

www.newriders.com

On our Web site, you'll find information about our other books, authors, tables of contents, indexes, and book errata. You can also place orders for books through our Web site.

Email Us

Contact us at this address:
newriders@mcp.com

- If you have comments or questions about this book
- To report errors that you have found in this book
- If you have a book proposal to submit or are interested in writing for New Riders
- If you would like to have an author kit sent to you
- If you are an expert in a computer topic or technology and are interested in being a technical editor who reviews manuscripts for technical accuracy

newriders-sales@mcp.com

- To find a distributor in your area, please contact our international department at the address above.

newriders-pr@mcp.com

- For instructors from educational institutions who wish to preview New Riders books for classroom use. Email should include your name, title, school, department, address, phone number, office days/hours, text in use, and enrollment in the body of your text along with your request for desk/examination copies and/or additional information.

Write to Us

New Riders Publishing
201 W. 103rd St.
Indianapolis, IN 46290-1097

Call Us

Toll-free (800) 571-5840 + 9 + 7494
If outside U.S. (317) 581-3500. Ask for New Riders.

Fax Us

(317) 581-4663